The Best Of
Alert Diver

THE MAGAZINE OF DIVERS ALERT NETWORK

BEST PUBLISHING COMPANY

Cover photo is a diver swimming into the wreck of the *RMS Rhone*, off the island of Tortola in the British Virgin Islands, by DAN Platinum Sponsor Chris Crumley, EarthWater Stock Photography.

Book design and layout by Doreen Wood

Edited by Renée Westerfield

Published 1997

ISBN: 0-941332-62-4
Library of Congress Catalog Card Number: 97-073096

Composed, printed and bound in the United States of America

Best Publishing Company
2355 North Steves Blvd.
P.O. Box 30100
Flagstaff, AZ 86003-0100 USA

Table of Contents

Foreword by DAN Executive Director Dr. Peter B. Bennett

The Best of Alert Diver
shows much of what's best at DAN

Dear Reader:

As many readers of this book will know, I initiated Divers Alert Network (DAN) in 1980. DAN's membership association, however, didn't start until 1983.

In the beginning the most important factor was DAN's emergency telephone assistance (the Diving Emergency Hotline), followed later by the advisory telephone services (Dive Safety and Medical Information Line). But soon there were sufficient members to merit a newsletter, so the first edition of *Alert Diver* was published in 1983.

Today, some 15 years later, bimonthly *Alert Diver* is an important part of every DAN member's service. From a brief newsletter format, it has blossomed into a 56-page multicolor award-winning magazine.

It has many facets, too, including letters from members, a bulletin board of news about DAN activities, information on DAN's many membership services, lists of DAN oxygen courses, diving accident insights, a list of DAN sponsors and details of the many DAN products available. But the most valuable parts of *Alert Diver* are the many articles by DAN staff and invited writers on diving safety, with great illustrations.

A wealth of information has been provided over the years. Much of this is very hard to find for recreational divers and is usually in a very technical form. At DAN, we try to break down the jargon so the articles are more readily understood. They address a wide range of the more common issues of importance to divers today.

Now we know that like all magazines, *Alert Diver* has a short lifetime, and only a few divers will keep all the issues. Thinking this over, I felt it was unfortunate that all this safety information was discarded; from this came the book *The Best of Alert Diver*.

In this volume you will have the very best of the last 15 years of *Alert Diver* to provide readily available advice, both for the experienced and the new diver. A wide range of diving medicine and related subjects of value to the diver are covered. If there is a question not answered, you can always call DAN and we will be happy to provide additional information.

I know that this is a volume that all DAN members will wish to have on their bookshelves. To those of you who are not yet DAN members, this book may stimulate you to join DAN, *Your* Dive Safety Association, operated by divers for divers.

With best personal regards,

Peter B. Bennett, Ph.D., D.Sc.
Professor of Anesthesiology
Senior Director, F.G. Hall Hypo/Hyperbaric Center
Duke University Medical Center
Executive Director, Divers Alert Network

ACKNOWLEDGMENTS

For their contributions to this book, we extend our thanks to Dr. Yancey Mebane, DAN's Associate Medical Director and Director of EMS Training (retired), Richard Dunford, Tony Almon, Karl Huggins, Dr. Paul Auerbach, Dr. Jolie Bookspan, Dr. Alfred Bove, Dr. Glen Egstrom, Cathie Cush, Dr. Jennifer Hunt, Dr. Philip J. Fracica, Karen Vick, Dr. Maida Beth Taylor, Dr. Kenneth Kizer, Dr. Bruce Wienke and Bob Rossier.

Our thanks to Chris Crumley, Don Jackson, Mike Webster, Eric Hanauer, Ken Bondy, Marla Tonseth, Denis Tapparel, Alese and Mort Pechter, Robert R. Clemons, U.S. Coast Guard, John T. Pennington, Sean Combs, Steve Barnett, Dan Orr and Jesse Cancelmo for their photos and illustrations.

Publications written or edited by Dr. Alfred Bove, Dr. Paul Auerbach, John Lippmann, Dr. Peter B. Bennett, Dr. Bruce Wienke, Dr. Richard Moon, and Dr. Jolie Bookspan are available through DAN.

NOTE: Medical standards change as information and equipment are updated and improved. If you have questions about current medical guidelines, call DAN or ask your dive instructor.

FROM THE DIVE GOODIE BAG

Putting the Squeeze on Barotrauma

BY RENEE WESTERFIELD, EDITOR, *ALERT DIVER*, AND
G. YANCEY MEBANE, M.D., DAN ASSOCIATE MEDICAL DIRECTOR &
DIRECTOR, EMS TRAINING

You're afloat in the warm, azure waters of the Caribbean, preparing to make that first dive of your long-planned vacation. You've had your dive equipment checked out, reviewed basic diving procedures, and listened carefully to the dive guide about the area you're diving. Last week's cold has left only a slight sniffle, and you're excited about your dive.

You make a last-minute adjustment to your mask, pop in your regulator and descend, eager to experience the depths. But wait. Your ears feel a bit too full. You alert your buddy, and, slowing your descent, perform your tried-and-true method of clearing your ears. It works on your left ear, and you begin a slow descent, working all the while on that stubborn right ear.

It'll clear in a second, you say to yourself. Just go slowly and keep at it: it's nearly clear. So you continue onward and downward, until the fullness in your right ear is punctuated by a sharp pain. You finally stop and signal your buddy that you're going back up.

In your haste to check out your external environment, perhaps you've neglected to consider your internal one. Last week's cold has become more than just a memory. What you've just experienced is called middle ear barotrauma, or ear squeeze, reported as one of the most common diving medical problems. As divers, we're all subject to ear squeeze whether commercial or recreational diver, deep or shallow diver, famous or not-so-famous diver.

Edmund Halley, the English astronomer best known for predicting the orbit of the comet that now bears his surname, was himself the victim of ear squeeze. In 1691, Halley patented a design for a diving bell. Halley made dives in the bell and reported that he suffered from ear pain throughout the dive.

What causes ear squeeze?

In medical terms, ear squeeze is the result of inadequate pressure equalization between the middle ear and the surrounding water. As a diver descends, the external pressure of the surrounding water becomes greater than the middle ear's pressure, compressing the air to the ear into a smaller overall volume (Boyle's Law). If the diver cannot voluntarily equalize these conflicting pressures and remains too long at depth, his body will eventually equalize these pressures involuntarily — sometimes at the expense of an eardrum, or worse. But ear squeeze doesn't have to have such dire consequences.

With a normal ear, the sole route to equalizing is through the Eustachian tube, which connects the middle ear to the throat, and whose primary job is to equalize middle ear pressures with outside pressures. It has a small opening into the throat which acts as a valve. Normally closed, it can be activated — usually by swallowing. It is this opening we use to equalize our ears when we encounter changes in pressure while flying, diving and even crossing mountains.

In some instances the Eustachian tube can fail to open sufficiently because of the rapid pressure changes encountered while scuba diving. This may happen for several reasons: the diver may descend too quickly; he may not make active attempts to clear his ears, or begin the procedure too late (deep); or he may have congestion and/or nasal inflammation and swelling. Any or all of these can result in increased negative inner ear pressure, which in turn intensifies the swelling of the Eustachian tube lining and further decreases the chance of adequate opening.

What are the symptoms of ear squeeze?

Pressures both inside and outside the ear are measured in millimeters (mm) of mercury (or Hg, as exemplified by the barometric pressure reports in weather forecasts). On the surface, the pressure rests generally at about 760mm. At a depth of 2.6 feet / .79 meters or deeper, without middle ear clearing, the difference in pressure between the middle ear and the surrounding water may be as high as 60mm.

This causes the eardrum — located at the opening of the middle ear — and the round window structure — located on the inner wall of the middle ear at the opening to the inner ear — to bulge inward, aggravating any swelling which may be present, causing more edema (swelling) of the mucosal lining and closing the Eustachian tube channel even tighter.

A sensation of fullness in the ear can develop at this point, accompanied by pain and some vertigo. A temporary hearing loss or a ringing in the ears (tinnitus) may also develop, though it isn't always obvious to the diver when underwater.

At a depth of approximately 3.9 feet / 1.18 meters (90mm Hg pressure differential), without clearing, it is usually impossible to voluntarily open the Eustachian tube. It is at this point both locked and blocked. More edema, additional inflammation and even bleeding from a ruptured eardrum can occur at this depth.

The eardrum has been found to rupture at depths from approximately 4 to 17 feet / 1.2 to 6.18 meters, depending upon the individual. The sharp pain of the rupture may be followed by vertigo, as cold water enters the middle ear. The dizziness will probably subside as the entering water is eventually warmed by the surrounding tissues.

If you attempt a forceful Valsalva maneuver in these conditions you may increase the pressure difference between the middle and inner ears to the point of even greater injury to your inner ear, such as can be seen with round window rupture.

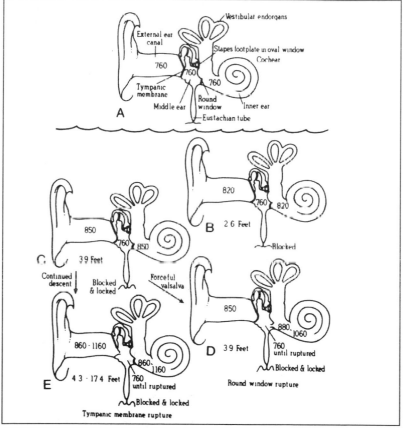

ILLUSTRATION COURTESY OF DR. JOSEPH FARMER OF DUKE UNIVERSITY MEDICAL CENTER, DURHAM, N.C. ADAPTED FROM DR. FARMER'S CHAPTER IN THE PHYSIOLOGY AND MEDICINE OF DIVING, 4TH EDITION, 1993, W.B. SAUNDERS COMPANY LTD., EDITED BY DR. PETER BENNETT, PH.D., D.SC., AND DAVID ELLIOTT, D.PHIL.

What causes sinus squeeze?

Although the ears are the most common site for injury because of pressure changes while diving, the sinuses are also frequently involved in the same process.

The sinuses are connected to the nasal cavity. The nasal cavity is separated by a partition called the nasal septum. The side (lateral) wall of the cavity is composed of three bony or cartilaginous structures covered by mucous membranes called turbinates.

Air conditioning is the primary function of your nose during normal respiration. The airstream passes over the turbinates, and in a 4-inch journey lasting about a quarter of a second, the air is cleaned, moistened and thermally adjusted. The humidity is raised to about 75 percent or more, the temperature is about 98.6°F / 37°C and all dust, bacteria and other particles have been removed

The paranasal sinuses are irregular air cavities which lie adjacent to the nose. There are about 12 sinuses on each side, which, according to their location, are divided into the anterior and posterior groups (front and back). The number of sinuses is variable and not always the same on the two sides. The anterior group includes the frontal, maxillary and anterior ethmoids. The posterior groups are the posterior ethmoids and the sphenoid.

The sinuses are lined with the same mucous membrane as the respiratory tract, though it is very thin in the sinuses.

The sinuses communicate to the nasal cavity through openings called ostia. Each ostium may not lie on the floor of the sinus but may lie high up on the wall. Fluids cannot drain out by gravity but are swept out as mucus.

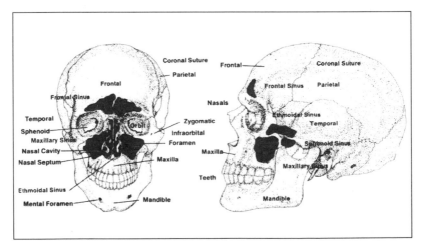

Sinus function & dysfunction

Theories abound as to the function of the sinuses, but none are conclusive. It may well be that the sinuses are a developmental accident and have no function. We become aware of these structures, however, when they become dysfunctional. Sinusitis refers to the inflammation of the mucosal lining of the sinus cavities and may be due to a chemical, bacterial or physical injury.

One type of injury occurs with the overuse of nasal sprays. When this happens, the mucous membrane of the nasal cavity and sinuses may become inflamed. The drug's effect on the nasal mucosa decreases, and a resultant rebound mucosal congestion occurs, leading to more frequent spray use. The spray soon ceases to be effective, and the mucosal congestion becomes persistent.

Upper respiratory tract viral infections (such as the common cold) lead to abundant nasal discharge and congestion. The sinus ostia may become obstructed, and secondary bacterial infection occurs, resulting in sinusitis.

Sinusitis may also be triggered by allergies. Allergic reactions may lead to swelling of the mucous membrane and reduced resistance to infection, allowing the development of sinusitis.

What are the symptoms of sinus squeeze?

Divers are susceptible to all of these causes of sinus squeeze and in addition must prevent barotrauma or pressure-related injury. Barosinusitis, or aerosinusitis, may be produced by rapid changes in barometric pressure. The result may be a swelling of the membrane lining the sinus, with bleeding into the cavity and subsequent sinusitis. This is more likely to occur if the ostium is already obstructed by changes in the membrane from infection or allergy.

When barosinusitis occurs during descent, the negative pressure in the sinus may be great enough to tear the mucosa away from the walls, causing hemorrhage into the cavity or beneath the mucosa (mucous membranes). This usually is quite painful and may continue as a dull ache several hours after the problem is corrected. The pain is located over the frontal sinus, less frequently behind the eyes, and may be in the maxillary (upper jaw) area or upper teeth, though this is uncommon.

During ascent, the pressure inside the sinus exceeds external pressure, which causes expansion toward the limit of the walls' elasticity. Pain occurs when this pressure change is severe and abrupt.

Sinus barotrauma of ascent may occur when there is a one-way blockage of sinus ostia by folds of mucosal tissue or sinus polyps (growths). The sinus may equalize on descent, but on ascent it is obstructed until the expanding gases blow out into the nasal cavity —

accompanied by blood and mucus. Pain may or may not be felt when this occurs, and the diver may be aware of the problem only because of the blood and the mucus found in the mask after surfacing. The frontal or maxillary sinuses are usually the ones involved.

Dive with care

Barotrauma can be easily prevented. Learn the skills necessary to equalize ear and sinus pressures during all phases of the dive. Descents and ascents should be slow, to allow sufficient time for equalization. Avoid diving if you have upper respiratory infections or chronic paranasal sinus disease. Avoid chronic irritants such as cigarette smoke, prolonged use of nose drops, and other noxious substances. When mechanical obstruction exists, it should be corrected by a physician.

Treatment may not be necessary for mild forms of barosinusitis. When symptoms persist or are severe, you should consult a physician. A return to diving should await healing of the injury. Air travel may be uncomfortable if the sinuses cannot be cleared.

As with most diving problems, prevention is much easier than treatment. Be careful and use good equalization techniques. If you have predive congestion, you will increase dramatically your chances of barotrauma. It's best to have a diving physician give you a predive evaluation if you have any concerns. And when you dive, do so with care.

— *From September/October 1993*

Ear-Clearing Techniques

BY RENEE WESTERFIELD AND JOHN ROREM, DAN COMMUNICATIONS

When you dive, water replaces air in your external ear canals. As you descend, the weight of the water pressing against your eardrums increases with depth. To avoid injury, you must equalize your ears every 1 to 2 feet / .3 to .6 meters, especially during the first 33 feet / 10 meters.

Barotrauma of *descent* results from under-pressurization of the middle ear because of its inability to take in more air to equalize disparate pressures. Nearly all cases of barotrauma are descent-related, and most ear-clearing techniques are geared to relieve this complication.

Barotrauma of *ascent* occurs when gases in the middle ear expand with ascent and become blocked, causing tissue damage similar to barotrauma of descent. This malady is less common, because, in all probability, any blockage will usually be felt first upon descent by blocking the Eustachian tubes.

The Eustachian tubes are small air tubes which connect the middle ear to the throat, making it possible to equalize pressures in both places. If these tubes are obstructed with mucus or inflammation, clearing may be difficult or impossible. This is why diving medical experts caution divers who have or who have recently suffered from cold or sinus congestion to avoid diving until they are healthy again.

You should begin clearing your ears as soon as you enter the water. If you do not adequately clear your ears, pain, fullness or a subsequent muffled hearing sensation may occur. If this happens, stop your descent and attempt to clear your ears. If this doesn't help, ascend a few feet until the pain or sense of fullness stops, and try equalizing again.

If your ears won't clear even after ascending a few feet or meters, discontinue diving that day and see a physician or a specialist in dive medicine. Continuing to dive despite growing ear pain could result in ruptured eardrums, leading to serious infection or possibly permanent damage of the inner ear. This could include vertigo with nausea and vomiting (possibly drowning) tinnitus (ringing in the ears) or permanent hearing loss.

All divers can suffer from barotrauma, no matter what the training or experience level. Here are some techniques which may help you conquer this common problem.

Valsalva Maneuver

Probably the most commonly practiced technique for ear-clearing is known as the Valsalva maneuver. To perform the Valsalva, simply pinch your nose shut and gently force air into your ears. Although this can be an effective ear-clearing technique, use it with care since it can increase the air pressure in the inner ear to the point of damaging the delicate internal ear. Because of this potential damage, most diving physicians recommend against using this method if your ears have failed to clear at depth.

Frenzel Maneuver

A lesser-known but safer technique is the Frenzel maneuver. This is accomplished by voluntarily closing your mouth, nose and glottis (throat) while placing your tongue against the roof of your mouth, and swallowing. The elevated tongue acts like a piston to compress air into the nasal cavities and through the Eustachian tubes without over-pressurizing your inner ear.

Yawn & Swallow Maneuver

The simplest maneuver is done with a modified yawn and swallowing. This action is accomplished by thrusting the lower jaw forward, slightly opening the jaw while keeping the lips pursed around the regulator, and swallowing.

Another method consists of moving the palatal muscles by raising the soft palate. This method can be easily mastered without the need to swallow or move the jaw. Another effective technique combines a gentle Valsalva combined with a jaw thrust.

Toynbee Maneuver

The Toynbee maneuver is done by swallowing while the mouth and nose are both closed. The inverse of the Valsalva maneuver, the Toynbee method has seen some success in relieving middle ear over-pressure, found in barotrauma of ascent.

— From September/October 1993

Uses & Abuses of Dive Computers

Are Computers Tricking Divers — or Do We Just Fool Ourselves?

BY KARL E. HUGGINS

Editor's Note: Dive computers continue to be the source of controversy among some in the diving field. There have been improvements in dive computer hard- and software since this article was written (1994). For example, more computers now have altitude capabilities, and most cannot sim-

DAN ORR PHOTO

ply be shut off to clear residual nitrogen time, as discussed in the article — now divers have to remove the battery.

Access to many computer algorithms is still limited, and none have statistically significant test dive data. It is timely to once again take a look at what we should know about computer use and abuse.

Ever since the introduction of microprocessor-based dive computers, divers have been coming up with imaginative ways of using them. Despite attempts to educate divers on dive computer limitations, and recommendations from agencies like the American Academy of Underwater Sciences (AAUS), divers are still abusing their dive computers.

General misuses are widespread. Some of these indiscretions are due to a general ignorance of computers and/or the perils of decompression illness, a little laziness on the part of some divers in learning the complexities of new technology, worship of the technology itself and trusting it implicitly, and just plain arrogance — the "not-me" method of thinking.

The results of computer misuses can be severe. Dive computers are only tools, and as such can be used to enhance the diving experience. They have limitations, as well, and divers must be aware of them. Manufacturers of computers should be more forthcoming with information regarding dive computer models and the testing done to validate them.

General Misuses of Dive Computers

There seem to be generalized techniques some overzealous divers have developed in order to squeeze out every second of dive time from a dive computer. Following are some of the most common errors:

Not reading the operating manual. It is alarming to see how many divers do not read the operating manuals for their computers prior to use. The manual should be thoroughly read before using the computer — and then should be reread on a regular basis.

Regularly pushing the unit to its limits. Many divers run their dive computers down to zero no-decompression time, ascend to a shallower depth, and then run the time back down to zero, pushing the decompression model in the unit to its limit.

Pushing the dive computer to its limit essentially indicates divers' ignorance of individual variation in susceptibility to decompression sickness (DCS). If they were aware that there is no real line, but a gray zone, they might have second thoughts before pushing a dive computer to the limit.

Using the computer outside its operating range. Some dive computers on the market are designed to be used only at sea level, or the first few thousand feet of altitude. However, some divers use the sea level dive computers at altitudes outside the model's operating realm. Another abuse is diving to depths that exceed the maximum depth range of the dive computer.

Diving outside of the tested envelope. Many divers routinely dive to depths which exceed the depths used to test the dive computer's decompression algorithm, and perform many more dives a day than were ever tested. In this type of activity, divers are basically performing uncontrolled human subject tests of the decompression algorithm.

From my personal perspective, another problem is that many divers have no urge to seek additional information on their dive computers. These divers make the assumption that their devices are "safe" and dive with them, not knowing the background or validity of their decompression models.

Even if divers do seek additional information, many times that information is not available. Dive computer decompression algorithms are considered by most manufacturers to be proprietary information, and therefore are not always available for public scrutiny. Human subject testing done on the actual dive computer algorithms is virtually nonexistent. Most of the algorithms have been "validated" by extrapolating tests of other tables or models. When asked at a 1991 AAUS workshop, "How do you validate your decompression models?" only one dive computer manufacturer indicated that it had performed any type of controlled human subject testing of its decompression algorithm.

Blind trust in numbers. Many divers think that because a dive computer is showing them exact numbers, these numbers are true. As pointed out at the AAUS workshop, "They are like small televisions, and people believe what they see on television."

The numbers produced by the dive computer are only a guide to a diver's decompression status. Divers must be aware of the other factors that may influence susceptibility to DCS and add their own safety factors. The dive computer's information is not gospel!

Turning decision-making over to a machine. Some divers do not want to worry or think about their decompression status, so they let a little box made out of silicon, metal and plastic take over their thinking requirements.

Ritualistic dances praising dive computers. Although this sounds silly, there is a videotape of a group of divers at Truk Lagoon performing a ritualistic dance on their dive boat with their dive computers. Even though this group's outlandish activity was all in fun, there are many divers who have personal attachments to their dive computers and will not dive without them.

Not reading, or ignoring, information. Some divers will just ignore the information provided by a dive computer if they don't like the information displayed.

Ignoring ascent rate warnings. Most dive computers assume ascent rates slower than the 60 feet / 18 meters sea water per minute, U.S. Navy standard. However, some divers do not want to follow these suggested ascent rates even though it may place them outside the tested limits of the model.

Violating decompression requirements. Some divers do not want to follow the suggested decompression requirements. They will surface before the dive computer indicates that it is safe to surface, based on its calculations.

Abusing safety features. Some dive computers have safety features that allow a diver to get out of situations outside of its model or electrical limitations. Case in point, the Edge dive computer by Orca has a maximum depth resolution of approximately 165 fsw / 50 msw. At that depth, the ambient pressure register is storing the largest number it can resolve. If the diver were to descend further, the dive computer would not be able recognize the fact that the diver was at a deeper depth. In the Edge, a safety feature was added that assumes the diver is at approximately 200 fsw / 61 msw any time the maximum depth has been exceeded. This assumption was designed to handle an accidental violation of the depth limit for only a moment or so. The diver, upon noticing the *faux pas*, could return to a shallower depth without having the unit stop its calculations. The Edge was not designed — or tested — to allow divers to dive to 200 fsw. However, there are divers who pervert this feature to make dives to 200 fsw. Some even use it to depths deeper than 200 fsw. Why? In some cases another diver has told them they could do it, while in other cases they have misinterpreted information presented in the manual.

Turning off the unit to clear residual nitrogen. Some divers who do not like the repetitive dive information being shown by their computers will actually turn them off to clear the residual nitrogen from the computers' registers, giving themselves more time on the repetitive dive. Clearing the residual nitrogen memory from the dive computer, however, does not clear it from the diver's body!

Continuing to dive with a dive computer that did not initialize on the first dive. There are cases where a dive computer did not initialize prior to the first dive. Upon surfacing, the dive computer concluded its initialization process and considered itself at the start of a new dive series, having no memory of the first dive. Some divers have actually continued to dive the computer to its limit on subsequent dives even though they were fully aware that the computer was not operating during the first dive.

"Hanging" the dive computer. This is one of the most ludicrous techniques observed. Some divers who violate the dive computer's ascent rate, or have surfaced while the dive computer still indicates required decompression, will tie a rope to the dive computer and hang it over the side of boat to clear the warnings and prevent the dive computer from going into ERROR mode. If the ceiling is shallow enough (1-2 fsw / .3-.6 msw) some divers "decompress" their computers in the rinse bucket on the boat.

What can you say? The computer understands depth and time. It has no idea if it is attached to the diver or not.

How Dive Computers Are Being Used

How are divers using dive computers in actual diving situations? In general, information on the actual dives being performed is hard to come by. Records of maximum depth and bottom time are virtually useless when you consider the computer's ability to handle multilevel dives.

Figure 1

New Time Limits for Hypothetical Dive Computer

Depth (fsw)	No-D Limit (min)	Percent Safety Margin				
		0% (min)	10% (min)	25% (min)	30% (min)	50% (min)
30	220	0	22	55	66	110
40	120	0	12	30	36	60
50	70	0	7	18	21	35
60	50	0	5	13	15	25
70	40	0	4	10	12	20
80	30	0	3	8	9	15
90	25	0	3	7	8	13
100	20	0	2	5	6	10
110	15	0	2	4	5	8
120	12	0	2	3	4	6
130	10	0	1	3	3	5

Two dives with the same maximum depth and bottom time can quite easily be vastly different dives. Currently, data is being collected in an attempt to understand the type of diving that occurs in the real world. (See Figure 1.) The DAN Doppler trips utilize dive profile recorders and, to date, have collected over 500 dive profiles. In addition, the Delphi and Suunto's SME-ML and Solution dive computers store dive profile information which, hopefully, will be made available to researchers.

Following are examples of some of the actual profiles and dive histories that have been collected regarding the use of dive computers in the field.

Galápagos

In 1987 a group of 10 sport divers was monitored during a 14-day dive trip to the Galapagos Islands. All the divers except one used dive computers. Following 76 dives, the divers were monitored using a Doppler ultrasonic bubble detector to check for "silent bubbles." On 65 dives the actual dive profile was recorded (maximum depth every three minutes).

When compared to the U.S. Navy tables, 52 of the dives indicated omitted decompression. The maximum omitted decompression time for a single dive was 71 minutes. The average was 23 minutes. For an entire day, the maximum omitted decompression was 145 minutes, and the average was 46.2 minutes. The maximum time extended past the U.S. Navy no-decompression limits was 55 minutes on a single dive.

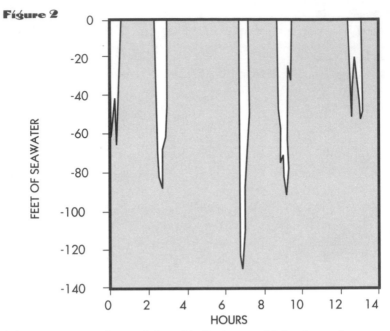

Figure 2

(The average time beyond the table limits was 23.8 minutes.)

The profile data indicated:

• 48.5 percent of the dive time was spent at depths which were between 75 and 100 percent of the maximum depth of the dive

• 26.2 percent of the dive time was spent in the range of 50 to 75 percent of maximum depth

• 16.3 percent of the time was in the 25 to 50 percent range

• Only 9.0 percent was spent in the shallowest quarter of the dive

This shows that, for this group of divers, the dive computers were not being used to make short excursions to deep depths, followed by the remainder of the dive in shallower water. Instead the computers were being used to extend dive time at the deeper depths.

Figure 2 shows the five dives performed by one of the divers in a single day. It is evident that the diver was not concerned about making the first dive of the day the deepest nor was there any indication of an attempt to perform the deepest part of the dive first and then work shallower. The diver was using the dive computer with no additional rules applied.

Little Cayman

One of the more frightening series of dives involves a diver on a liveaboard boat off Little Cayman who made a series of three dives to 190 fsw / 58 msw within a period of six hours. The first of the three dives appears as a straightforward decompression dive with all of the decompression requirements taken at 30 fsw / 9 msw.

The second dive, however, is a different story. The diver repeated the initial deep dive after a short surface interval. In addition, the diver proceeded back down to 105 fsw / 32 msw after reaching 30 fsw / 9 msw. Why? These are questions only the diver can answer. Following these two dives with another 190 fsw dive simply violates any and all sense of diving safety. It is a certainty that it would be very difficult to try to get a profile like this approved for human testing, though this diver chose to ignore standard diving practices.

What was the outcome of this dive series? Fortunately, the diver did not report any symptoms of DCS, and Doppler monitoring showed only the mildest grade of bubbles following the last two dives.

Bonaire

Another series involves a diver in Bonaire who performed three dives in excess of 130 fsw / 40 msw in a period of about six hours. The difference between this diver and the one from Little Cayman is that this diver tended to do a deep bounce and then spend the remainder of the dive in shallow water without returning to deeper depths. The only time there tends to be a deeper return is on the third dive, when there was a quick excursion from 45 to 70 fsw / 14 to 21 msw. This diver is at least attempting to add a bit of safety to the use of the computer by spending lots of time at the end of the dive in shallower waters.

Wreck of the *Andrea Doria*

Researcher Mike Emmerman reported dive profiles that were being used on the wreck of the *Andrea Doria*. What he observed was frightening. Divers were doing 210 fsw / 64 msw dives, waiting four to six hours, and then performing the same dive over again. Some would do two dives a day, and others did three. This was done three days in a row. More than 50 percent of the divers used dive computers. Some used dive computers that had maximum depth ranges that were shallower than the depths of the dives. Of the 16 divers on the trip, six of them presented definite signs and symptoms of DCS. The six did express some concern for their condition, but at the time none of them sought treatment.

Finally, there are those divers who do not push the dive computer to the limit, but still end up with problems.

Wreck of the *Regina*

This case involves a 53-year-old experienced female diver in excellent physical condition diving on the wreck of the *Regina* in the Great

Lakes. She performed three dives to depths of 70 to 80 fsw / 21 to 24 msw using a dive computer. (Note: pressure was calibrated in feet of sea water, although the dive was done in fresh water.) At no time was there less than five minutes of no-decompression time remaining on the dive computer. However, on the second dive, her drysuit sleeve ripped, exposing her arm to very cold water. Following the dive she had pain in her arm, but attributed it to the exposure to cold water.

The suit was fixed, and, using a dive computer, she performed the third dive. Later that evening, the pain in her arm became so severe that she could not tolerate it, and she sought treatment. A major extenuating factor, besides exposure of the arm to very cold water, was that she had no hydration during the day. (When she finally passed urine it was dark brown.) There was no way for the dive computer to know that the dry suit had ripped or that the diver was dehydrated.

The Diver's Responsibility

Divers need to realize that they have to take responsibility for their actions. They must acknowledge the fact that every time they dive there is risk involved. One of these risks is the possibility of developing DCS. A diver needs to make a risk/benefit assessment of the dive that is being planned. The goal of the assessment is to maximize the benefit while minimizing the risk.

The operations and limitations of the dive computer being used need to be understood. The more the diver understands about the equipment being used, the more educated the decisions will become.

Adding Safety Factors

Much has been said about divers adding safety factors while diving. But just how is this done with dive computers? Some divers utilize the practice of allowing no less than five to 10 minutes of no-decompression to be displayed on their dive computers. This method ensures that the algorithm is not pushed to its limit. However, this does not provide the same level of safety margin for every depth.

If the no-decompression time displayed by a dive computer for 130 fsw / 40 msw is 10 minutes, then a 5-minute safety margin will give a 50-percent safety margin. While at 30 fsw / 9 msw, where the no-decompression limit is 220 minutes, the same five-minute margin will only provide a 2.3-percent safety margin. In other words, the 5-minute margin will allow the model to be pushed to 50 percent of its limit at 130 fsw and to 97.7 percent of its limit at 30 fsw.

A method of maintaining a constant safety level margin has been proposed by Paul Heinmiller of Orca. It involves multiplying the no-decompression limits at each depth by the safety factor desired. If the diver wants a 10-percent safety margin, then all of the no-decompression times scrolled by the dive computer need to be multiplied by 0.10. This will give the shortest time permitted at each depth in order to maintain this margin. Using the previous example, the 130-fsw limit would be one minute, while the 30-fsw limit would be 22 minutes.

Diving until the no-decompression time equals zero places the diver at the actual limits of the model. Diving up to these new limits will push the model to 90 percent of its limits.

Figure 1 shows the no-decompression limits of a hypothetical dive computer and the remaining time limits required to reach various levels of the model's limits.

Once the limits have been calculated for the specific dive computer and safety level, they can be transferred to a slate and taken on the dive. The diver then makes sure that the remaining no-decompression time at any specific depth does not fall below the new time limit.

Editor's Note: Although adding a five-minute decompression stop and/or reducing dive time increases the dive safety margin, one cannot accurately express the reduced risk in quantitative terms.

Conclusions

The advent of reliable dive computers should not give people in diving an excuse to avoid teaching tables. Neither should the use of computers lend lazy divers an excuse to not learn tables or practice using them. I have talked to instructors who would have no qualms about having their student strap on a little black box that "tells their decompression status" so that they would not have to learn dive tables.

There are also cases where students show up for their first pool sessions wearing dive computers. In these cases we must ask: "What incentive do they have for learning the concepts and use of dive tables?"

No dive table or computer is 100 percent effective.

Common sense and understanding must be part of the equation. Dive computers are tools, and as such can be used to enhance the diving experience. But they are only tools — not demigods to be worshipped and followed religiously. You do not want to end up like the diver being treated for DCS who, when asked, "What type of dive computer were you using?" answered "It was yellow."

— *From March/April 1994*

AAUS Recommendations

The AAUS has held workshops dealing with diving safety and dive computer use. The following are recommendations for general diving practices compiled from three of its workshops:

• All divers relying on dive computers to plan dives and indicate or determine decompression status must have their own unit.

• On any given dive, both divers in the buddy pair must follow the most conservative dive computer.

• If the dive computer fails at any time during the dive, the dive must be terminated, and appropriate surfacing procedures should be initiated immediately.

• Divers should not dive for 24 hours before activating a dive computer to use it to control their diving.

• Once a dive computer is in use, it must not be switched off until it indicates complete outgassing has occurred or 24 hours have elapsed (whichever comes first), or if no more dives are planned over the next few days.

• When using a dive computer, non-emergent ascents are to be at the rate(s) specified for the table, or by the make and model of dive computer being used.

• Ascent rates shall not exceed 60 fsw / 18 msw per minute.

• A stop in the 10- to 30-fsw / 3- to 9-msw zone for three to five minutes is recommended on every dive.

• Repetitive and multilevel diving procedures should start the dive, or the series of dives, at the maximum planned depth, followed by subsequent dives of shallower exposures.

• Multiple deep dives should be avoided.

• Breathing 100 percent oxygen above water is preferred to in-water air procedures for omitted decompression.

• It is recommended that divers' attention be directed to emphasis on the ancillary factors to decompression risk such as: fitness to dive, adequate rest, hydration, body weight, age, and especially rate of ascent — which should not be more than 60 feet / 18 meters per minute.

• Divers are encouraged to learn and remember the signs and symptoms of decompression illness and report them promptly. This enables them to receive effective treatment as rapidly as possible and helps prevent residual injury later on.

• Breathing oxygen on the surface whenever possible via a demand regulator mask system (to ensure the highest percentage of oxygen to the patient) is recommended while awaiting treatment if decompression illness is suspected. The use of 100 percent oxygen in the water while awaiting treatment is not recommended.

Drowning in a Sea of Tears

BY G. YANCEY MEBANE, M.D.,
DAN ASSOCIATE MEDICAL
DIRECTOR & DIRECTOR,
EMS TRAINING

MIKE WEBSTER ILLUSTRATION

When down her weedy trophies and herself
And, mermaid-like, awhile they bore her up;
Which time, she chanted snatches of old lauds,
As one incapable of her own distress,
Or like a creature native and indued
Unto that element; but long it could not be
Till her garments, heavy with their drink,
Pull'd the poor wretch from her melodious lay
To muddy death.

— from Hamlet, Act IV, Scene VII, by William Shakespeare

For most people, drowning is something that happens to someone else on the evening news. Yet drowning accounted for 61 percent of all diving fatalities reported to DAN in 1991. In those states with mandatory child restraint laws, drowning has replaced motor vehicle accidents as the leading cause of accidental death among children.

Although the mechanism of drowning may be radically different between divers and children, the stages ultimately leading to these deaths are similar.

The diver with perfect buoyancy control has the most important skill to make the weightless experience of diving a pleasure. More importantly, this skill will produce an automatic response to a problem rather than an alarm response leading to panic and loss of control.

Although experienced divers do suffer drowning mishaps, there are more fatalities involving new or inexperienced divers. These divers seem to follow the same pattern of being unable to cope with a simple problem, which quickly escalates into panic, inappropriate behavior and catastrophe. Dropping a weight belt and inflating a buoyancy compensator are very simple operations, yet nearly all drowning victims, when recovered, still have their weight belts on and their BC uninflated.

Our goal is to eliminate drowning from diving. This is not an impossible task, and it can be accomplished through education. All divers must learn and relearn the skills of diving so well that they automatically maintain good buoyancy control and can immediately respond to problem situations.

Breathhold Diving

Before discussing the mechanism of drowning, an understanding of breathhold diving is useful. The breathhold diver immersed in water experiences physiologic stresses which are magnified in the drowning victim.

We humans are relatively poor breathhold divers when compared with other mammals such as whales, dolphins, seals and walrus. Yet we've been breathhold diving probably as long as we have been on earth, for one reason or another. Even today, the greatest population of commercial divers in the world are the breathholding women divers (the Ama) of the western Pacific.

An expedition of physiologists studied these divers several years ago. At that time the Ama technique was to free-dive with masks, but rarely with fins. The husband operated the boat and watched the operation. The wife descended to the bottom by holding a heavy weight released on a line. Within seconds she was at 100 feet / 30 meters where she would swim along the bottom gathering seaweed or other items. At a certain pre-arranged time the husband would wind the wife back in, followed by the weight, and the whole operation would then be repeated. This would continue for two to three hours, followed by a two- to three-hour break for rest, rewarming and nourishment. These female divers have contributed a great deal to our knowledge about breathhold diving.

Apnea (Not breathing)

The changes occurring with breathholding are a prompt decrease in the amount of oxygen in the arterial blood and an increase in carbon dioxide. Exercise increases these blood gas changes by increasing oxygen consumption and carbon dioxide production.

During breathholding, the muscle oxygen content drops rapidly, but muscle is designed to operate briefly without oxygen. The muscles consume oxygen rapidly until the stores are exhausted. However, muscles are able to keep working for a time without oxygen by using another energy source which produces lactic acid. This metabolism is inefficient, but it allows the muscle to work. As the lactic acid build-up continues, a point is reached which inhibits muscle action. Fatigue is due in part to the lactic acid accumulation, causing acidity in the muscle, which inhibits muscle action.

When breathing resumes, a tide of lactic acid comes out of the muscle and enters the bloodstream. This lactic acid must be largely eliminated before another breathhold dive can be performed. A diving mammal has an obligatory surface interval to get rid of lactic acid and recover oxygen before diving. Whale hunters take advantage of this because they know a whale coming up from a deep dive must stay near the surface and breathe for a time.

The same thing happens in humans, but not as dramatically. That's why repeat breathhold dives become more difficult.

Immersion & Increased Ambient Pressure

The heart, blood vessels and lungs are the major target organs of the effects of immersion and pressure. Breathhold divers often breathe between dives through a snorkel or while immersed to the neck.

Snorkeler — When breathing through a snorkel, the airway remains at atmospheric pressure, while the chest is subjected to the weight of the surrounding water. This produces a pressure gradient from the chest wall to the airway. The effect is to reduce the volume of the lungs and to impair ventilation. The snorkel increases dead air space, furthering impairment. The work of breathing increases because of the weight of the water surrounding the chest and the increase in airway resistance.

Pressure — The hydrostatic compression of the body and loss of gravitational forces leads to a few generally favorable changes. The compression of the limbs by water pressure leads to a large central shift in blood volume, dilating the central veins and increasing blood return to the heart. This autotransfusion plus negative pressure breathing increases the output of blood from the heart. The left atrium becomes distended (due to increased venous return and central blood pooling), which has been implicated as the cause of increased urine production.

The effects of pressure on air spaces in the body result from the principles expressed by Boyle's law. The pressure increase results in decreased volume of non-rigid gas-filled spaces. As the breathhold diver descends, the lungs and chest wall begin collapsing, resulting in less water displacement, and the diver becomes negatively buoyant.

When the diver's lungs are compressed to the smallest possible volume, there can be no further compression, and continued descent leads to lung damage. The depth limit of breathhold dives seems to be related to the ratio of total lung volume to residual volume (lung volume at maximum exhalation). Thus, an individual with a large total lung volume and a small residual volume would be able to achieve greater depths because of that.

The most complicated physiological process to understand in breathhold exposures is related to Dalton's law of partial pressures. As the total pressure of a gas mixture increases, the partial pressure of each gas increases linearly, therefore there are marked changes in partial pressures in the alveoli during deep breathhold dives.

Alveolar pressures during dive — As the diver descends, the partial pressure of oxygen rapidly increases despite the increased oxygen consumption of exercise. Likewise, the partial pressure of carbon dioxide rises, and it is rapidly driven into the bloodstream.

As carbon dioxide is highly diffusible and soluble, it may be stored in the periphery in great quantities. There will be minimal carbon dioxide elevation, but the diver can easily suppress the urge to breathe for a while because of the high partial pressure of oxygen in the lung. Thus, the diver is able to prolong breathholding the deeper he goes. At some point in the dive, his total carbon dioxide level rises until breathhold breakpoint is reached.

On ascent both the carbon dioxide and oxygen levels fall quickly so that the diver may have a decreased urge to breathe and may become unconscious because of the low oxygen content. As there is no significant carbon dioxide elevation to stimulate the respiratory center, the problem of breathhold dives becomes one of available oxygen. During descent, the oxygen is readily delivered to the tissues because of the steep partial pressure gradient. On ascent, the available oxygen falls rapidly and there is sudden oxygen deficiency.

Hyperventilation & Drowning

Most swimmers know that underwater swimming can be extended by hyperventilating. This works because the respiratory drive comes from carbon dioxide levels in the bloodstream and hyperventilating lowers the level. The hazard is the possibility of running out of oxygen before the carbon dioxide rises enough to trigger respiration. Consequently, hyperventilation before breathhold diving is extremely dangerous and a common cause of drowning.

Now that you've seen some of the demands placed on us by breath-hold diving, you should understand the similarity with the drowning process, which occurs in stages:

1. At first the victim fights to stay afloat while hyperventilating, resulting in negative buoyancy. At this moment a panic state has developed so that self-rescue is impossible.

2. Submergence occurs, and reflex breathholding begins. The compression of the chest by water pressure increases negative buoyancy, and the urge to breathe becomes stronger and stronger as the victim consumes the remaining oxygen.

3. After one to three minutes, the combination of cerebral inhibition by oxygen lack and the strong urge to breathe caused by carbon dioxide excess causes the victim to breathe underwater. The individual is semiconscious, but begins to swallow water reflexively in order to prevent entrance of water into the lungs. Consequently, most victims will have a stomach full of water.

4. As oxygen deficiency worsens and carbon dioxide increases, the urge to breathe becomes stronger. Reflex swallowing gives way to a strong, deep breath. The lungs then fill with water causing the individual to become more negatively buoyant while continuing to breathe unconsciously.

5. The oxygen deficiency becomes profound and brain function becomes depressed, resulting in inhibition of respiration. The heart rate slows, and ultimately a cardiac arrest occurs with a terminal seizure.

For resuscitation, it is very important to identify the time that the individual was last seen breathing. After the victim submerges, underwater breathing will begin in three to four minutes. If the victim is recovered before underwater breathing begins, resuscitation may be accomplished with little difficulty.

After another three to four minutes, profound oxygen lack occurs leading to cardiac arrest. Following cardiac arrest another four to six minutes may elapse before brain tissue is damaged past the possibility of recovery. The total time of submergence with chance of recovery then can be expected to be 10 to 12 minutes at most. *However, because of thermal considerations, this is not always correct.*

Possibility of Resuscitation

The critical factor in determining the possibility of resuscitation is the length of time without oxygen. For that reason, ventilation and circulation must be accomplished as rapidly as possible. It is unlikely that a victim who has experienced long submersion and prolonged resuscitation attempts will survive. However, a number of victims have been successfully resuscitated with full recovery following long submersions in extremely cold water. If rescuers do not have an accurate time of submersion, it is reasonable to attempt resuscitation at the scene unless there are obvious physical signs of death.

The outlook is poor in persons who have a core temperature below 82°F / 28°C; have been immersed more than 50 minutes; have life-threatening injuries; or are more than four hours from definitive care. In such a situation CPR might be discontinued before definitive care is available if, in the opinion of the most qualified medical person present, the response to resuscitation has been inadequate.

The *Mammalian Diving Reflex,* which is present to some degree in all mammals and is well-developed in animals such as seals, whales and walrus, has been offered as a partial mechanism for survival after long immersion in cold water. This reflex, which produces slowing of breathing and pulse, is triggered by exposure of the face to cold water and causes shunting of blood from the gut, skin and muscles to those tissues very sensitive to the lack of oxygen, such as the brain, heart and lungs.

This has been a well-publicized response which has been given credit for a few "miraculous" recoveries, but its significance in humans above the age of 2 is questioned by many authorities.

Equally important in survival in cold-water drowning are the effects of cold water on the body. Immersion hypothermia is marked by cooling of the brain, slowing of circulation and slowing of metabolism. Hypothermia can kill, but it can also protect.

The areas of greatest heat loss are the head, neck and groin, due to the large surface area with arteries close to the skin. The brain cools faster than other tissues, causing a drop in oxygen requirement. As hypothermia reduces oxygen needs dramatically, the available oxygen can supply the body's needs for a longer period of time. The maximum length of time is unknown, but at present CPR is advised for underwater exposures up to one hour. Attempts past one hour are valid, but generally unsuccessful so far.

Among the factors that influence successful resuscitation is age. The younger individual is more apt to recover since the Mammalian Diving Reflex is most active in the young. Also the rate of temperature fall is maximal because of a relatively larger surface area and lack of adequate insulation. A short exposure means a better chance at survival, but there are reports of survival after 40 minutes of exposure.

Death from immersion hypothermia can occur in several ways. The sudden shock of entering ice-cold water can result in immediate ventricular fibrillation before cooling has occurred. An example might be the good swimmer who falls into icy water and never surfaces. The involuntary deep breath on sudden cold-water exposure may occur underwater and cause drowning.

More commonly there is the relentless reduction of core temperature from surface cooling, with delirium and unconsciousness, followed by drowning. Death is preceded by moderate levels of immersion hypothermia so that prolonged submersion can be compatible with complete recovery.

Occasionally someone supported by a personal flotation device in cold water may lose consciousness and develop cardiac arrest from hypothermia without asphyxiating. Such individuals can sometimes make a full neurological recovery after prolonged exposure.

Circulatory arrest may occur from cooling and drowning separately, simultaneously or sequentially. Each process is distinct and may require different management.

The Mammalian Diving Reflex is not operative in water temperatures above 70°F / 21°C. Fortunately, most U.S. waters are below 70°F, except in the South during the summer; and even there below 10 to 15 feet / 3 to 4.5 meters, the water temperature remains below 70°F most of the year. Clean water is an important factor, since badly polluted water also decreases the chances of survival.

Immediate and efficient CPR is the most important survival factor. When the face of the victim is taken out of the water, the protective Mammalian Diving Reflex shuts down. Intact survival depends on immediate resuscitation at the scene of the accident. Even a few minutes' delay may be critical as far as recovery of the brain is concerned. Mouth-to-mouth resuscitation should be instituted in the water and closed-chest massage as soon as possible.

Immediate management should be to maintain ventilation, oxygenation, and circulatory support. At the scene, the airway must be secured. It is extremely important to remember that the hypothermic individual is very susceptible to severely abnormal heart rhythms, particularly if the airway is disturbed.

The ABCs of CPR (maintenance of Airway, Breathing and Circulation) apply to near-drowning victims. The airway should be assessed and cleared of any debris or vomitus by the finger-sweep maneuver. Due to the risk of vomiting and aspiration, the Heimlich abdominal thrust should not be done unless the airway is obstructed.

Do not try to rewarm the victim at the scene or in transport by external heat sources. The victim should be provided with insulation in the form of blankets, dry clothing or other materials so that passive rewarming may occur. It can be very dangerous to rewarm a body from the outside. Sudden circulation from the extremities may flood the heart and lungs with stagnant, cold blood.

What about the near-drowning victim who was rescued and required little or no resuscitation and now appears normal? Any near-drowning victim who was submerged for more than a minute, was cyanotic or required resuscitation should be transported to a hospital for observation. Even a victim who did not require resuscitation, but did require rescue, should be carefully observed. There are many reports of near-drowning victims, who appeared normal on initial assessment, and even had normal chest X-rays, yet developed fatal complications as long as 12 hours later.

Though we have reviewed the process of drowning, we have not solved the puzzle of prevention. That solution will require us to become better skilled divers, instructors, diving technicians and physicians.

— *From March/April 1993*

The Occidental Tourist

BY G. YANCEY MEBANE, M.D.,
DAN ASSOCIATE MEDICAL
DIRECTOR & DIRECTOR,
EMS TRAINING

CINDI COURTER PHOTO

Every year thousands of divers travel to exotic locations throughout the world to experience the pleasure of diving in a remote, unspoiled area. However, many of these divers visit countries where tropical diseases are endemic.

Frequently, information on avoiding diseases during the trip is not part of the diver's preparation. If you are planning such a trip, spend a little time (and money) to acquaint yourself with health information for the traveler.

We will review briefly some of the health concerns you may encounter on your trip and suggest resources for further information.

There are an increasing number of travel clinics (a branch of medicine known as emporiatrics) which offer counseling and preventive treatment. You may find such a clinic listed in the yellow pages for your community. A pretravel visit to a travel clinic will help you to be prepared for the health conditions in the areas you visit.

The destination will determine the health risks, as it is certain that a visit to Hawaii or Lake Superior has different risks than a visit to Malaysia. The health hazards likely to be encountered in a developing nation include the exposure to bacterial, viral and parasitic disease as well as limited medical resources for treatment. You may avoid these problems by appropriate preventive measures.

Immunizations

The most important pretravel precaution is to obtain appropriate immunizations. All standard immunizations should be brought up to date. The World Health Organization actually recommends that a five-year booster schedule be followed for routine immunization rather than the five- to 10-year schedule as followed in the U.S. These include: tetanus and diphtheria, measles, mumps, rubella and polio.

Other immunizations will depend on the destination. Certain countries and travel areas have specific requirements. Smallpox vaccination is no longer required and is not given. Yellow fever vaccination is required by some countries for travelers arriving from an area known to harbor yellow fever. Yellow fever is a viral illness transmitted by mosquitoes. There is no known treatment and fatalities do occur. Some countries also require cholera vaccine, but the vaccine is not very effective and not medically advised. Americans practically do not get cholera in endemic areas (risk is 1/500,000 travelers).

Hepatitis A is a viral illness of the liver and is a worldwide problem associated with food and water contamination. Prior to your trip, consult with your physician on the latest and most effective protection. The quality of the travel setting may not be protective, as the world-class hotel may be just as likely a source of exposure as the street vendor.

Hepatitis B is transmitted by certain body fluids and the vaccine is advised for anyone who will have close personal or sexual contact with persons who may be carriers of the virus. Ordinary tourists may not need the vaccine unless they are going to be sexually active or they are health care workers.

Typhoid fever is a risk in some areas, but there is a well-tolerated, oral vaccine which is very effective. It should be considered if you will be exposed to food or water in rural areas for a long period of time. The oral vaccine is given as a single capsule taken every other day for four doses. There are no reactions and immunity lasts about four years.

Rabies is a risk in villages in Africa, Asia, and Central or South America. Consider the vaccine if planning on an extended trip into the villages of these areas. Your personal physician may advise pneumococcal and influenza vaccines.

Other vaccinations will depend on the itinerary, lifestyle, and length of the trip.

Malaria

The most serious health hazard to the tropical traveler is malaria. Malaria is an organism transmitted to humans by the bite of an infected *Anopheles* mosquito.

Malaria endemic areas occur worldwide and prophylaxis is essential for travelers to these areas. There are medications which offer protection. The most commonly used drug is choloroquine phosphate which is safe, highly effective and well-tolerated. There are resistant strains to choloroquine in some of the major tourist areas around the world and other medications are needed. Further information can be obtained from the Centers for Disease Control and Prevention (see Resources). Personal protection is probably the best way to prevent malaria as well as other diseases transmitted by the mosquito. When outdoors in a mosquito area you should wear clothing that covers most of the body and use an insect repellent that contains at least 30 percent DEET. Stronger concentration can be used with caution. Between dusk and dawn remain indoors in a well-screened area and use mosquito nets and repellents for sleeping.

Schistosomiasis

The *Schistosoma* parasite is a fluke which has a life cycle involving a freshwater snail. The disease is found in rural tropical and subtropical areas including the Middle East, Africa, eastern South America, and parts of the Caribbean. A person bathing in or drinking fresh water harboring the snail may encounter the free-swimming larvae which can penetrate unbroken skin. The disease which may result can have serious consequences. Chlorinated and salt water are safe for swimming, but swimming or bathing in freshwater in endemic areas is not safe. Water for bathing should be heated to above 122°F / 50°C for more than five minutes or allowed to stand for more than 48 hours or chemically treated.

Traveler's Diarrhea

Traveler's diarrhea is the most common complaint of the tourist and may be encountered anywhere in the world.

All travel involves a risk of diarrhea. Certain areas are very high risk, and the risk may reach 50 percent. Your best defense is to develop safe eating and drinking habits when in high risk areas. A safe food is one that is steaming hot (not merely cooked), has a high acid content (like citrus), has a high sugar content (jellies and syrups) or one that is dry (bread). Anything that is moist and warm or at room temperature is unsafe. This includes sauces, salads, and anything on a buffet. Citrus fruits and all fruits that you peel yourself are safe. (Be sure your hands are clean). Unpeelable fruits (e.g., grapes, berries) are not safe. An unpeeled tomato is not safe; a peeled tomato is safe. Watermelon is sometimes injected with water to make it heavier and may be unsafe.

Untreated water is not safe, but bottled drinks, wine and beer can be considered safe. If you purchase bottled water, be sure that the seal is intact. I have seen children refilling water bottles at a town well which they then sold to unsuspecting tourists as safe water.

Eating Abroad

Peace Corps Rule — Boil It, Cook It,
Peel It or Forget It.
Hot and steaming is safe.
Bread is safe.
Rice and noodles are safe if cooked and hot.
Fruit is safe if peeled by you.
Water may not be safe, even for brushing teeth.
Sealed bottled water is safe.
Sealed carbonated drinks are safe.

These simple precautions will give you a much better-than-even chance that you will avoid diarrhea even in the worst circumstance. There are medications that can slightly improve your chances, but not without risk. Sixty percent of travelers who do not take preventive medications in high risk areas do not get diarrhea. Not taking a medication has many advantages. It is convenient, avoids drug side effects and doesn't cost anything. The disease you are trying to prevent is uncomfortable, but not life-threatening, is easily treated, and will go away without any treatment. Most travel physicians do not advise antibiotics to prevent diarrhea because serious reactions to the antibiotic are about as common as serious diarrhea.

Self-treatment of the disease, if it occurs, is possible with a little preparation. You should have the following in your travel gear: a thermometer, an antidiarrheal and an antibiotic prescribed by your physician. React quickly at any sign of illness.

Traveler's Checklist

Malaria prophylaxis
Traveler's diarrhea kit —
    antibiotic (prescribed) & antidiarrheal (prescribed)
General risk avoidance
Insect precautions
Medical assistance abroad
Safe eating and drinking habits
Safe sexual practices
Traveler's health insurance
Traveler's medical kit

Vaccinations / Immunizations

Routine — diphtheria-tetanus, measles-mumps-rubella, & poliomyelitis

Travel-specific — cholera, yellow fever, hepatitis A, hepatitis B, meningococcus, rabies, typhoid fever

If you have a watery stool, take your temperature. If you are feverish (100°F / 37.7°C) or have a bloody stool take only the antibiotic. If you do not have a fever or bloody stool take both the antibiotic and the anti-diarrheal. This will usually have you back in action in about 12-15 hours. If symptoms do not improve within about 48 hours you will need medical attention because of the possibility of a parasitic infection.

Sexually Transmitted Disease

The traveler who practices high risk behaviors may encounter a number of sexually transmitted diseases. The World Health Organization estimates 10 million adults infected with HIV [*Note: There are 25.5 million estimated adult HIV infections as of mid-1996. —Ed.*] Hepatitis B, syphilis, gonorrhea and other sexually transmitted diseases are widespread. Treatment is frequently complicated by drug-resistance on the part of the organism or the lack of any effective treatment at all.

Be aware of the risks of these diseases. If sexual contact is expected or possible, take latex condoms. Abstention is a prudent alternative.

Airline Travel

There are certain illnesses which make travel on a commercial aircraft difficult. However, the same illness probably prevents the person from diving. You should be aware of the restrictions on flying after diving because of the exposure to altitude.

Long international trips result in more than usual fatigue for several reasons. The sudden shift in time zones results in the well-known jet lag. In addition, the noise, low humidity, irritants in the cabin air, and inactivity all contribute to a feeling of fatigue. There are a plethora of remedies for jet lag, none of which are particularly effective.

Avoiding alcohol and caffeine, and using a sedative for sleeping will help to minimize the problem. It is wise to plan on resting the first day after traveling through multiple time zones.

Motor Vehicle Travel

Motor vehicle accidents are the leading cause of death for the traveler. Nonfatal injuries occur about once for every 500 travelers. The risks in a developing nation may be increased because of inaccessible medical care and the possibility of contaminated blood, instruments, and needles in medical facilities. HIV infection has been reported several times following hospital treatment for motor vehicle injury.

Insurance for medical evacuation in the event of a major injury or illness is very important.

— From September/October 1992

Resources

Questions / Emergencies / Medical / Insurance

Divers Alert Network (DAN)
The Peter B. Bennett Center
6 West Colony Place
Durham, NC 27705

Questions / Medical Information Line
(919) 684-2948

Dive Emergencies
(919) 684-8111 or (919) 684-4DAN (-4326)

Dive Insurance
(800) 446-2671

Books, Publications and Other Sources of Information

**Centers for Disease
Control and Prevention (CDC)**
*Traveler's Information
Hotline* (404) 332-4559

DAN TravelAssist *From the US,
Canada, Puerto Rico, the Bahamas,
British and U.S. Virgin Islands call
(800) 326-3822 or (800) DAN EVAC
(202) 296-9620 (collect from anywhere in the world)*

**Health Information
for International Travel**
HHS Publication No. [CDC]
90-8280
Supt. of Documents,
Government Printing Office
Washington, DC 20402
(202) 783-3238

**International Association for
Medical Assistance to Travelers
(IAMAT)**
417 Center Street
Lewiston, NY 14092
(716) 754-4883

**A Medical Guide to
Hazardous Marine Life**
Paul S. Auerbach, M.D.
DAN Products
(800) 446-2671

Travelers' Health
Random House
201 E. 50th St.
New York, NY 10022

**International Travel
Health Guide**
Stuart R. Rose, M.D.
DAN Products
(800) 446-2671

**DAN Dive & Travel
Medical Guide**
Available to DAN members
800) 446-2671

An Introduction to Stinging Marine Life Injuries

BY PAUL S. AUERBACH, M.D., M.S.

The comments I offer here are not based solely on my own reflections, but represent discussions that are ongoing among medical experts who treat patients with marine stings and who study the animals that generate these injuries.

First, a sting is not a sting. That is, while there are certain circumstances in which the tentacle "prints" are so classic in appearance that they implicate a specific creature and preclude any other (such as with the typical frosted and cross-hatched skin lesions from *Chironex fleckeri* — the box jellyfish), this is often not the case. Therefore, unless the animal is positively identified, the person stung makes a presumption of what has "gotten" him, based upon the geographic location, season, nature of injury and common fauna of the marine region. That's why it is very important for divers to learn how to identify potentially dangerous animals at their diving destination.

One of the messages is that an allergic reaction is possible to virtually any foreign substance (commonly a protein) to which a human has been previously sensitized. Therefore, every diver with known sensitivities should consider carrying an allergy kit with epinephrine and an antihistamine and know how to use it.

This brings us to the matter of first aid. There is a perpetual controversy over what to use to immediately (at-the-scene first aid) counteract jellyfish (or fire coral or anemone) venom. The experts have been wrestling with this one a long time, because we want to give people the best advice. Unlike man, all jellyfish are not created equal. The venoms they produce carry many chemical structural similarities, but there are also differences which cause the venoms to withstand various decontaminants used by rescuers.

Some jellyfish venoms seem to be neutralized better with acetic acid (vinegar) than with alcohol, and some better with bicarbonate (baking soda) than with acetic acid. Many people claim that they have obtained relief with the application of meat tenderizer (papain), raw papaya or papaya latex, diluted ammonia, urine, benzocaine and numerous other substances. Who can argue with success?

Then there's the question, "Does fresh water improve or worsen a sting?" I have personally watched a woman stung by a Portuguese man-of-war in the waters off Hyannis, Mass., be driven from a mild to a severe reaction with shock by the casual application of cold, wet towels. The pain was relieved instantaneously with isopropyl (rubbing) alcohol sponging. But some Australian investigators have watched nematocysts (stinging cells) under the microscope fire off their lethal darts during application of alcohol, while they are paralyzed by acetic acid. To make it even more confusing, lifeguards in Florida report that a brisk freshwater shower controls the stings of certain jellyfish, while it worsens the stings of others. Some Australians apply cold packs to jellyfish stings for pain relief.

The best we can do right now is make recommendations that will get the greatest number of persons stung out of distress while putting the least at risk. Take these suggestions to heart, learn the pressure immobilization technique for venom containment and know how to call for an evacuation to a facility that stocks antivenin. (And remember, as a DAN member, if you ever do need an evacuation due to a marine-life injury, that evacuation is covered by your DAN *TravelAssist* benefits. The phone number is on your membership card.)

Scientists in the field on marine-life injuries are learning all the time. For example, we have received recent information from multiple investigators concerning the true nature of "sea lice," which is the misapplied term used by divers to describe what the medical community accurately calls "sea bather's eruption." Sea lice are parasites that feed on fish, not people, and sea bather's eruption is caused by larval and juvenile forms of anemones, jellyfish and other coelenterates.

One day we are hopeful that marine biologists will be able to test every species of jellyfish and nematocyst-armed stinging creatures with a broad spectrum of chemical decontaminants, so that we can tell you what works and what doesn't for each animal. Until then, learn how to identify the primary offenders, pursue training in first aid for marine-life injury injuries and learn how to dive without touching fragile, and potentially dangerous, marine animals.

— *From January/February 1994*
Edited for inclusion in The Best of Alert Diver

Things That Stings

BY JOLIE BOOKSPAN, PH.D.

— CARTOON FROM SEPT/OCT 1995

What's the difference between poisonous and venomous? Here's a hint: Pufferfish are poisonous but not venomous; stonefish are venomous but not poisonous.

Give up? Here's another hint: Have you ever heard of a venomous mushroom?

Probably not, because a venomous creature has a specialized anatomy to deliver the mixture of chemical compounds called venom. A poisonous beastie, on the other hand, can only produce and store the stuff, so you must eat it in order for it to do any harm.

Pufferfish, like porcupine fish, ocean sunfish and filefish, manufacture a poison that accumulates in the tissues — particularly in the gonads and liver. Even though illness and death have occurred from eating them without careful preparation, divers handle them safely, frightening them into hapless basketballs for entertainment. Not so for the stonefish, which is safe to eat but whose sting can kill.

Why Do They Sting Us?

To answer this question, you have to look at the end that's doing the stinging.

Stings can be for offense or defense. Offensive stinging is used to kill prey. The venom delivery system is generally located near the mouth, as with the anemone and sea snake.

Defensive venoms guard against attacks by predators and are located around the tail, such as is found in the stingray. Since defensive venoms evolved as deterrents, they usually pack less punch than the offensive sting.

Hollywood aside, fish don't go and bite us for fun. Venomous creatures are almost always slowpokes or fixed to the bottom. (The term for this is *sessile* animals.) They sting defensively as a last resort if they're stepped on or cornered. Those who sting offensively for food usually want morsels smaller than themselves.

That's not to say that offensive systems won't sting unintentionally. Jellyfish can swim weakly by jet propulsion but mostly drift around with current, tide and wind. When a diver swims into jellyfish, stinging cells called nematocysts trigger automatically. These cells continue to deliver venom until they are exhausted, as long as they maintain contact with the diver's skin — even after the diver has left the water. When jellyfish wash ashore, their nematocysts can brave many hours drying in the sun and still fire upon contact.

What Happens When They Sting Us?

Venoms are unstable mixtures of pieces of protein molecules called peptides and large protein molecules called enzymes. Enzymes are present in all living things, controlling the speed of the biochemical reactions that go on all the time in every cell. The foreign enzymes of a venom can upset the human enzymes' ability to control reactions in the body. When the respiratory, nervous or circulatory systems are affected, the consequences are severe.

When foreign proteins enter the body, they are referred to as antigens. The body responds by producing its own proteins called antibodies, which react specifically with the invading antigens. Powerful venoms, however, overload the antigen-antibody reaction and can affect the body's systems.

A diver's reaction to a venom can be classified as allergic, toxic or sensitized. *Allergic* means that someone is hypersensitive to a substance that is harmless to others. The term *toxic* is more universal. *Sensitization* suggests high susceptibility to a second sting at a later date from the first — when the first sting caused no serious symptoms.

When the body is sensitive or allergic to a foreign substance, it releases a substance called histamine. Histamine is present in all tissues of the body all the time and is a breakdown product of histidine, a common amino acid. Normally histamine works to dilate small blood vessels.

When a reaction releases lots of histamine, blood vessels become more permeable, which in turn allows fluids to escape from blood plasma. This problem, called extravasation, results in swelling. Blood vessel dilation increases local blood flow and causes the warmth and redness associated with stings. Pain is believed to come from the injury itself, from chemical substances released and from local pressure of swollen tissue. These four characteristics, medically termed tumor (swelling), calor (warmth), rubor (redness) and dolor (pain) are the hallmarks of inflammation. A substance that blocks the inflammatory effects of histamine is called antihistamine.

How Do You Treat Stings?

The most common stings are by coelenterates (pronounced: sell-EN-tuh-rates). Coelenterates are the almost 10,000 species of invertebrates like jellyfish, anemones, hydroids and corals. Only a dozen or so of the more than 500 species of jellyfish are venomous, and of those, only a few have potent stings

The term "coelenterate" means "hollow cavity" because these beasties are constructed of only a mouth and a way to get food into it. Their feeding mechanism consists of cooperating tentacles liberally armed with nematocysts. There are more than 30 kinds of nematocysts, but two main types concern us. One is a cell with a miniature harpoon inside. A hair protruding from each nematocyst fires the stinger when touched. The other type clings to the skin by a sticky mucus and then deposits venom. Each can only fire once, but there may be millions of nematocysts per tentacle.

Jellyfish

The composition of the tentacles of jellyfish, like the Portuguese man-of-war and the sea wasp, is very close to that of sea water, which makes them translucent and hard to see. Their tentacles trail in the water in clusters from a few inches to 100 feet / 30 meters in length. Fish and divers swim into them and don't know it until a reaction begins soon after contact.

Divers fare better than the fish who are paralyzed, drawn into the mouth by the tentacles and eaten. Reaction to coelenterate stings is dose-dependent and subject to individual variation. The first response is pain or a prickly sensation, then an itchy rash, blistering and swelling from histamine release. The characteristic welts left by the jellyfish called lion's mane are familiar to fans of Sir Arthur Conan Doyle, whose story "The Adventure of the Lion's Mane" recounts a man's injury and subsequent death after his encounter with the creature. The man-of-war and Australian box jellyfish (called the *Chironex fleckeri*) stings are serious. Pain can be severe enough to knock divers unconscious, causing them to drown. Effects range from nausea, fever and delirium, to paralysis, respiratory difficulty and death from cardiorespiratory collapse. If someone is stung by an Australian box jellyfish, be prepared to inflate the person's BC, get them back to safety and, for extreme cases, administer artificial respiration or CPR.

According to Dr. Paul Auerbach's *A Medical Guide to Hazardous Marine Life,* whether you're in Australia or Aruba, once you've stabilized a diver suffering from a jellyfish sting, here are some general first aid guidelines:
• If necessary, rinse the affected area with sea water. (Do not use fresh water, because in some cases it makes the nematocyst cells fire.)
• Soak the injury with vinegar. (In some cases, baking soda will work well.)
• Remove any large tentacles with forceps. (Don't try to remove them with bare hands.)
• Rinse the area well, then apply shaving cream and shave the affected area. This helps get the remaining nematocyst cells off the skin.
• Soak the area again with vinegar, then apply a thin coating of hydrocortisone lotion or cream.

Venoms lower local tissue resistance to bacterial infection. That and the high humidity in ocean areas may make a small sting fester for a long time, so keep the wound clean and dry. Applying a thin layer of antiseptic ointment would also be appropriate. Anesthetic creams help reduce pain, and hydrocortisone topicals may reduce the itch; however, steroid preparations should not be used if there is any sign of an infection. Divers with sensitivities or allergies should see their doctors for a prescription antihistamine and epinephrine for their dive first-aid kits. Take a first-aid class. Keep your tetanus shots current, too.

Hydroids and Fire Coral

Stinging hydroids look like fluffy plants but are animals. Fire coral is not a coral at all — it's a stationary hydroid colony. Both hydroids and fire coral are more closely related to jellyfish than hard or soft corals. Treat hydroid and fire coral stings the same way as jellyfish stings.

Corals

Coral polyps have plenty of nematocyst cells along their tentacles, but most often it's their hard external skeleton that gives divers problems. This skeleton easily cuts bare skin, and the wound infects just as easily from bits of organic matter and water-borne bacteria pushed under the skin. Clean out coral cuts with soap and clean, fresh water, then hydrogen peroxide. After that, apply a thin layer of bacitracin ointment and cover the wound. You should continue to monitor and clean coral cuts on a daily basis.

Sponges

Sponges don't have nematocysts, but sharp spicules that puncture the skin, making entry portals for toxins, irritants and germs. Sponges may produce their own toxins or get them from the bacteria, fungi and algae that colonize them. First aid is similar to jellyfish stings (except instead of shaving the area, apply tape and pull it off to get the spicules out), though with sponge-related injuries, you're likely to suffer a more prolonged skin irritation that may require medical attention.

Venomous Fish

Of the more than 200 known species of venomous fish, four are most common: stingrays, lionfish, stonefish and catfish. First aid for all these animal injuries is similar, but stingrays deserve a closer look, because they pose a triple threat.

Stingrays cause tissue damage with their sharp tails, which can hold from one to four spines. The jagged cut from a ray's tail is prone to infection. The spine, located in the base of the tail, is covered with a membrane called an integumentary sheath that tears to release venom from ventrolateral grooves along the side of the sheath. Venom releases as long as bits of the sheath remain in the wound. A blue area often surrounds the wound because of the swelling from the venom.

Keep the unlucky person quiet — activity circulates the venom — and flush the wound with clean, fresh water. Next, soak the wound in nonscalding hot water for 30 to 90 minutes. Venom proteins are unstable compounds and are easily denatured, or permanently changed in composition, by heat. When soaking the wound(s), water temperatures should not exceed 113°F / 45°C. Don't get carried away by getting the water too hot, or you'll treat a burn next. The best way to test the water temperature is to use your hands. (Avoid, if at all possible, using the injured person's extremities for the temperature test because the sting may have affected his/her nervous system and he/she might not be able to distinguish temperature effectively.)

Removing the barb is no mean feat. The retropointed barbs may tear on the way out, but if any can be removed easily, it will be more comfortable in the long run to do so. Leave the barb in place if it is located in the chest or neck. Don't tape or sew the wound shut unless it's absolutely necessary to stop bleeding. And in any case, when you've been barbed, so to speak, see a doctor right away.

How Do You Prevent Stings?

When in doubt, don't touch. Better yet, don't touch anyway. Don't handle the reef — doing so destroys it. Listen to pre-dive environmental briefings. Keep hands out of rocky holes — somebody venomous may live there. If you're wading, shuffle feet on sandy bottoms to warn buried stingrays. A sponge won't jump off a rock and bite you, so take its picture — don't squeeze it. You'll be considerate to the reef and to your immune system.

Protective clothing thwarts most stings. But there are exceptions to the rule: The spines of stonefish, stingrays, sea urchins and starfish, such as the crown-of-thorns starfish, can pierce most protective clothing. And the man-of-war has nematocysts which can pierce a rubber glove.

In Australia, lifeguards had been known to use pantyhose before the diveskin was developed. Most divers, however, prefer diveskins or light wetsuits, which are also good against sunburn. But don't consider that a license to go dragging your body all over the reef. Besides being impolite, breaking up coral stirs up larval forms of stingy things that lodge under bathing suits and sting away.

Also, nix tormenting the reef creatures. If you frighten them, they may defend themselves. And remember to watch the end that does the stinging.

— *From January/February 1994*

HEALTH AND FITNESS

Fitness and Diving

Buddied up, they make a safer, more enjoyable pastime —
and contribute to the overall quality of your life

BY G. YANCEY MEBANE, M.D., DAN ASSOCIATE MEDICAL DIRECTOR &
DIRECTOR, EMS TRAINING

Fitness and diving; fitness for diving; fitness in diving; fitness to dive. As divers we've heard these expressions in our training classes, in dive publications and in discussions among our fellow divers. Although stated in a slightly different fashion in each case, we are essentially linking the ideas that physical conditioning and scuba diving, like good dive buddies, work better when they're paired up.

STEVE BARNETT PHOTO

Good physical conditioning is invaluable to us as scuba divers — and, quite simply, as human beings. The truth is, when we feel good, we perform well, no matter what we're doing. And the way we feel — both physically and mentally — may directly affect us when we dive.

Not all diving requires measures of great strength or endurance. Unlike commercial divers, recreational divers may select the time and place for their dives to match them to their own strengths and skills. We all agree, however, that no matter how simple and easy the dive, physical fitness actually adds to the pleasure and safety of the event.

Every dive requires some degree of work and exercise, which is often greater than the everyday demands on a body. This intensified muscular activity in turn increases the work of the heart in delivering oxygen and fuel to the exercising muscles. The heart and blood vessels respond to this increased load by adjusting blood flow and increasing its output via the heart.

Activities associated with diving — carrying heavy gear, climbing ladders and swimming — all require increased oxygen consumption. The normal heart has considerable reserve to help meet these demands, but in order to maintain this reserve at high levels you must maintain a program of "physical fitness."

ERIC HANAUER PHOTO

What Is Fitness for Diving?

What do we mean by physical fitness? Very simply: It is endurance or aerobic capacity measured by your response in oxygen consumption to an increasing work load. Your fitness level is determined primarily by your cardiovascular system. It is possible to have great musculoskeletal strength (as in a body builder) but still have poor cardiovascular reserve.

Near the age of 30, both physical strength and exercise capacity begin a decline which continues throughout the remaining lifespan. The body's ability to achieve maximum use of oxygen in energy production reaches a peak in the late 20s and then begins a decline. This deconditioning is the result of many causes. Some are fundamental changes in physiology that come with aging. And if you follow an inactive lifestyle, these changes may be accelerated.

This reduction in physical fitness may be rapid or slow, depending on each individual's physical condition and endurance training. The decline in physical endurance can be slowed, however, by certain conditioning programs. Known as the training effect, regular aerobic exercise programs augment and improve general physical performance.

You can measure your cardiovascular reserve with an exercise stress test. This usually involves exercise on a treadmill or a stationary bicycle while response to the exercise is monitored with an electrocardiogram. Sometimes oxygen consumption is also measured. This test is often used to detect coronary artery disease, but it is quite useful to assess overall exercise capacity and to determine the response of the heart to increasing work load. Although the exercise associated with diving may use different muscle groups than those used in walking or bicycling, the cardiovascular load is similar for each activity.

Six Steps To Start Up

Dr. Cooper lists these guidelines for a safe exercise program:

- Have a checkup by a physician.

- Prepare with a proper diet, proper clothing and equipment and proper workout conditions.

- Warm up thoroughly, stretch adequately.

- Choose your proper performance objective and avoid overexertion.

- Monitor your exercise and recovery pulse regularly.

- Cool down thoroughly.

Are You in Shape?

The question may be easy to answer — or it could be difficult. Begin by asking yourself about those risk factors which are well recognized to be associated with heart disease:

KEN BONDY PHOTO

- *Does anyone in your immediate family have a cardiovascular disease?* Try to remember if a close relative has died prematurely of heart attack or stroke.
- *Are you a male?* Cardiovascular disease appears earlier in men than in women, but as both sexes become older the incidence tends to even out.
- *How do you react to stress?* Stress and stress-producing personality behavior patterns may place a strain on the heart. The body's hormonal systems behave today just as they have done since the Stone Age: When faced with a challenge, they speed up the heart rate and increase blood pressure to get you ready for "fight or flight." If you don't fight or flee, these hormones remain in the bloodstream for a time and keep the heart and blood vessels under a constant, low-grade pressure.

- *Are you an active person?* Inactivity is clearly associated with heart disease, according to many research studies. Active people have better hearts than do sedentary people.

Other equally important factors are high blood pressure, an abnormal resting electrocardiogram, obesity, elevated cholesterol and diabetes. Cigarette smoking is a vital factor in determining overall fitness. If you want to achieve maximum fitness levels, avoid tobacco.

How About Some Exercise for Dessert?

Now, since you've made it this far, it's time to ask yourself, "Am I ready to start an exercise program?"

If you have identified your risk factors and developed a plan to deal with those which can be changed, you have one more thing you should do before beginning an aerobic exercise program: a physical exam. Here are some guidelines:

- If your age is less than 30, you are still not immune to heart disease although your risk is lower than for older persons. You should have had a complete medical history and physical examination sometime in the 12 months before you begin your exercise program.

- If your age is between 30 and 35, you should have had a complete history and physical examination including a resting electrocardiogram sometime within six months before you kick off your program.

- If you are over 35, the examination should have been done within three months before beginning your new protocol. The examination should include an exercise test with monitoring by electrocardiogram, or a stress ECG.

To determine if your heart has problem areas, it is essential to see how it performs when challenged by exercise. Although there may be some difficulties which don't show up when the heart is functioning at a high rate of speed under a load, the test will give a good assessment of overall exercise capacity and will likely indicate most problems.

The principle is the same as taking your car up to highway speeds to determine how well it performs. Exercise stress tests are available nearly everywhere; your personal physician can arrange one for you and then interpret the results for you.

Beginning an Exercise Program

You've identified your risks. Now you can begin your exercise program. How do you start?

You may be fortunate enough to have a physician interested in aerobic training — one who can give you an "exercise prescription." This prescription outlines a training program in detail for you. Other resources are available at sports medicine clinics, which usually have someone qualified to direct an exercise program.

If these resources are not available to you, then you may "do it yourself." Start by obtaining one of the books on aerobic conditioning found in most bookstores. Kenneth H. Cooper, M.D., has written a series of these books which are now offered in inexpensive paperback editions. These books provide detailed instructions on starting an exercise program safely while avoiding injury.

Remember, though, that you still require a medical evaluation before you start an exercise program unless you are already conditioned. There are many choices for exercise, so you can pick an activity you enjoy.

Swimming is a popular choice for divers, but running, tennis, squash, stair-climbing and many others are also options.

Keep in mind that some recreational activities are enjoyable but have little or no benefit for your cardiovascular system. The weekend round of golf, the after-dinner stroll, bowling, stationary weightlifting, horseback riding (it's the horse who gets the exercise, not you) and other nonaerobic exercises don't count in cardiovascular and pulmonary conditioning.

Maintain Your Program

It's very important not to get ahead of your exercise charts. Your program is designed to gradually increase the energy requirement as you increase your fitness. If you skip stages, you may wind up exhausted, injured or discouraged and quit your program.

On the other hand, if you approach your program on a gradual, step-by-step basis, you'll be surprised to find that you'll look forward to your exercise time as you improve. The positive feelings you will obtain from exercise after you have achieved fitness will motivate you to continue. It appears that exercise and cardiovascular fitness also affect your mental health. Numerous studies have confirmed a link between physical health and psychological well-being.

Fitness is our natural state. Watch young children at play: nearly everything they do is aerobic. Only later do they learn to spend hours in front of the television screen and begin the sedentary lifestyle which can follow them into adult life.

If you're out of shape, you're out of sorts with yourself. Take better care of yourself, get fit and enjoy this great sport of ours.

— *From September/October 1994*

Get Fit For Diving

BY ALFRED A. BOVE, M.D., PH.D.

There is a myth among recreational divers that diving is a non-strenuous sport; therefore, divers do not need good physical conditioning. I maintain that divers must be in good physical condition to dive safely. The most compelling reason for insisting on fitness is to be able to respond to stressful situations with the necessary physical exertion to avoid an accident.

This means that you should be able to swim a reasonable distance with diving gear, without getting severely short of breath, and be able to help a partner who has been injured or who develops a cramp in the water to return to land or a boat. Fitness provides the strength and endurance to climb up a boat ladder in rough seas, to walk the needed distances carrying diving gear to get to a boat or shoreline without becoming totally exhausted, and to have some reserve energy after a day of diving.

There are numerous ways that fitness can be defined. First, you must be in good health. Chronic or acute illness causes a loss of fitness, and diving shouldn't be done when acutely ill (with a cold, for example). With chronic illness, special consideration must be given to the type of illness and the current state of health of the diver.

We usually define fitness as the ability to do physical work. The best measure of fitness is the maximum oxygen consumption. This measure shows how much oxygen is taken in during exercise at the highest level of work that is tolerated. Testing for maximum oxygen consumption requires an exercise machine (treadmill or cycle), and a special analyzer to determine the amount of oxygen taken in during different work loads of increasing intensity.

The graph on the following page shows the amount of oxygen taken in during a graded exercise test. There is a maximum level of oxygen that is reached by everyone at high levels of exercise. At the maximum oxygen uptake, exercise cannot be continued for more than a few minutes, before exhaustion occurs.

We usually define workloads for any individual as a percent of the maximum. If a certain task requires 100 percent of maximum, it is certain that the work cannot be sustained for more than a short burst, before exhaustion occurs. This is very obvious to anyone who tries to swim against a fast current. The work will quickly rise to maximum, exhaustion will occur, and the diver may panic from

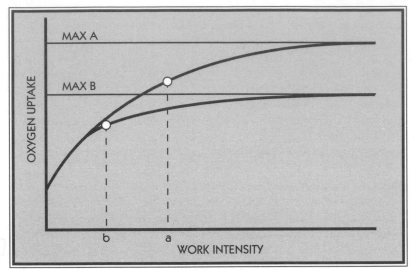

the severe shortness of breath that accompanies working at maximum capacity.

On the other hand, when you only need to perform at 40 percent of maximum, the work is easily tolerated for long periods of time, breathing is comfortable, and a degree of confidence is achieved that prevents panic.

Based on this concept, there are several ways to match your fitness level to the work required for diving. The first (not recommended) is to avoid *any* hard work during diving. Nowadays, this is possible because many of the diving resorts and dive boats have eliminated all of the labor involved in preparing for diving, and getting in and out of the dive boat.

Another means of adjusting to the fitness needs of diving is to carefully plan your dives to avoid situations where excess physical exertion may tax your exercise capacity. This approach is helpful for elderly divers, or for divers who have chronic illnesses which limit exercise capacity.

The third method of adjusting your fitness to diving is to exercise regularly so that you are in good physical condition and capable of handling the diving contingencies that can arise in a sport diving environment. This is the best approach for divers who are in good health and who wish to be able to dive in a wide variety of environments. If you plan to dive in distant dive locations where the diving environment is not certain, then being in good physical condition is the best insurance against problems or accidents.

Getting in Shape

It is not necessary to become a world-class marathoner to be in good shape for diving. A moderate exercise program that can be pursued constantly four or five days a week is adequate for fitness for diving. There are many ways to exercise for fitness. Swimming is an excellent exercise, and a necessary one for divers. You should be able to swim comfortably with diving gear, and the only way to become comfortable while swimming is to swim as part of your fitness training. You can walk, jog, bike, or row in addition to swimming. All of the exercises cause your pulse rate to increase, your breathing to increase, and your oxygen intake to rise. The graph shows how your body takes up oxygen with increasing workloads.

As your effort increases, there is an increase in the oxygen intake that is directly related to the effort intensity. The higher the intensity of your work, the higher the oxygen intake. Note that there is a maximum intake (labeled "max"), where the oxygen intake no longer increases. When you perform work at or beyond the maximum oxygen intake, the body must do some of the work without oxygen to supply the energy. This type of work is called anaerobic because it is done without oxygen.

The work done along the sloped portion of the graph is called aerobic since adequate oxygen is supplied to do the work. In diving you should not get into a situation where anaerobic work is needed. This level of exercise is very intense, and usually cannot be sustained for more than a few minutes. Most scuba regulators would be hard breathing at maximum oxygen intake.

Conditioning improves your maximum oxygen intake. The A curve of the figure shows how a conditioning program would affect your ability to exercise. Your maximum would shift upward (Curve B to Curve A), and you would improve your capacity at 70 percent of max from B to A. You can expect to improve by about 25 percent if you are not in shape now and undertake an exercise program. A 25 percent increase will allow you to tolerate higher intensity work without feeling the discomfort that goes with working near the maximum.

A Training Program

You should exercise five or six days a week to improve your state of conditioning. This should be devoted to aerobic exercise, and the intensity of the exercise should be determined by counting your pulse rate during the exercise and establishing a target heart rate. The target heart rate can be determined by the formula:

$$target\ heart\ rate = (220 - age) \times 0.70$$

Subtract your age from 220, multiply by 0.70 and you will have an estimate of the heart rate that you should achieve when exercising for fitness. For example, if you are 35 years old, 220 - 35 = 185, multiply times 0.70 and you arrive at a target heart rate of 130 per minute. When you exercise, you

Calculate Your

Target Heart Rate for Peak Fitness

Age	Target Heart Rate*
10	147
15	143
20	140
25	136.5
30	133
35	129.5
40	126
45	122.5
50	119
55	115.5
60	112
65	108.5
70	105
75	101.5
80	98

* $THR = (220 - age) \times 0.70$

should aim for a pulse rate of 130. You should follow an exercise plan like the one shown in the graph on the next page.

There should be a five-minute warm-up period which can include stretching exercises, and which should also include beginning your usual exercise slowly for a few minutes. After the warm-up period, there should be a 30-minute continuous exercise period where you maintain a steady pace. At the end of the steady exercise period, there is a cool down period which allows your body to adjust to the cessation of exercise. When you begin a program of exercise, you must adjust the pace initially to get your pulse to the target rate.

Exercising Safely

There is little risk in exercising this way to improve your conditioning if you are in good health. However, if you have a chronic illness, there may be a risk. The most important and serious risk occurs when you have coronary artery disease. This disease causes the arteries of the heart to narrow, and may go undetected in its early phase, especially if you are not physically active. The risk for coronary disease is increased if you smoke cigarettes, if you have high cholesterol, if you have diabetes, if you have high blood pressure or if you have a history of coronary disease in your family. If you are over 35 years old, have not exercised in several years, and have one or more of the risk factors for coronary disease, you should have a medical evaluation before beginning an exercise program. The evaluation should include an exercise stress test. This test shows whether exercise is safe for you, and provides the doctor information to establish a more accurate exercise prescription.

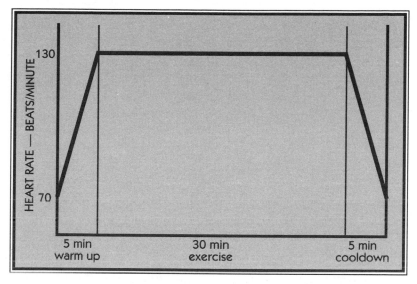

Once you have been cleared for safe exercise, you should start slowly. A common problem that occurs at the beginning of an exercise program is the development of an injury. If you are injured early in your fitness program, you will not be able to continue. It is easy to become discouraged, and give up permanently if an injury stops the program at its beginning. Ankles, knees, shoulders or back problems can stop your activity before any benefit accrues. The secret to avoiding injury is to start your program gradually. Tendons, ligaments and muscles all gain strength as you train. At the beginning, though, they may be weak, and prone to injury. By allowing yourself to increase gradually, these structures can be strengthened at the same time as you develop better aerobic conditioning.

If you have not exercised for several years, you should take two to three months to build your activities to the target. Once you have taken the time to get your body into shape, you can maintain a steady level, or even go beyond to higher levels of intensity if you wish.

Keeping Fit

Fitness is a state that requires a constant commitment to training. If you stop training, you will return to a state of low fitness, and need to retrain again to achieve a higher level. The program of 40 minutes, five days per week will keep you at a level of fitness that will provide safe and enjoyable diving.

The fitness program can be varied between different types of aerobic exercise and sports that require reasonable physical exertion. You cannot stay in shape by diving unless you are diving every day, and even

Cardiac Vital Statistics — the Heart Facts

BY ROBERT HULS

WEIGHT — 10.5 ounces (slightly less than a canned drink).

SIZE — Equal to a clenched fist.

LOCATION — Left of chest's center, nestled between the lungs and protected by breastbone and ribs.

RATE — 60 to 100 beats per minute in the adult, faster in infants and children.

LONGEVITY — Based on 72 beats per minute, a heart beats 4,320 each hour; 103,680 times each day; and, during a 72-year life span, 2,724,710,400 times!

MAKEUP — Composed of inherently contracting cardiac cells — in tissue culture even a fragment of heart muscle continues to pulse rhythmically — arranged in bundles that efficiently wring blood out of the heart.

FORMATION — Embryo's heart develops from a mere thickening of cells into a tube that eventually folds upon itself to produce the heart's four chambers.

WORK — Quantity of blood pumped each day: 2,500 to 5,000 gallons (enough to fill 50 to 100 bathtubs).

VELOCITY OF BLOOD — Travels from heart to big toe and back — its longest circuit — in less than a minute.

BLOOD VESSELS — Combined length of arteries, veins and capillaries: more than 60,000 miles — one-fourth of the distance to the moon!

then, some type of additional exercise program is needed to maintain conditioning. Your fitness program will become easier to maintain the longer you continue. Most people who maintain programs for a long time find it difficult to stop the program because of the feeling of better health that comes from a continuous fitness program. Once you get to that point in your program, it will be easy to maintain.

For improved general health, as well as safer and more enjoyable diving, it is worthwhile to maintain fitness by a commitment to a long-term exercise program. These programs can be done safely by almost anyone, but you should have a medical evaluation before starting if you fit the categories of high risk as noted above. Diving will always be safer and more enjoyable if you are fit.

— From July/August 1992

Are You Ready to Dive?

Diving fitness involves more than just getting into good physical condition

BY GLEN H. EGSTROM, PH.D., DAN BOARD OF DIRECTORS

Diving responsibly encompasses a number of factors — among them, keeping dive profiles that fit your level of experience in diving, maintaining your dive equipment in prime working order and, perhaps most importantly, keeping in tune with your personal well-being.

Our bodies are among the most complex organisms in the animal kingdom.

And they're very accommodating. The human organism is capable of making highly specific adaptations to the many demands imposed upon it. For divers, this understanding begins with the recognition that diving fitness is an involved issue not well-suited to a simple solution.

In a day-to-day environment, the human organism constantly adapts to all manner of stresses that are placed upon it by a variety of environmental and behavioral variables. One of the rules of nature itself is the tendency toward balance: There is a continual striving for equilibrium within a given environment. The resulting longer-term adaptations develop a higher order of fitness for each new level of performance.

Individuals, then, tend to become more fit for a particular activity by increasing the demands which are specific to that activity. This resulting adaptation to a higher level of achievement leads to a greater enjoyment of the activity and an enhanced level of comfort with it. For divers, concerns about fitness must also be based on an understanding of the specifics of the adaptation that lead to the goals identified by the diver.

The scuba diver who wishes to become a safe, effective denizen of the deep accepts certain challenges, both physical and mental. I choose to categorize the pathway to the goal of enhanced diver fitness as this broad challenge: overcoming barriers to improved performance in diving. These barriers may be grouped into broad categories of challenges: biomechanical, physiologic, methodologic and psychologic.

BIOMECHANICAL BARRIERS

The biomechanical aspect of fitness implies that the diver is capable of handling his equipment as if it were a second skin. The old saying, "A man in armor is his armor's slave" is particularly appropriate to illustrate this challenge.

Biomechanical barriers are best identified by their ability to limit the diver's performance by restricting his movement. How so? The typical diver adds equipment to the body with little regard for the consequences on performance. These additions increase diver drag, reduce range of motion and can result in greater workloads.

And there is a price tag — which requires payment — for every item of equipment that a diver utilizes. Dive gear involves a great deal of commitment: It must be transported to the water; moved through the water once donned, attached or carried; and it must be returned to the surface. The components of the price tag include energy cost, strength, endurance and mental commitment. And this is just the beginning.

Resistance is a drag

A corollary of diving fitness requires that all biomechanical restrictions be reduced to a minimum. Anything that increases drag carries a price that must be paid with every single kick the diver makes. Despite this, divers usually hang any number of auxiliary devices onto the framework of their dive equipment. The diver, while moving through the water, uses energy to overcome resistance; doubling his speed through the water increases the resistance fourfold.

To reduce drag and increase range of motion, loose straps and hoses should be reconfigured. Selecting and configuring proper-fitting equip-

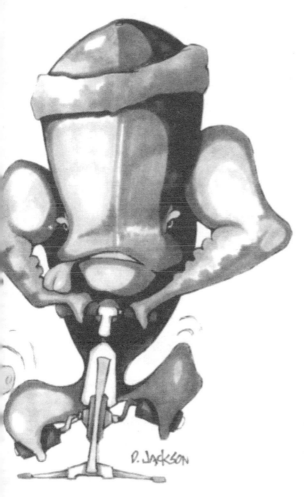

P. JACKSON

ment reduces drag and work effort while increasing range of motion. This in turn improves diver fitness.

But other factors must be considered. A diver normally wears a mask covering both eyes and mouth. Not only does the mask cause tunnel vision and change the drag configuration of a diver's head, it turns him into a mouth-breather. Add a snorkel to this, which further changes the head configuration and creates additional drag with every kick. Combine this with a small amount of additional breathing resistance to every breath on the surface, and you have an assortment of challenges already.

Thermal protection has its ins and outs as well. Some kinds of thermal protection cause the diver to become more buoyant; at the same time decreasing the range of motion of most of the body's joints, while adding more drag. The addition of weights to compensate for this additional buoyancy augments the workload.

Fins, which divers wear to generate more thrust force, add significantly to the energy cost. The tank, regulator, hoses, gauges and buoyancy control devices not only create more drag surfaces, but also increase breathing resistance, decrease range of motion, add to the workload and raise the center of mass, resulting in a diver that is less stable in air. Additionally, it's advisable to find user-friendly locations for all equipment controls that require monitoring or adjustment during the dive.

Not only does diving have physical considerations, but mental and emotional issues are also part of the fitness equation. Diving is filled with risks which must be weighed and accepted by the diver prior to each dive. Any physical or mental condition, or an injury that limits range of motion — whether it is permanent or temporary — should be recognized, put into realistic perspective and evaluated for the dive being planned. Any limiting factors like these must be considered a calculated risk for the planned dive.

Divers who accept risks without adequate information are not necessarily fit for diving — far too many accidents result from the diver making mental appointments that the diver's body cannot keep.

PHYSIOLOGIC FITNESS

Physiologic fitness centers on an individual's development to achieve adequate levels of strength and endurance to meet the demands of any dive — with sufficient reserves to cope with an emergency situation.

Every activity involves strength and endurance, to some degree, and will have a particular pattern of intensity, rate and duration associated with it. Some activities, like walking five miles, are lower-strength and higher-endurance types, while others, like lifting a heavy barbell one time, are higher-strength and lower-endurance. Diving is interesting in that the diver out of the water is usually using more strength and less endurance than will be needed once the diver enters the water and becomes neutrally buoyant. Strength then becomes a lesser issue, while endurance becomes key to a successful dive.

Overexertion often leads to a loss of control, especially in divers who are not used to being in the water. Strength and endurance levels are quite specific to the various requirements of diver performance, and each type of requirement needs attention before it becomes a problem. When in doubt, sort it out. Fortunately, there are some skills that can help to reduce the workloads; unfortunately, they must also be in place before any problem develops.

Progressive overloading

Developing your strength is a must for good diving fitness. As a rule, strength is best gained at that point in the range of motion where the highest resistance is met during the activity. For example, fin swimming imposes loading on the leg musculature that is unlike nearly all other activities. The development of the strength for fin swimming requires that the functional muscles used to move the fins be subjected to progressively increasing resistive loading.

Called the progressive overloading concept, the development of endurance requires that continuation of an activity be progressively extended until the diver is comfortable with the workload. Rate is usually not a major concern, since the pace underwater is normally rather slow and steady. The progressive overloading concept is twofold in nature: You must perform slightly more repetitions during each successive training session, and you must move the functional muscle groups in an identical fashion to the way they are used in the activity.

Overloading progressively while wearing the fins is quite probably one of the better ways to prepare for diving. Specific adaptation can result in two to three weeks of appropriate training, providing valuable, "cheap" insurance for safe diving. This concept can be applied to other aspects of diving as well.

As a diver, your conditioning activities should, insofar as possible, duplicate the functional mechanics of diving with progressive workloads. This concept is based on what is known as identical performance elements. Underwater swims with the mask, fins and snorkel will provide a better specific adaptation than swimming laps using the crawl stroke or jogging around the park.

Medical fitness

A subset of physiologic fitness, medical fitness becomes a large factor in diving responsibly. This is a vital factor, since many divers are apparently unaware of — or choose to ignore — the potential risks associated with the failure to have an adequate medical evaluation prior to diving. The late Dr. Jefferson Davis, a pioneer in diving medicine, labored for several years — with the assistance of nearly 100 medical experts from most of the medical specialties — to provide an easy-to-understand consensus guideline on the medical examination of scuba divers.

Sometimes individuals who dive find they must limit their diving or suspend it altogether. The challenges and risks which must be appreciated by individuals with significant medical problems may well create problems that limit their ability to adapt effectively to the diving environment.

On the other hand, individuals considering diving may sometimes accept the risks without the knowledge to make an informed decision regarding their personal diving fitness. This is true particularly in areas such as asthma, diabetes, epilepsy and advancing cardiovascular disease. Those who choose to dive — whether in ignorance or apathy — can be a threat to their own welfare, as well as the welfare of the buddies with whom they dive and others who become involved.

METHODOLOGIC FITNESS

Methodologic fitness is associated with the development and use of proper techniques to ensure effective, efficient performance while diving. As the sport of diving has become more and more diversified in equipment configurations, training techniques and diver goals, this aspect of fitness has assumed even more importance.

In the early days of diving, things were simpler, with fewer choices than today. In terms of techniques and methodology, there was "the bible" (the *U.S. Navy Diving Manual*), diving equipment that generally looked and functioned generically, and an almost standardized list of skills that every diver was expected to be able to perform. Today we see an explosion of diving literature filled with a plethora of divergent views, diving equipment that is remarkable for its variations, and diving behavior that varies significantly with the divergent goals of the training given to divers.

The techniques used in modern diving are largely different in terms of the specifics of their application during the dive — such as the use of personal diving equipment. A quick inspection of 20 divers on a resort boat would probably reveal about 20 significant variations of devices that impact upon emergency procedures. One could expect four or five air-sharing configurations, eight or 10 buoyancy control variations, two or three weighting configurations, and six or eight different personal computers. Problems can arise when these divers cannot or will not take the time to familiarize themselves with their buddy's equipment, much less that of the other divers with whom they interact during an emergency.

At a minimum, methodologic fitness requires that individual divers are comfortable with the techniques that they have learned, and that they can quickly and effectively utilize their own equipment. At the same time, they should be able to interact with their buddy's diving techniques and equipment during an emergency.

It is unlikely that diving equipment configurations will ever be standardized. Because of this, individual divers should consider adopting the habit of familiarizing themselves with the two (hopefully not more) sets of equipment that will be involved in their dive.

PSYCHOLOGIC FITNESS

Psychologic fitness for diving implies that the diver is able to think and solve problems while relaxing and enjoying underwater experiences. This is often difficult for the novice diver, who is confronted with the challenge of a relatively unknown environment. Each dive, for some, is victory over adversity, and the sense of exhilaration that follows the dive is the reward for survival. For others, the challenges of the deep include avoiding dangerous marine life, avoiding diving illnesses, overcoming sea conditions and generally making it through the ordeal. As the comfort level increases, however, the diver becomes a "waterperson," and the interaction with the underwater challenges becomes routine. At this point, stress is minimal, and the fear of the unknown is replaced with anticipation of another great dive.

As a subset of psychologic fitness, the diver should be concerned about overlearning critical skills. Overlearning results when a skill has been practiced so often that little or no conscious effort is needed to perform the skill effectively and efficiently.

Many years ago, our UCLA underwater research team conducted an experiment to determine the number of trials needed by basic, or open-water, students to establish a minimal error rate on the skill of buddy breathing while swimming around the pool underwater.

It was found that 17 to 20 trials were needed for the particular beginning class of about 24 UCLA students. Following a three month period where minimal diving was undertaken, a number of the class were tested again and found to need additional reinforcement of the skills in order to reach the previous level of proficiency.

There is a learning curve and a decay curve for all skills. Many critical skills — particularly those associated with emergency procedures — are rarely overlearned and even more rarely practiced outside of training situations. Psychologic fitness requires that the diver be able to think and solve problems during an emergency while using critical skills.

A responsible diver should be able to take the time, without embarrassment, to reinforce skills which may make it more likely that he and his buddy will enjoy a comfortable dive. Divers cannot afford to lose self-control during a dive — panic behavior can have damaging results. Psychologically fit divers are far less likely to panic if they have overlearned and reinforced critical skills.

Conclusion: Adaptation is the key

The successful adaptation to each of these aspects of fitness depends, in a large measure, on the individual's ability to establish a rather wide array of newly imposed demands of both the internal and external environments. The normal equilibrium that an individual enjoys within his environment is the result of effective responses to a large number of stressors, such as temperature, barometric pressure, humidity, workload, tools, etc. The presence of any stressors sets up a disequilibrium which requires adaptive change from the individual in order to establish a new equilibrium.

As an example, the diver who gets a new pair of fins that is longer and more rigid than the well-worn older pair will encounter new demands on the muscles during normal kicking cycles. Since we gain strength in that portion of the range of motion where we encounter increased resistance, we will, during the times we use the new fins, establish new and appropriate levels of strength to meet the new workloads.

A careful analysis of the pattern for the summation of forces during a movement will inform us about the speed of the movement, where in the range of motion the muscles are loaded, and the duration time of

---

Staying fit

It's obvious that the best way to stay fit for diving is to dive on a regular basis.

For many divers, this is not feasible, since weather, location and lack of motivation can interfere with the best of intentions.

Here are some suggestions in preparing for a dive trip following a layoff in activity:

1. Ask yourself what kind of diving you will be doing:
   - identify the kind of equipment you will be wearing
   - estimate the environmental conditions of the dive
   - try to gauge the level of exertion that will be required
   - review the need for emergency procedures
   - review any areas of concern you might have for the dives
2. Ask yourself whether you really want to do the dives. A yes indicates that you are confident that you will be fit at the time of the dive.
3. Prior to your diving excursion, dedicate at least 30 minutes a day every other day for two to three weeks for exercise that will focus on the use of the mask, fins and snorkel.

Usually, most divers know they'll be diving well in advance of any diving trips; and many live near a pool facility they could use. Hopefully, just prior to the trip, a pool session with full gear and your diving buddy can be used to review your emergency procedures.

---

the movement. This analysis can tell us not only about the functional muscle groups which are operating, but also what intensity, rate and duration parameters should be considered when preparing a fitness program or an exercise routine geared to bring about change.

This concept will operate with any new set of imposed demands on the diver. If we fail to adapt to the new conditions, we should not be surprised when we are unable to perform as well as we would like. Fortunately, most of the adaptations that we do make take place without major effort, and we are not conscious of the change taking place. Unfortunately, the adaptations can also move in a negative or undesired direction.

The failure to maintain fitness can result from a condition where the demands on the individual are reduced to levels below current levels — adaptation will be reduced to the level of the new demands. Getting "into" or "out of" shape is a simple matter of re-establishing equilibrium with a new set of demands, whether they are positive or not. A period of reduced activity for two to three weeks may result in significantly reduced levels of fitness for the activity. Conversely, increasing the demands can result in significant improvement in fitness over the same time span. The key to change is to properly and regularly utilize progressive amounts of appropriate training over an extended period of time. The individual must make a decision with regard to the specific performance goals to be met.

Fitness and health concerns are closely related. Freedom from debilitating disease, which may limit diving performance, is a clear function of fitness for diving. But what about relative fitness? One of the most hazardous marine animals is a diver who behaves irresponsibly. If every diver would dive within his or her personal limits of fitness, there would be a marked reduction in diving accidents.

The American College of Sports Medicine, in cooperation with other fitness-oriented groups, produced a statement in 1993. It points out that a persuasive body of scientific evidence accumulated over the past several decades indicates that regular, moderate-intensity exercise confers substantial health benefits. A primary benefit is protection against coronary disease; other benefits include a degree of protection against several other chronic diseases, such as adult-onset diabetes, hypertension, certain cancers, osteoporosis and depression.

While there are no guarantees, it appears that the majority of the adult population, particularly the older members, are in need of more physical activity. Divers would benefit tremendously by concentrating a portion of their regular exercise on the issue of fin swimming — hopefully underwater.

If a pool session just isn't possible, stretch and exercise the functional muscle groups that you use in the activity through the same range of motion that they must pull through in order to accomplish fin kicking.

This concept of training by using identical elements involved in diving with nondiving exercises requires some understanding of how the body works. For example, muscles pull — they never push — to exert force. They may, however, pull by shortening, lengthening or by holding tension without movement. When you analyze a movement, think of functional muscle groups that pull to develop the movement. Simply ask: "How do the muscles pull to get the job done?" It is not necessary to know which muscles, only that they pull together to create the movement.

Another example: When you kick with fins, the muscles that flex and extend the hip, knee and ankle through the range of motion during the kick cycle are encountering the resistance of the water. Functional groups on either side of the joint operate to pull the upper leg relative to the hip joint, the lower leg relative to the knee joint and the foot relative to the ankle joint. If you cannot use the water and fins for resistance, you may be able to go to the gym and locate different resistive exercise apparatus that will allow you to duplicate the movements of fin swimming under an increase workload.

Increasing the resistance against functional muscle groups which are doing the same movements that you would make during fin swimming will improve your strength for that movement, and moving at similar rates for longer duration will improve your endurance. It is certainly not rocket science, but it can improve your fitness for using fins, and thereby improve your fitness for diving.

The enjoyment and the preservation of the underwater world is markedly enhanced for the diver who enjoys total fitness for diving. The development of the fine controls that enable the skilled diver to move through the water with relative ease is the result of paying attention to the details of diving. Making the appropriate specific adaptations to the demands of the underwater environment can result in improved diving fitness.

Develop and maintain your specific adaptations for diving. It will change your life.

— From May/June 1995

The Straight Scoop
on Spinal Care for Scuba Divers

BY CATHIE CUSH WITH PHOTOS BY MARLA TONSETH

Your mother was right! Long before you ever strapped a tank to your back, she had the key to an often-overlooked aspect of scuba-related safety. If you want to dive – or do much of anything else, for that matter – without injuring your spine, you have to...

SIT UP STRAIGHT!

It's simple, straightforward advice. Granted, it's not as sexy as, say, "Avoiding High-Pressure Nervous Syndrome" or even "The Advantages of Oxygen Decompression." But, for most divers, the topic of back pain hits closer to home.

In fact, lower back problems affect an estimated 80 percent of adults at some point in their lives. According to the 1992 edition of *For Your Back* by H. Dwayne Saunders, MSPT, Americans lose 93 million work days a year to back pain and spend $17 billion a year on back-related injuries. With those statistics in mind, anyone participating in a recreational activity that involves handling at least 50 pounds of gear should sit up and take notice — make that sit up straight and take notice.

Lifting the proverbial straw

Just lifting a tank or a weight belt usually isn't enough to cause a back injury. But lift it wrong enough times, and that's another story.

"Most injuries aren't from a specific event. The primary cause of back pain is cumulative microtrauma. It's a result of all the times that you use poor body mechanics, poor posture," explains Marla Tonseth, a physical therapist in practice since 1977 and a NAUI dive instructor. Tonseth has lectured on back health and body mechanics for hospitals, home health agencies and the Undersea and Hyperbaric Medical Society. Eventually, she says, all those little insults add up. "The 15,000th time, you sit down and can't get up again."

To understand what causes back problems, take a look at the backbone, or spine. The spine consists of individual bones called vertebrae. Each vertebra has a solid cylindrical section called the body, or centrum, and a hollow section called the neural, or vertebral, arch, which has bony projections on either side and the center. The nerves of the spinal cord run through a channel, or foramen, in the vertebral arch; individual nerves branching off the spinal cord pass through notches in the vertebrae.

The eight to 10 vertebrae that make up the sacrum and the coccyx, or tailbone, are fused together. Losing one's balance on a rocking boat deck and landing heavily in a sitting position could injure the coccyx, causing extreme short-term pain and potential longer-term complications. Falling while wearing equipment is an obvious potential problem, and most divers take steps to prevent it. Far more insidious are the repeated small injuries we inflict on the flexible parts of our spines during the course of a dive day.

Twenty-four of the vertebrae are connected by strong ligaments, enabling the back to bend and twist. In between each of the vertebrae is a disc made of cartilage, which has tough and fibrous rings around the jelly-like nucleus pulposus. These intervertebral disks act as shock absorbers.

"With good posture, the stress is transmitted along the lines of the rings," Tonseth says. "When you slouch or arch your back too much, the nucleus is pushed, and it puts pressure on the rings."

Imagine a water balloon between two books. Pressure coming straight down on top of the books causes the balloon to flatten, distributing the added weight evenly. But push down on one edge of the book, and the balloon will bulge toward the opposite side. Bending at the waist and slouching are like pushing down on the edge of the book. Every time we bend to strap on a fin or put something in a gear bag, we put stress on the disks. Particularly vulnerable are the disks in the lumbar spine, the five vertebrae in the lower back, which are most often involved in bending and twisting. People bend forward more often than backward, and the ligaments at the back of the spine are not as strong as the ones in front. Consequently, 95 percent of disk problems appear in the posterior, or back, part of the spine.

The disks' inner rings have no nerves, so when problems begin to develop, the individual usually has no discomfort.

"When the outer ring is affected, you get pain," says Tonseth. Frequently the result is a sharp pain down the leg, a condition known as sciatica because it involves the sciatic nerve. The good news, according to Tonseth, is that exercise can correct about 80 percent of these problems. If the problem goes uncorrected, it can result in a ruptured, or herniated, disk — a condition which almost always requires surgery.

Learn to lift it right

If we wanted to spend all our time with both feet solidly planted on the floor, we probably wouldn't be divers. We can't eliminate stresses on the spine, but we can minimize them by using proper body mechanics.

"Anything you lift should be lifted correctly," Tonseth says. "It's not so much the weight that matters as the postures." For instance, as she illustrates, divers or crew members may have to lift tanks into or out of a hold.

"Most people will lean from the waist instead of bending from the knees. When you're bending over into the hold, you may lift to a certain extent with your arm, but when you straighten, you're using your back." Instead, "you should lift with your quads and your glutes — the two largest muscles in the body," she says, referring to the quadriceps and the gluteus maximus, the muscles in the front of the thigh and the buttocks, respectively. In both men and women, those large muscles provide power. Back muscles, in contrast, are only meant to provide postural support.

Stress also occurs when lifting and turning at the same time. Commonly, groups of divers will take a "pass-the-bucket" approach to loading or off-loading a boat. Divers should pivot when passing items along like this rather than twisting at the waist.

Holding an object at arm's length increases the stress on the spine seven to 10 times. "For example, a 2-pound/0.9 kg weight held away from you puts the same stress on your spine as a 20 pound/9-kg weight," says Tonseth.

This is especially true when objects are lifted above the head. In many areas, the dive boat and the dock may be at two different levels, depending on the tide. Items should be held close to the body. When moving equipment from a vehicle to the boat or beach, Tonseth suggests carrying a tank on the shoulder so the weight pushes straight down or cradling it across the chest with both arms. If a diver wants to carry two tanks, they should be balanced — one in each arm. Wearing the tank in the BC and carrying gear bags backpack-style is another good choice.

The best option is to move heavy items with a handtruck or cart if available. Making several trips with smaller loads,

DO:

A good lifting position requires that you bend from the knees, keeping the object you're hoisting close to your body.

DON'T:

When lifting an object, don't hold it out from your body — it increases stress on the spine many times over.

rather than a few trips with heavier loads, is also preferable. If you can't lift an item without straining, don't lift it.

"You should be able to lift it with a smooth motion," the physical therapist says. "If you have to make quick, jerking motions, it means that it's too heavy for you." It is also important to be aware of head posi-

---

Better Body Mechanics

- Hold objects close to the body when lifting them.
- Bend at the knees, not at the waist.
- Maintain the normal arch in your back.
- Keep your ears in alignment with your shoulders.
- Pivot on your feet instead of twisting at the waist.
- Don't strain when lifting.

Bad Back or Bends?

Pain in the leg... Numbness... Is it a disk problem or decompression sickness? One involves tissue around the spinal column; the other affects the nerves of the spinal cord. Although the two maladies may seem to mimic each other, there are differences.

A few key observations can usually help with an accurate differential diagnosis, according to Joel Dovenbarger, R.N., Director of Medical Services at DAN.

"Numbness, tingling, pain or loss of sensation can be either one. One tip-off is symptoms that come and go," Dovenbarger says. "That's generally not DCS."

If the pain and numbness can be produced with movement, it's probably not a decompression problem, either. Two other conditions that seem to be unique to a back injury are shooting pains or a burning sensation.

"This is just a personal observation," Dovenbarger cautions, "but you rarely hear of a spinal DCS victim complain of a burning sensation. Both DCS and back injury victims will sometimes complain of a cool or cold sensation. There is no evidence that a back injury increases one's susceptibility to DCS.

"Unfortunately for the diver with a history of back problems," notes Dovenbarger, "if you have symptoms in the back or lower extremities after your dives, it's going to call for a trip to your doctor for evaluation and/or treatment. DCS can fool you. It can coexist with other symptoms of back injury.

"Don't diagnose yourself," concludes Dovenbarger. "If you're unsure about any condition before or after your dive, call DAN, or get evaluated by medical professionals."

---

tion when lifting in order to avoid problems with the vertebrae in the neck.

"When your ear is in front of your shoulder — rather than in line with it as viewed from the side — it increases the stresses in the cervical spine three times," Tonseth notes. "Your head weighs about 12 pounds/5.4 kg, but when you lean it forward or backward, the stress on your neck is as if it weighed 36 pounds/16 kg.

Bend over backwards to help yourself

Divers should be aware of their spinal alignment whether lifting a tank or climbing a ladder to get back on the boat. Good posture is the key to preventing back problems — and not just on the days we're toting dive gear.

"Look at how you are in the mundane activities," Tonseth counsels. It's best to keep your back in a neutral position, with its slight natural arch. Sitting is even more critical than standing, because it puts more pressure on the disks. Muscle tension can aggravate disk problems, so stress management is important. Also, she says, studies show a relationship between cigarette smoking and back problems, because decreased oxygen circulating in the blood slows disk healing.

Tanks, weight belts, gear bags and coolers all take their toll. And the spinal column isn't the only part of the back that's at risk.

"You can have a problem if you overload a muscle," Tonseth notes, although a muscle spasm is not nearly as serious as a herniated disk. A muscle spasm occurs when muscle fibers contract suddenly, which can decrease blood flow to an area.

Fortunately, prevention for both types of musculoskeletal problems is the same: exercise. Strengthening and stretching back and abdominal muscles makes them

DO:

Carry your load close to your body, with your back in a relaxed position, and your ears and shoulders in a vertical alignment.

DON'T:

Bending at the waist and the off-center position of his body all add up to potential back injury for this man lifting a tank.

DO:

A backpack can help transport your tank from your vehicle to the beach with minimal pressure on your back.

less prone to injury themselves and better able to provide support for the spine. An exercise program for an individual without any symptoms of back pain could incorporate crunches, knee-to-chest lifts and slow, straight leg raises. These should be complemented by exercises that arch the back in the opposite direction: press-ups, prone arching and leg lifts on the stomach. To build strength, gradually increase frequency and repetition.

If your back aches after a day of diving, says Tonseth, "your muscles are working overtime. Get yourself on an exercise program."

If the pain is more acute, it needs more attention. Rest in a position that allows a normal arch in the back. Ice the sore area for 24 to 48 hours and, if necessary, take an anti-inflammatory drug, such as aspirin or ibuprofen. After 24 hours, heat may also be helpful.

"The latest recommendations are to resume normal activity as soon as possible," Tonseth reports.

If the pain is severe or lasts longer than 48 hours, see a doctor. This is also the course of action if the pain runs down one leg or the other, because sciatica usually indicates disk involvement. Treatment may include prescription pain relievers or muscle relaxants and a program of physical therapy.

"In a PT (physical therapy) evaluation, we use certain test motions. Your responses determine what way you need to move to reduce the problem," explains Tonseth. Heat, cold, ultrasound and electrical stimulation (often called TENS, for transcutaneous electrical nerve stimulation) may all be used to manage the pain, but not to fix the problem.

"Once you know what the proper motions are, the exercises correct the problem. It's the mechanical process of putting the disk back into place and holding it in place."

So, you can exercise now, or you'll have to exercise later. Just carrying tanks down to the beach and back once a week isn't enough. But standing up straight, using proper lifting techniques and staying in shape can go a long way toward eliminating missed dive days due to bad backs.

— *From March/April 1996*

Mind & Body

The treatment for decompression illness should go far beyond simple physiology.

BY JENNIFER HUNT, PH.D.,
AND BILL CLENDENEN, DAN DIRECTOR OF TRAINING

Editor's Note: In the following article, a predictable case of DCI is one in which the diver violated known rules of diving safety as understood within his relevant diving milieu — commonly referred to as a "deserved" injury (or "hit"). An unpredictable case of DCI is one in which the diver followed known rules of safety — usually known as an "undeserved" hit. The use of these alternative terms by the authors — "predictable" and "unpredictable" — are not meant as indications of mathematical probability but rather are designed to take the moral stigma out of terms like "deserved" and "undeserved" injuries.

For most divers, decompression illness (DCI) is fortunately something that will never occur. Yet, for those who are injured in a diving accident, the primary concern is usually the medical treatment of the physical manifestations of DCI. The diver's mental state is an often-omitted consideration, because it is viewed by many in the diving community — including the injured diver — as irrelevant, inconsequential or otherwise unworthy of attention.

It is the mind, not the body, that interprets and acts on illness information and determines how it is experienced and managed. It is important, then, for any caregiver — whether it be a dive buddy at the scene, EMS personnel or the attending physician — to try to understand the diver's mental state, if appropriate treatment and recovery are to take place.

THE MANY FACES OF DENIAL

Divers' psychological reactions to decompression illness differ depending on a number of variables, including: the diver's personality, systems of social support, the circumstances surrounding the incident, and the severity of the injuries. But regardless of whether the injury is mild or severe, "predictable" or "unpredictable," a distinct complex of psychological responses in injured divers is possible.

With the onset of DCI symptoms, divers may experience a "signal" of anxiety which is barely perceptible. They then mobilize a variety of psychological defenses to protect them from experiencing a flood of unpleasant emotions, such as anxiety, panic, shame, embarrassment, weakness, anger and depression.

A person's psychological defenses are normal mechanisms of the mind which provide a means of protection against external and internal threats to their psychological and/or physical well-being. Under some circumstances, however, defenses can become maladaptive.

Defenses which result in delays in appropriate medical or psychological treatment can compromise a diver's long-term physical and psychological welfare.

WHEN IT'S OBVIOUS

When the symptoms of DCI are so severe they can no longer be ignored, divers will call for assistance. Serious symptoms like those caused by lung-overpressurization (arterial gas embolism, or AGE) and neurological decompression sickness (DCS) necessitate prompt calls for assistance. But 50 percent of the injured divers suffering from mild or pain-only DCS (with painful joints, fatigue and nausea) frequently wait over 12 hours before seeking help, and a total of nearly 20 percent wait four or more days to call for assistance. [Based on statistics from

DAN's *Report on Diving Accidents and Fatalities* for 1994. — *Ed.]*

The diver's ability to deny injury can be affected by the nature of the illness. Many symptoms of DCS (as with pain-only DCS) are subtle and resemble numerous other ailments such as tennis elbow, lower back problems, colds and the flu. (See DCI quiz, page 76). Sometimes DCI occurs arbitrarily, and because of this, it can be easily dismissed through a process of rationalization. For example:

- Dive tables and computers ("But I was within my limits").
- Buddies ("I can't be bent because my buddy's not bent").
- Prior dive experience ("I've done that same dive 100 times").
- Acceptable dive practices ("I haven't done anything wrong").
- The diver's own sense of infallibility. ("This can't happen to me — I'm a good diver.")

PSYCHOLOGICAL DEFENSES

Denial is one of many defenses divers use to protect themselves from the flood of unpleasant feelings that accompany injury. Often called "the first symptom of decompression illness," denial occurs when divers fail to recognize the significance of symptoms — they may deny their existence altogether. They may attribute them to aches and pains associated with diving-related strenuous activity such as lifting tanks and heavy gear. They may also minimize the seriousness of symptoms by engaging in seemingly inappropriate behavior such as joking, exercising or drinking alcohol.

Displacement involves a diver's shift of concern from the significant point of anxiety (the diver's injured body) to something outside himself or herself which doesn't evoke the same degree of fear. Divers may focus concern on the feelings of other people who may be upset if they learn their colleague is injured, or they may become preoccupied with broken equipment or the cost of treatment. In some instances, attempts to displace anxiety may be grounded in certain social realities — for example, the cost of treatment may be a serious concern for the diver who has no insurance.

Projection is a defense used by injured divers to attribute feelings and fantasies onto others which may be intolerable to themselves. This is often used to neutralize the feelings of shame, embarrassment and anger which may accompany DCI. By doing this, divers can avoid full acknowledgment of painful feelings by projecting them on to others whom they believe are angry with them or see them as weak, incompetent and deserving of punishment.

Externalization is another defense divers frequently use to minimize anxiety and self-blame. Injured divers may shift responsibility for their injury on forces outside of their control, including narcosis, fatigue, medications, menstruation and dehydration. They may also blame other people, such as a dive buddy or a divemaster who they believe led them astray or did not provide sufficient protection by preventing their engagement in high-risk behavior.

Attacks on the self are often used in conjunction with externalization. Some divers cannot tolerate the rage they feel toward others, and they may experience guilt about it. They then turn their aggression inward, engage in self-recrimination, and punish themselves for their rage.

EMOTIONS

Divers use a variety of defenses to reduce anxiety associated with fears of paralysis and death; loss of the ability to dive, loss of friends or loved ones; and they may even fear loss of their own identities as competent and morally worthy persons. These defenses also help protect them against feelings of shame — injured divers may feel they have done something bad and deserve to be disciplined. Some may even perceive their injuries as punishments for having too much fun.

Feelings of shame and humiliation may be accompanied by a transformation in body image. After injury, once-invulnerable divers may think they are weak and damaged.

Divers with unpredictable cases of DCI may feel as though they have no control of their bodies, which seem to act in irrational, unpredictable and painful ways. They may also experience humiliation because their apparently fragile physiques seem to get hurt in ordinary circumstances.

"I am ashamed of myself," says one diver with an unpredictable hit. "It would have been more glorious being bent doing that outlandish dive to 200 fsw [61 meters] which we did in Papua New Guinea ... terrible, terrible. It was sordid for me to get bent in a disgusting [shallow dive]. It is like a race car driver having an accident sitting in his own car getting rear-ended by a truck."

Divers typically experience depression during and after their injuries. The depression may last for weeks, months or even years. Symptoms of depression include low self-esteem, fatigue, frequent periods of sadness, irritability, anger and an inability to experience pleasure. Depressed persons may have short-term memory loss and difficulty concentrating. Their speech and movements may be slow. They may lose their appetites, or they can overeat. Some have trouble sleeping, awaken early, or sleep too much. They may also be preoccupied with thoughts of injury, violence or death.

"I have memory loss now," says one injured diver. "I cannot watch anything violent — I cry immediately. . . . I am a happy person, but I can't be bothered with anything to do with diving now."

SILENT ECHOES

The crystallization of feelings and fears that are mobilized in the face of injury may link to thoughts from the present and the past about which divers are not fully aware. These "silent echoes" serve to intensify and reinforce anxiety and depression. The content of the unconscious thoughts varies depending on individual character and personal history.

Take the case of a diver whose difficulty acknowledging the serious-ness of mild symptoms of DCI was rooted in her childhood relationship with both parents.

The diver grew up in a household in which her father was critically ill and could die suddenly. As a result, her own childhood illnesses were viewed as insignificant and given little attention. Her mother was also a hypochondriac who feigned illness to spoil the diver's fun and keep her close. This often occurred when the diver planned an exciting sports vacation. The mother would then use illness to convince her daughter to interrupt her trip and come home. When the diver was bent, she did not perceive her injury as worthy of attention because she was not paralyzed or near death, like her father.

She also defended herself against angry feelings toward her mother by projecting her rage onto diving colleagues with whom she identified. Thus, she did not want to tell them she was hurt because she feared they would be angry at her for ruining their trip, just as she had been toward her mother. Denial of the seriousness of her injury also protect-ed her against an ambivalent identification with her mother. If she announced she was sick with only mild symptoms, she felt as though she was like her mother — a hypochondriac and spoiler.

SOCIAL REACTION

Diving injuries take place in a social context in which divers' fears and fantasies may be magnified. Many members of the diving commu-nity believe that DCI occurs only when mistakes are made and rules of safety are violated. As a result, the person with DCI can be stigmatized and viewed as incompetent, unworthy, a safety risk, a poor diver, an "accident waiting to happen," a deviant or even crazy. While divers who "push the envelope" or violate known safety rules may be particularly vulnerable to stigmatization, those with unpredictable injuries may also have to endure negative social reactions.

"It is not black and white, and nobody knows the answers for everything," notes an instructor who sustained an unpredictable hit. "The fact that my students might think they are in danger of getting bent, or that I might be less [than what they thought] irritates me. . . . If you get bent, you made a mistake, and you are guilty, and that is the story. . . ."

While some colleagues react critically to announcements of DCI, others may help with the divers' effort to deny the seriousness of their injury.

Friends may confirm divers' beliefs that their post-dive nausea, fatigue, aches and pains are caused by the flu. Diving colleagues may discourage injured divers from asking boat captains or airline attendants for oxygen because "they have to save it for the real emergencies."

The immediate concern of medical specialists when they are presented with an injured diver is to alleviate the physical symptoms of the injury. As a result, they may be unaware of the diver's psychological state and unintentionally respond in ways which increase anxiety and depression.

Since the diving community as a whole believes that most injured divers have caused themselves harm by taking excessive risks and are deserving of reprimand, some in the community may develop callous attitudes and lose their ability to empathize with injured divers.

THE RESULT OF STIGMATIZING

The stigmatizing of injured divers is troublesome for many reasons. It perpetuates the myth which assigns blame to the innocent and increases their feelings of shame and incompetence. All diving involves some degree of risk. The only way divers can actually prevent the possibility of getting decompression illness is to literally stop diving.

Stigmatization hurts individuals who are psychologically vulnerable and already engaged in self-punishment. It also serves to confuse the diver by verifying in reality his or her fantasies that injury will result in lost friends and a ruined reputation. Injured divers may then have difficulty distinguishing what people are actually saying about them from what they think and feel. Their maladaptive defenses may then be bolstered as protection against both external and internal attacks.

Divers who are stigmatized may become unable to let down their guard to reflect on the meaning of their symptoms, or to explore how and why they got hurt. Without a full understanding of the psychological dynamics of their injuries, divers are more likely to experience long-term psychological suffering and repeat patterns of behavior which may increase their chances of getting DCI again.

Divers who are subject to negative social reactions or hear about the bad experiences of others may be hesitant to seek treatment if and when they are injured. This can delay treatment, compromising recovery.

BEHAVIORAL REACTIONS TO INJURY

Divers demonstrate a number of behavioral reactions to their injuries. Some are able to handle the physical and psychological consequences of decompression illness with minimal internal conflict. They quickly recognize the meaning of their symptoms and seek immediate treatment. They are able to tolerate the unpleasant feelings and thoughts which typically accompany DCI, reflect upon the circumstances surrounding their injury, and gain insight into its physiological, psychological and social dimensions. Divers who develop new insights about themselves, their diving and the dive community are less likely to engage in patterns of behavior that could increase their risk of DCI.

Other divers react to decompression illness by going back to diving before they are physically or mentally prepared. They may avoid interrupting their vacations and continue to dive hours or days after recognizing symptoms. (Approximately 20 percent of divers with DCI reported to DAN in 1993 had symptoms prior to their last dive.) They may seek treatment, wait a few weeks and jump back in the water — with or without medical clearance. Action can provide a substitute for painful thought and a means to conceal underlying anxiety and/or depression. It also serves to minimize an injured diver's feelings of passivity. Only by action do some divers believe they can prove themselves competent and physically fit.

Divers who prematurely resume diving are flirting with additional injury — not only are they physically more susceptible to DCI, they may also be unconsciously prone to engaging in behaviors which increase risk. Some divers who sustain multiple accidents may attempt to protect themselves from anxiety and/or social criticism by boasting. They view DCI as a medal of honor that defines them as "real divers," forming a vicious cycle in which progressive injuries are risked in false attempts to prove worth or status. The result is: multiple incidents of DCI which can cause serious, irreversible physical problems.

Another group of divers may experience symptoms of decompression sickness, may or may not recognize them, and sooner or later seek recompression. Due to a variety of physical, social and psychological issues, their injuries appear to mobilize painful affects (emotions) and thoughts that lie stagnant or intensify with the passing of time. These divers' attempts to rehash events, understand what happened and resolve relevant psychological conflicts are often unsuccessful.

Test Your DCI-IQ

Since many illnesses and injuries have similar signs and symptoms as DCI, try to match the signs and symptoms with the associated illness or injury.

A. Angina
B. Heart Attack
C. Stroke
D. Hypoglycemia (low blood sugar)
E. Fracture
F. Chest Injury
G. Decompression Sickness (DCS)
H. Arterial Gas Embolism (AGE)
I. Flu

1. Dizziness, loss of function or paralysis of extremities, numbness, headache, nausea, loss of bladder/bowel control, lowered conscious level
2. Headache, blurred vision, fever, fatigue, numbness
3. Radiating pain to upper extremities particularly shoulder, arm and elbow, shortness of breath, nausea
4. Painful or difficult breathing, coughing up bloody froth, distended neck veins, tracheal deviation, cyanosis
5. Difficulty breathing, chest pains, numbness, unconsciousness, paralysis, blurred vision, convulsions, headache
6. Pain, numbness, fatigue, dizziness, headache, nausea, unconsciousness, paralysis, itching
7. Anxiety, marked discomfort, sweating, difficulty breathing, denial, pain under chest which radiates to arms, neck or jaw
8. Pain, tenderness, loss of function, loss of sensation, numbness, tingling
9. Dizziness, headache, change in behavior, seizures, hunger, cold, clammy and pale skin, unconsciousness

As you can see, the signs and symptoms of diving illnesses resemble many other common injuries and illnesses. If you experience any sign or symptoms of DCI, seek medical treatment immediately. While denial of the injury may prevent panic, it's important to recognize the need for appropriate medical care.

Answers: 1 (C, G); 2 (C, G); 3 (A, B); 4 (F); 5 (G, H); 6 (C, G); 7 (A, B); 8 (E, G); 9 (C, D, G, H)

If they dive after their injury, these divers may or may not put themselves at risk. They may or may not take their psychological conflicts underwater and expose themselves to additional injury. However, in many cases, their experience with DCI has left them with psychological scars which inhibit their full enjoyment of relationships, work and play.

SEEKING HELP

Any diver who has suffered decompression illness may find psychological treatment helpful. Divers who are unable to resolve their psychological conflicts and continue to suffer anxiety and depression would benefit greatly from good treatment. Action-oriented divers who tend to put themselves at risk of injury might also gain from consultation with a psychotherapist, if they are able to subordinate action to thought long enough to allow for self-reflection.

A well-trained psychotherapist can provide a safe and comfortable setting to help explore the feelings and thoughts which link the injury and its aftermath. Psychotherapy and/or other appropriate treatment can relieve symptoms, pave the way for the resolution of relevant psychological conflicts and help divers gain the psychological independence and self-liberation which will allow them to accomplish their goals with maximum pleasure and minimum risk.

SOLUTIONS & RECOMMENDATIONS

While DCI injuries are rare (approximately 900 reported accidents a year out of an estimated 3-4 million certified divers in the United States), the resulting physical and psychological consequences can be severe. For the diving community, it is frequently easier to treat the physical manifestations of DCI, because they seem obvious and unambiguous once diagnosed. In contrast, however, psychological reactions may appear untreatable because they can be subtle, confusing, mysterious and seemingly irrational at times.

The diving community should recognize a number of aspects of DCI: It is a medical illness which can have serious psychological implications; divers with DCI may deny illness and delay treatment, resulting in permanent physical disability; divers may engage in dangerous diving patterns and/or prematurely go back underwater after being injured; and injured divers with untreated psychological conflicts may suffer debilitating anxiety and depression.

The diving community as a whole should consciously work on developing a more empathetic attitude to those who suffer from DCI. Decompression illness is not a moral disease and should not be treated as one: Many divers who suffer injury violate no known safety rules.

Divers who sustain DCI — both predictable and unpredictable cases — all experience unpleasant emotions and thoughts. Negative social reactions to injury tend to bolster maladaptive defenses and undermine divers' physical and psychological welfare.

A more empathic approach to DCI will help encourage divers to take appropriate action sooner — and avoid future injury. Those with predictable hits will be more likely to initiate exploration of the motivations behind their risk-taking behaviors with a resultant decrease in dangerous diving behavior. Divers with unpredictable incidents of DCI will be better equipped to face the anxiety and depression which accompany their injuries and so reduce their suffering. Those who are able to examine the psychodynamics of their diving, the feelings and thoughts surrounding their injuries, and/or other relevant personal conflicts will enjoy safer and happier recreational — and professional — lives.

Some members of the diving community may view psychological treatment as a crutch which defines its recipients as weak and dependent. This attitude is troublesome, not only because it discourages individuals from seeking treatment, but also because it can perpetuate additional injury. It's easier for most divers to gear up and go back in the water than attempt to penetrate and master the unlimited and cloudy depths of the mind. It takes courage to look at and take responsibility for psychological conflicts — which can compromise the diver's own and others' safety, as well as inhibit the enjoyment of relationships, work and other leisure activities.

Sometimes insight into diving injuries can be gained independently, and at other times it can't. Psychological exploration resembles advanced diving in wrecks or caves — it involves the use of special equipment, a guideline, and a professional partner or team to successfully and safely accomplish the challenge.

— From July/August 1995

HEALTH CONDITIONS

Diving After Radial Keratotomy

DAN polls its members for their personal experiences.

BY DONNA M. UGUCCIONI, M.S., DAN RESEARCH, AND
JOEL DOVENBARGER, DAN DIRECTOR OF MEDICAL SERVICES

Good vision is essential to good diving — and for enjoying the underwater environment. For those divers who require vision correction, many options are available to ensure good vision. However, not all divers are willing to invest in a corrective lens for the faceplate, and others worry about mask flooding and the loss of a contact lens or the consequences of diving at some depths with contacts.

Because of these considerations, some divers have chosen another option — Radial Keratotomy (RK). This is a popular procedure to correct nearsightedness (myopia) by making radial incisions (to a 90-percent depth) in the cornea of the eye. RK has become popular with individuals who have trouble with or cannot wear contact lenses and don't feel that glasses are an acceptable solution.

But what about RK for scuba divers?

"Can I dive after RK surgery?" and "How long should I wait to return to diving?" have become commonly asked questions for DAN medical specialists. In order to gather information about diving with RK and the suggested waiting period after surgery, DAN has asked for the personal experience of DAN members with RK surgery and diving.

This request was published in the September/October 1994 issue of *Alert Diver*. At that time, DAN membership was over 105,000. DAN received 60 responses to the request through November 1994 and did a follow-up questionnaire with the respondents during the spring of 1995.

The average age of the survey respondent was 40, with an average of 10 years of dive experience. Some had 100 dives or more since surgery. Of the 60 respondents, only nine (15 percent) reported having any problems while diving. Of the 15 percent who had problems, only five divers had an associated mask squeeze, and only one of those had any accompanying eye pain. Two individuals had problems with stinging in their eyes, while one individual had vision change associated at depth.

Eighty-five percent of the respondents reported no problems while diving after RK surgery. In fact, those with no problems commented on how pleased they were with the surgery and how it increased the pleasure of their dive experience. Many had previously worn contact lenses or prescription lenses and enjoyed the freedom of having to wear neither. They also noted they were pleased they didn't have to worry about their masks flooding and the subsequent loss of a contact lens, or worry that their expensive prescription lenses might be broken.

Recreational divers thus far have not seen any strong recommendations about diving and RK. Not so for the military. The U.S. Navy has strict regulations regarding RK surgery, and individuals who have had this type of myopia correction have historically been prohibited from diving. Other branches of the service may also limit diving after RK. In a review by Captain Frank Butler, M.D., an eye surgeon and medical diving doctor for the U.S. Navy, several researchers recommended that military divers not be allowed to dive after RK surgery because of the possible complications and possible barotrauma-induced rupture of the corneal incisions.

On paper, Butler has summarized the theoretical data that supports the potential complications and ruptures, but to date no such occurrences have ever been reported. Butler has examined three U.S. Navy divers and one U.S. Coast Guard diver who had had bilateral radial keratotomy following completion of their initial dive training. All had returned to diving shortly after undergoing RK surgery. All

TABLE 1

Doctors' recommendation for safe return to diving after RK surgery

Time Interval	Total	Percentage
0-1 month	19	31.7
2-5 months	17	28.3
6-10 months	8	13.3
Until healed	1	1.7
No recommendation	14	23.3
Blank	1	1.7
TOTALS	**60**	**100.0**

had been diving for four to 10 years since surgery without any corneal wound problems or other adverse effects.

How long should recreational divers wait to resume diving after RK surgery?

This is a question asked by both divers and their ophthalmologists. Some doctors believe diving should be stopped altogether, while others have a more open approach, but vary in their recommended time intervals until returning to diving.

Like most medical procedures, there are other possible complications and side effects after RK surgery. These include:

- corneal weakness due to the incisions
- a perceived halo or glare around lights at night
- farsightedness
- the possibility of a corneal rupture with trauma to the eye

Because there is little available data on the subject, many physicians are unsure of recommending a specific waiting period for divers. Most physicians do feel, however, that once there is no risk of infection and the corneal incision sites have healed, diving may be considered.

The Butler review recommended that individuals who have had RK surgery which doesn't involve full-thickness incisions may return to diving after three months. The major risk for damage after surgery would be from direct pressure to an incision site where some weakness might exist. The difference of opinion about when to return to diving is most likely to be based on the physician's experience of when a corneal incision is considered completely healed.

TABLE 2
How long divers wait to return to diving after RK surgery

Time Interval	Total	Percentage
0-2 months	28	46.7
3-5 months	9	15.0
6-8 months	12	20.0
9-11 months	1	1.7
12 months or longer	10	16.7
TOTALS	**60**	**100.1**

There are no published guidelines on the time required for wound healing prior to resuming diving. The recommendations of ophthalmologists from the DAN study can be seen in Table 1. Some doctors (23.3 percent) made no recommendations on returning to diving. The majority of doctors' recommendations (60 percent) allowed diving within five months of surgery, while others recommended waiting at least one year.

According to the survey, most divers seemed to wait up to two months after the operation to resume diving. Only 16.7 percent of the divers surveyed waited longer than one year. The length of time a diver waited after RK surgery can be seen in Table 2.

In diving, the increase in pressure across the cornea is usually not significant except in the case of a face mask squeeze. Mask squeezes are uncommon in diving. To avoid a mask squeeze, all divers need to do is exhale into the mask to equalize the pressure. While there is a great concern for a potential corneal rupture when diving following RK surgery, its occurrence is uncommon. Most ruptures occur from a direct, blunt blow to the eye.

Conclusions

The decision to have radial keratotomy may differ among individuals and physicians. DAN does not recommend RK surgery, but it is clear from the DAN survey results that some divers are successfully participating in scuba diving with increased enjoyment and limited difficulty. Although there is some concern for a potential corneal rupture when diving following RK surgery, an actual occurrence to date is uncommon.

There are several other, newer corneal refractive surgery options for divers, including photorefractive keratectomy (PRK), which uses a cold (excimer) laser. These procedures do not involve corneal incisions.

The options to invest in corrective lenses for a face mask or wear contact lenses, especially disposable ones, are still choices for those who do not consider surgery an option.

Physicians and anyone else who would like more information on the effects of diving after eye surgery and on disorders of the eye may wish to review the article "Diving and Hyperbaric Ophthalmology," by Captain Frank Butler, M.D, in the March/April 1995 issue of *Survey of Ophthalmology*.

— From March/April 1996

The authors thank Captain Frank Butler, M.D., Christopher Debacker, M.D., and Dr. Gary S. Gerber for their invaluable assistance.

Patent Foramen Ovale

What is it, and what are its implications for scuba divers?

BY RICHARD E. MOON, M.D., DAN MEDICAL DIRECTOR,
AND JOHN ROREM, DAN COMMUNICATIONS

As scuba divers, we are aware of the pressures our bodies are subjected to at depth. We know the dangers of decompression illness (DCI) — that's why we strive to dive conservatively, abiding by the limits set by dive tables and dive computers. And that's why we read, with great interest, accounts of divers and DCI. Who gets bent and why?

We know the lungs and all body tissues are involved in DCI, but what other factors are there to consider? In answering this, researchers have found that the heart is one important place to start.

Recently, there has been interest in the anatomic variant of normal in the human heart: It is termed patent foramen ovale (PFO — pro-

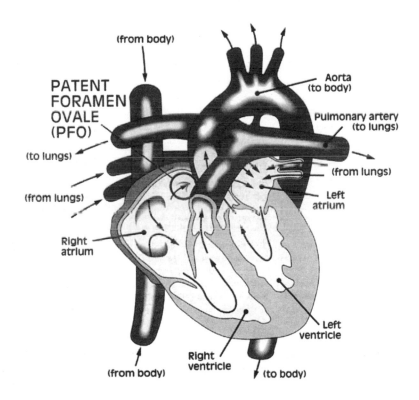

nounced PAY-tent fore-A-men O-val-eh), and through research, DAN is exploring its possible importance for scuba divers.

What is patent foramen ovale? The foramen ovale is an opening, or communication, between the right atrium and left atrium in the heart. (*Foramen* is Latin for opening, or aperture; *ovale* is, appropriately, Latin for oval, indicating the shape of the aperture.) The normal passage of blood in the adult human is from the great veins of the body, through the right atrium into the right ventricle, and then via the pulmonary artery to the lungs. Blood returns via the pulmonary veins into the left atrium. It is then pumped into the left ventricle and via the arteries to the various tissues of the body.

In the developing fetus, however, the lungs are not functional. Blood, therefore, bypasses the lungs predominantly through the foramen ovale, directly from the right atrium to the left atrium. After birth, the foramen ovale closes, allowing blood to be pumped through the lungs for oxygenation.

The foramen ovale is initially closed by a "flap valve," similar to a spring-loaded door. The valve remains closed because the pressure in the left atrium is slightly higher than the pressure in the right atrium. In most people, the flap valve actually seals over, and the foramen ovale completely disappears. In a small percentage of individuals, however, there is incomplete sealing of the valve.

This incomplete seal is what is termed patent foramen ovale, although it remains closed because of the pressure differential between the two atria. (*Patent* is Latin for open, indicating the incompleteness of the seal.) In rare instances, the foramen ovale remains completely open — this condition is more pronounced and is called atrial septal defect.

Why should the presence of patent foramen ovale be important? It isn't to a nondiver. People with patent foramen ovale are completely unaware of it and will go through life completely free of any symptoms related to it. For a diver, it could theoretically be important. The reason is that some divers, depending on depth and duration of their dives, produce bubbles in their venous blood during and after decompression (ascent from the dive). These bubbles are small, usually relatively few in number, and do not give rise to any symptoms since they are trapped by the small blood vessels in the lungs and filtered out of the circulation.

Recent evidence suggests that after decompression, many normal scuba dives, with no symptoms of decompression sickness, may produce bubbles in the venous blood. Why is this important for a diver with patent foramen ovale? It has been found that some people with patent foramen ovale may actually pump leak quantities of blood from the right atrium to the left atrium. This suggests that divers who have patent foramen ovale who also have venous gas bubbles during decompression may pass gas bubbles directly into the left atrium, bypassing the lungs. Gas bubbles in the left atrium are then carried to the body tissues, where they could cause symptoms.

Do we know if this actually happens? We have no direct evidence of this yet. What we do have is some preliminary data suggesting that patent foramen ovale may result in the bends in some individuals. The evidence is this: We have made use of a diagnostic test which can provide a very accurate image of the beating heart (two-dimensional echocardiography). Using this technique, the flow of blood within the heart can be demonstrated by injecting a tiny quantity of microscopic bubbles suspended in saline solution into a vein. These tiny bubbles are then carried to the heart and can be visualized on the echocardiographic image.

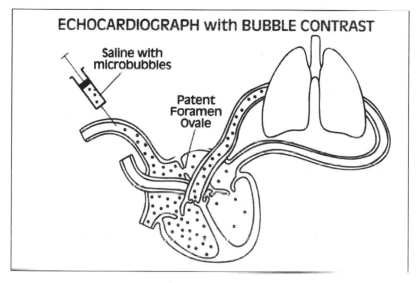

ECHOCARDIOGRAPH with BUBBLE CONTRAST

Saline with microbubbles

Patent Foramen Ovale

We have examined with a two-dimensional echocardiogram 91 patients evaluated and/or treated for decompression sickness at Duke University Medical Center. Of these 91, 39 had PFO. Sixty-four of the 91 patients had more serious symptoms (weakness, dizziness or symptoms of brain abnormalities) and 32 of these 64 had patent foramen ovale (50 percent). This percentage is higher than one would expect in a normal population (10 to 20 percent).

Does this mean that the presence of patent foramen ovale may cause decompression illness? No, it does not. The data we have are merely

DAN Gets to the Heart of Things

In the pursuit of more data on diving and PFO, two studies on seven men and four women were recently conducted at the F.G. Hall Hyperbaric Center and Echocardiography Laboratory of Duke University Medical Center. These studies looked at the effect of both exercise and immersion in water upon right-to-left shunting (the passage of blood from the right side of the heart into the left) through a patent foramen ovale.

The conclusion was that while immersion in water may cause the heart to enlarge, neither immersion nor exercise affected the right-to-left shunting through a patent foramen ovale. DAN will continue to expand its database in its efforts to better understand the relationship between PFO and diving.

suggestive. The number of patients we have checked is too small to draw any firm conclusions. One issue which needs explanation is that whereas 10 to 20 percent of the normal population may have patent foramen ovale, less than 0.1 percent of divers get the bends. In order to form firm conclusions, we must examine many more patients.

Also, the normal populations with which we are comparing our data have been obtained from other laboratories. In order to be absolutely certain of the relationship between patent foramen ovale and the bends, we must investigate many more patients with decompression sickness and also a group of normal volunteers in the same age range as our divers.

What should be done in the meantime? Nothing yet. Diving is a relatively safe sport. We recommend safe diving practices to make the sport even safer. If specific recommendations need to be made about testing divers for patent foramen ovale, we will make this known to you as soon as possible.

— From March/April 1995

Pulmonary Physiology and Problems

BY PHILIP J. FRACICA, M.D.

One of the important considerations in evaluating an individual's medical fitness for diving is the status of the lungs.

The key to understanding why this is so lies in knowing basic lung structure and function, how diving stresses the lungs, consequences of failure of the lungs to meet the stresses of diving, what types of conditions can lead to diving lung injuries, and what methods may be useful in evaluating individuals suspected of lung disease.

Pulmonary Structure and Function

The lungs are contained within the chest cavity With each breath the chest cavity expands, the lungs expand with the chest cavity and a slightly negative air pressure is created within the lungs. Air then flows down the respiratory passages to fill that vacuum.

At the end of a breath, the breathing muscles of the chest cavity relax, the chest decreases to its resting dimensions and creates a slightly positive pressure. The air then exits the lungs. This cycle of inspiration and expiration is *ventilation*.

The lungs are branching structures of tubular air passages, known as the *bronchial tree*. However, these bronchial passages are not rigid tubes. They are surrounded by circular bands of involuntary muscle which can relax or constrict, and they have a mucous membrane lining which can swell and secrete mucus under various conditions. The bronchial tubes become narrower and more numerous as they branch deeper into the lungs.

The ends of the smallest branches terminate in clusters of microscopic balloon-like air sacs called *alveoli*

An upside-down tree is a good analogy for this structure. Imagine the solid branches representing the hollow bronchial passages and the leaves representing the alveoli.

Deoxygenated blood circulates through a fine branching network of blood vessels in the walls of the alveoli, where oxygen is absorbed into the bloodstream and carbon dioxide is eliminated from the blood into the alveoli.

How Diving Stresses the Lungs

If a gas-filled balloon is placed underwater, it will shrink and grow in size, depending on the depth. This phenomenon is a basic gas law, which is known as *Boyle's Law.*

As the depth increases and the surrounding water pressure increases, the volume of gas within the balloon shrinks and the pressure within the balloon increases to match that of the surrounding water.

Similarly, as the depth decreases and the water pressure decreases, the gas volume expands and the pressure drops to match the decreasing surrounding water pressure.

If the balloon was filled with pressurized gas at depth and brought to the surface, it would expand until it became overdistended and, possibly. rupture. However, if the gas were vented out of the balloon as it ascended, then overexpansion, overpressurization and possible rupture would be avoided.

The air-filled lungs of a diver at depth is analogous to the balloon. As the diver ascends, the gas in the lungs will expand. The air needs to be steadily and evenly emptied from each of the millions of alveoli that lie at the end of the branching bronchial tree.

Anything that impairs this emptying can lead to localized overdistension and lung injury. Injury to the lung occurring from overdistention and overpressurization is referred to as *barotrauma.*

HEALTHY LUNG

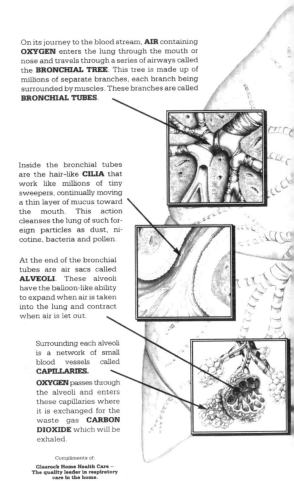

On its journey to the blood stream, **AIR** containing **OXYGEN** enters the lung through the mouth or nose and travels through a series of airways called the **BRONCHIAL TREE**. This tree is made up of millions of separate branches, each branch being surrounded by muscles. These branches are called **BRONCHIAL TUBES**.

Inside the bronchial tubes are the hair-like **CILIA** that work like millions of tiny sweepers, continually moving a thin layer of mucus toward the mouth. This action cleanses the lung of such foreign particles as dust, nicotine, bacteria and pollen.

At the end of the bronchial tubes are air sacs called **ALVEOLI**. These alveoli have the balloon-like ability to expand when air is taken into the lung and contract when air is let out.

Surrounding each alveoli is a network of small blood vessels called **CAPILLARIES**.

OXYGEN passes through the alveoli and enters these capillaries where it is exchanged for the waste gas **CARBON DIOXIDE** which will be exhaled.

Compliments of:

Glasrock Home Health Care –
The quality leader in respiratory
care in the home.

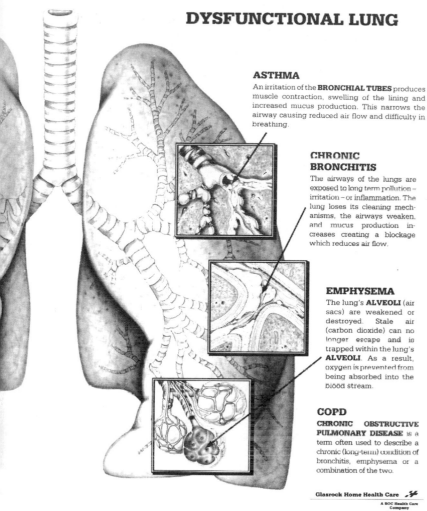

DYSFUNCTIONAL LUNG

ASTHMA

An irritation of the **BRONCHIAL TUBES** produces muscle contraction, swelling of the lining and increased mucus production. This narrows the airway causing reduced air flow and difficulty in breathing.

CHRONIC BRONCHITIS

The airways of the lungs are exposed to long term pollution – irritation – or inflammation. The lung loses its cleaning mechanisms, the airways weaken, and mucus production increases creating a blockage which reduces air flow.

EMPHYSEMA

The lung's **ALVEOLI** (air sacs) are weakened or destroyed. Stale air (carbon dioxide) can no longer escape and is trapped within the lung's **ALVEOLI**. As a result, oxygen is prevented from being absorbed into the blood stream.

COPD

CHRONIC OBSTRUCTIVE PULMONARY DISEASE is a term often used to describe a chronic (long-term) condition of bronchitis, emphysema or a combination of the two.

Glasrock Home Health Care

A BOC Health Care
Company
Critical Care
Worldwide

ILLUSTRATION COURTESY OF GLASROCK HOME HEALTH CARE

For individuals with normal lungs (who don't breathhold while ascending), the expanding gas will be vented from all areas of the lungs by normal exhalation. By contrast, the lungs of some individuals are unable to adequately empty with exhalation and may be susceptible to barotrauma.

Consequences of Diving-Induced Pulmonary Barotrauma

The most straightforward consequence of pulmonary barotrauma is a *pneumothorax,* which refers to air within the chest cavity but outside the lung.

If the expanding gas ruptures through the lung tissue and exits the surface of the lung, it will accumulate within the chest cavity. The right and left sides of the chest cavity are normally separated by the heart and other anatomical structures, so the trapped gas is usually confined to one side of the chest cavity.

As more gas accumulates with ongoing leakage or from gas expansion (with decreasing depth), the lung will collapse as the gas volume between the outside of the lung and the chest wall increases.

A pneumothorax will usually produce sudden chest pain and shortness of breath. The greater the degree of lung collapse, the more severe the shortness of breath. In the most severe cases, even if the affected lung completely collapses, the gas volume may continue to increase. That increased pressure may push the heart into the other side of the chest, which can impair heart function and limit the normal expansion of the other lung. This is referred to as a *tension pneumothorax.* This is a true medical emergency and can rapidly become fatal.

Management of a pneumothorax depends on how large the air collection and lung collapse is, and how well the affected individual tolerates it.

With a small well-tolerated pneumothorax, no treatment may be necessary, as the air will gradually become reabsorbed by the body. However, a large tension pneumothorax will require evacuation of the trapped air with a needle or a surgically placed chest tube.

If significant disruption of pulmonary blood vessels occurs, as the expanding air ruptures lung tissue, then lung hemorrhage (bleeding) can occur, which can be quite dangerous as well.

In some cases when the expanding air ruptures through the alveoli it can travel along other routes in addition to gaining access to the chest cavity.

The gas can travel towards the center of the chest and then up into the tissues of the neck. If this happens, neck or facial swelling may occur. Palpating (touching) the skin around the face and neck may reveal a "crunching sensation." This condition is known as *subcutaneous emphysema.* The crunching sensation, or crepitus, is caused by compression of numerous tiny air pockets in the tissue like popping "bubble" packing material.

Subcutaneous emphysema, while not dangerous in itself, should still be considered as evidence of lung barotrauma and will require prompt medical evaluation.

One of the most dangerous manifestations of pulmonary barotrauma occurs if the expanding gas enters the blood vessels of the lungs as it rips through the lung tissue.

These gas bubbles can enter the arterial bloodstream and block arterial blood flow to vital organs. This is known as *arterial gas embolism*. The bubbles can be carried to the brain causing stroke-like symptoms and seizures, and to the spinal cord causing numbness and paralysis.

Lung Conditions That Can Lead to Pulmonary Barotrauma

One common type of lung disease is *obstructive airway disease*. This describes a condition in which inhaled gas can easily enter the lungs but cannot be exhaled easily from the lungs. This occurs because there is a tendency for the bronchial passages to narrow during exhalation.

This expiratory obstruction to air flow is increased in several lung diseases resulting in slower, less even air evacuation from the lung and increasing the possibility of areas of air trapping.

Lung diseases that have significant obstruction include emphysema, chronic bronchitis, and asthma.

Asthma is a source of some disagreement among members of the diving medicine community. This is because asthma is a disease of variable severity from one individual to another and from one moment to another in a given individual.

In asthma there is an abnormal tendency of the muscle fibers surrounding the bronchial passages to constrict and cut off air flow. This constriction, once triggered can occur quite rapidly. An individual can go from normal breathing to labored breathing in just a few minutes.

Constriction of the airways can be provoked by many factors including exercise, choking on water, and in some cases, anxiety.

Wheezing is often a prominent symptom of asthma and represents the sound of air whistling through the narrowed respiratory passages. However, many asthmatics may have other symptoms such as chest tightness, dry cough, or shortness of breath as the major manifestations.

For the severe asthmatic there is no debate — that person shouldn't be diving. But what about the prospective diver that isn't on medication, and had their last wheezing episode perhaps·months or years ago? This individual may be totally asymptomatic on an everyday basis, but what would happen if they breathed irritating cold dry gas, or if they choked on a mouthful of water? This could trigger an attack. Such individuals would have an increased risk of pulmonary barotrauma. If there is any question, such cases should be evaluated by an expeirnced dive medicine physician on an individual basis.

Besides obstructive lung disease, the other major risk factor to consider is spontaneous pneumothorax.

This refers to the spontaneous occurrence of a pneumothorax not provoked by any unusual overdistension or overpressurization of the lung. Such an individual may have an inherent weakness of the lung tissue, and would be at an increased risk of a pneumothorax triggered by diving-related pressure changes.

There are a myriad of other diseases of the chest which may theoretically increase risk. Many have never been systematically studied in significant numbers of individuals. Again, such cases should be individually evaluated by a qualified physician.

Methods of Pulmonary Diagnostic Evaluation

A good medical history and physical examination are always important. Specific tests that might provide additional information about the status of the lungs include chest X-rays and pulmonary function testing.

Chest X-rays can show evidence of many types of lung disease including emphysema. Pulmonary function testing measures the ability of an individual to inhale and exhale air, and can also detect individuals with obstructive lung disease.

Asthmatics who are not actually having an attack can have fairly normal pulmonary function tests. However, if significant asthma is suspected, various types of "challenge" tests can be performed where the individual is exposed to a substance which provokes airway constriction. An asthmatic individual will show an enhanced sensitivity, and their bronchial passages will constrict more easily than a normal individual.

Editor's Note: For the most current information on diving with asthma, see "Asthma and Diving," by Dr. Guy deLisle Dear, from the January/February 1997 issue; p. 107 in this book.

Conclusion

Even divers with apparently normal lungs can experience pulmonary barotrauma. However, with many forms of lung disease the risk of pulmonary barotrauma substantially increases.

In view of the potentially devastating consequences of diving related pulmonary barotrauma, it is my opinion that in cases where doubt exists, a cautious approach will best protect the health of the prospective diver.

— *From September/October 1991*

Hypertension Under Pressure

BY KAREN VICK, M.S., R.PH.

Hypertension, or high blood pressure, is the most common adult medical problem in the modern world.

Estimates indicate that over 60 million Americans suffer from this malady. Untreated, many may go on to develop more serious complications such as coronary artery disease or stroke.

The etiology (cause) of hypertension is unknown. Patients generally exhibit no symptoms. If treatment with medications are necessary to control blood pressure, therapy is generally lifelong.

Numerous medications are now available to treat hypertension. These antihypertensives act by a variety of mechanisms to decrease blood pressure.

Selection of the "best" product for an individual is based on other underlying health problems, severity of hypertension, the development of adverse drug reactions, cost of therapy, and compliance with the medication regimen.

This brief drug review will outline possible physiological alterations in the response of individuals when exercising or diving. In general, divers taking anti-hypertensive medications may have a significant inhibition of normal physiologic control mechanisms in the cardiovascular system.

Poor exercise tolerance is often noted by patients receiving these medications. The development of syncope (fainting) is also commonly reported. Individuals frequently describe limitations during exercise due to the development of generalized weakness, orthostatic hypotension (rapid blood shift), shortness of breath, dizziness or an abnormal heartbeat.

Medications, such as diuretics, inhibitors or peripheral antagonists, e.g., increase the ability of the vasculature (blood vessels) to dilate, inhibiting blood pressure rises during exercise and may lead to exertional syncope. Additionally, an increased loss of body fluids can occur with use of these medications.

Calcium channel blockers can produce these same types of general adverse effects under pressure. Changes in heart rhythm and rate of heart muscle contraction can also occur. Careful exercise screening of an individual should therefore occur prior to approval for diving with any of these agents.

Centrally acting agents act at the level of the brain stem to reduce heart rate and decrease vasoconstriction in peripheral blood vessels. Because of the action at the level of the central nervous system, sedation, dizziness and confusion have been reported with their use. Use of these agents in the underwater environment may be dangerous for patients experiencing this side effect.

Beta blockers pose additional concerns for the diver. These medications reduce blood pressure by reducing heart rate and enhancing dilation of blood vessels. Patients receiving beta blockers may also have a significant inhibition of heart rate response to exercise. This can produce severe fatigue and a reduction in maximum exercise performance. Exercise testing may be appropriate prior to a dive for individuals receiving beta blocking agents.

Discontinuation of antihypertensive medications prior to a dive is not recommended without consultation from a diving physician. Often a "rebound" phenomenon is seen with the abrupt cessation of therapy. Rapid increases in blood pressures have been reported. Contact your physician before initiating any changes in your current drug therapy.

Antihypertensive agents have a direct effect on the cardiovascular system. Other effects on the central nervous system and fluid balances assist in managing blood pressure. Divers must be aware of the problems associated with the inhibition of these physiologic mechanisms and the risks of diving while using these medications.

Please contact your physician to assess your physiologic response to exercise before attempting a dive if receiving any of these medications.

— From July/August 1991

Common Categories of High Blood Pressure Medications

Classification	Generic —	Trade Names
Diuretics	Hydrochlorthiazide	
	Furosemide	Lasix™
	Bumetinide	Bumex™
Beta Blockers	Propranolol	Inderal™
	Metoprolol	Lopressor™
	Atenolol	Tenormin™
	Nadolol	Corgard™
	Timolol	Blocadren™
Calcium Channel Blockers	Verapamil	Calan™, Isoptin™
	Diltiazem	Cardizem™
	Nifedipine	Procardia™
	Nicardipine	Cardene™
Peripheral Antagonists	Prazosin	Minipress™
	Terazosin	Hytrin™
	Hydralazine	Apresoline™
Centrally Acting Agents	Clonidine	Catapres™
	Guanabenz	Wytensin™
	Guanafacine	Tenex™
ACE Inhibitors	Enalapril	Vasotec™
	Captopril	Capoten™
	Lisinopril	Prinivil™, Zestril™
Other Agents	Labetolol	Trandate™

Diabetes & Diving

*Current practices demonstrate
that many with diabetes do take the plunge
The question DAN wants to explore is: How safe is it?*

BY GUY DELISLE DEAR, M.B., FRCA, DAN ASSISTANT MEDICAL DIRECTOR

Diabetes and Diving Get New Scrutiny

The traditional view of diving physicians has been to ban individuals with diabetes from diving. Dive medical researchers discussed the topic of diving with diabetes at the May 1996 meeting of the Undersea and Hyperbaric Medical Society (UHMS). The workshop, "Some Diabetics Are Fit to Dive, But Who?" convened to discuss the issue. Researchers discussed the possibilities that the ban on divers with insulin-dependent diabetes mellitis (IDDM) may be too severe, noting that hypoglycemia while underwater or on the surface may be less common than previously believed.

The undisputed risk remains, however, that divers with diabetes who experience a hypoglycemic attack while underwater risk drowning. At the same time, they can endanger their buddies, since diving is a shared responsibility.

DAN statistics reported at the UHMS meeting showed that of 550 fatalities reported to DAN from 1989 to 1994, seven had diabetes mellitus, which may have contributed to their deaths. Eight of the 2,400 episodes of decompression illness reported were divers with diabetes. This is in line with the expected numbers in the general population.

In the DAN survey reported on in the January/February 1996 issue of *Alert Diver* ("The Diabetes Question," page 101), 164 divers with diabetes completed the questionnaire, noting they had made hundreds of dives safely. The majority of those who responded (129 divers) were IDDM divers.

Dr. George Burghen, Chief of Endocrinology and Metabolism at the University of Tennessee, a committee member in the American Diabetes Association, has developed procedures and special training for divers with diabetes. He presented evidence that selected individuals with diabetes could be allowed to dive under specified conditions.

This view was endorsed by Dr. Chris Edge of the UK Sports Diving Medical Committee. In England, he notes, the diver with diabetes has the responsibility of running the training program for his respective club.

The selection of the diver with diabetes and the pre-dive, in-dive and post-dive procedures have been precisely defined by the UK Sports Diving Medical Committee. The committee has nearly 100 divers registered in its database that is designed to record any incidents that occur during or after the dive. The good news is that to date they have registered no incidents in divers with diabetes.

At the UHMS meeting, Dr. Michael Lerch, researcher with the Department of Diabetology, Protestant Hospital, Witten, Germany, presented data from seven IDDM divers. Blood glucose levels were measured before and after every dive, and in no case did the blood sugar levels rise or fall excessively. One factor he did find to be a problem was that dehydration was more noticeable in his diabetic group.

Challenges

The problem of diving with diabetes is threefold.

• The effect of diving on blood sugar levels is not known with confidence. Although persons with diabetes may participate in strenuous sports above the water, little data have been gathered on the true incidence of hypoglycemia during scuba diving.

• The procedures by which divers with diabetes can dive safely have not been defined.

• The numbers of divers on whom appropriate observations have been made is insufficient to draw firm conclusions regarding the safety of diving for individuals with diabetes. Very small numbers of divers with diabetes have been studied in the field.

DAN's new field study in divers with insulin-dependent diabetes will log approximately 400 dives and record blood sugar levels before and after multiple dives during a multiday dive period. This should enable the study of a fairly wide selection of divers, and hopefully, some insight gained into the variation blood sugar levels in IDDM divers.

What exactly is diabetes?

Diabetes mellitus (DM) is a disorder of the endocrine system, manifested by one of two things:

• an insufficient production of insulin, or
• the resistance of the body's cells to the actions of insulin, despite normal or high levels.

Persons with DM often have excessively high blood glucose (BG), called hyperglycemia, or a very low BG, better known as hypoglycemia.

Diabetes mellitus itself has two major forms:

- Insulin-dependent diabetes (IDDM) in which insulin must be given by injection to control blood sugar levels, and
- Non-insulin-dependent diabetes, which may be controlled by diet or by oral hypoglycemic medications.

Who gets diabetes?

IDDM may occur in any age group from childhood to adulthood. The prevalence of diabetes in the United States population has been estimated to range between 2 percent at age 20 to 17.7 percent at ages 65-74. These rates include undiagnosed diabetes as well as previously diagnosed diabetes (*Diabetes*, 1987).

The main risk to the diver is the occurrence of hypoglycemia, or low blood sugar levels, which may manifest as confusion, sweating, rapid heartbeat, unconsciousness and even death.

High blood sugar levels, or hyperglycemia,

DENNIS TAPPAREL PHOTO

may also cause unconsciousness although this usually develops much more slowly than with hypoglycemia. Impaired consciousness underwater can lead to almost certain death. Although hypoglycemia occurs most commonly in IDDM, it can also occur in individuals taking oral hypoglycemic medications.

Although hypo- or hyperglycemia can occur daily, other problems can develop in diabetes over the long term, including:
- retinopathy (alterations in visual acuity)
- disorders of the kidneys
- coronary artery disease
- changes in the central nervous system including abnormal nervous conduction, and
- atherosclerosis, causing poor circulation in the limbs.

UHMS Conclusions

The UHMS workshop did come up with some important conclusions by a consensus of the diving physicians present. These were summarized by Dr. David Elliott, diving physician and physiologist and civilian consultant to the Royal Navy:

- Divers with diabetes are at risk of sudden loss of consciousness. As divers, this carries the ultimate risk of drowning and implies additional risks for their healthy buddies.

- Individuals with diabetes, however well the diabetes is controlled, should not be passed as fit to dive without restriction.

- Individuals with diabetes who meet certain criteria can dive provided they dive in accordance with detailed procedures, such as those of the UK Sports Diving Medical Committee.

- Divers with diabetes should be examined periodically for complications of their disorder that disqualify them on the grounds of additional risks.

- Hypoglycemia in deep dives could be wrongly perceived by a diver with diabetes as nitrogen narcosis.

- Many questions remain unanswered — additional data collection in the field is essential.

— From January/February 1997

Sources

Prevalence of diabetes and impaired glucose tolerance and plasma glucose levels in the U.S. Population age 20-74 years. Diabetes April 1987.
Alert Diver. Jan-Feb. p.21-23, 1996.

Edge C. The Diabetic Diver in Medical Assessment of Fitness to Dive. Proceedings from the International Conference at the Edinburgh Conference Center. Pressure 25(4 July/August) 1996.

The Diabetes Question

"Diving safely" and "insulin-dependent" may not be mutually exclusive terms.

BY DONNA M. UGUCCIONI, M.S., DAN RESEARCH,
AND JOEL DOVENBARGER, DAN DIRECTOR OF MEDICAL SERVICES

Who wouldn't want to go to summer camp on the island of St. John in the U.S. Virgin Islands? In a heartbeat, most of us would sign up for a camp where you can scuba dive, snorkel, hike, sea kayak and sail.

This camp, however, is specifically designed for adolescents and young adults with diabetes. Divers Alert Network was invited to observe the 1995 session at Camp DAVI and collect data on persons with diabetes involved in scuba diving.

Camp DAVI, which represents the Diabetic Association of the Virgin Islands, was begun in 1990 to guide young, active persons with their diabetes. The camp, structured for eight to 12 campers — men and women — ranging in age from 12 to 40, allows persons with diabetes to combine exercise and active watersports with education about diabetes.

Founded by Stephen Prosterman, who also has diabetes, the camp staff includes a medical doctor and a nurse practitioner. Prosterman is the organization's president, as well as the dive supervisor for the University of the Virgin Islands. Camp DAVI is also sponsored by the University and is held annually at the Virgin Islands Environmental Research Station (V.I.E.R.S.) at Lameshur Bay.

The camp's goal is to provide an additional resource on diet, regular exercise and blood glucose monitoring. Five camps have convened since 1990, involving approximately 50 persons with diabetes. All participants have had the opportunity to experience scuba diving, and a number have gone on to receive their dive certification.

Camp DAVI in Action

At [the 1995] camp, there were a total of 10 insulin-dependent persons with diabetes, including Prosterman; Dr. Doren Fredrickson, the camp doctor; and Rebecca Winsett, a family nurse practitioner. The team collected data on the diet, exercise, insulin use and blood sugars of all campers, and also acted as a resource for glucose control during aerobic exercise activities.

Camp DAVI's daily schedule is full of activities. Breakfast is at 7 a.m., followed by a one-hour aerobic activity such as jogging, hiking or swimming. Morning activities, which include snorkeling, sailing, hiking and windsurfing, follow. Afternoon activities are usually dedicated to scuba diving. Group discussion follows dinner each night and covers a review of the day's activities and the campers' personal experiences, and medical and health issues relating to diabetes.

Data Collection on Divers with Diabetes

The dedication of Prosterman and the uniqueness of a Camp DAVI experience caught DAN's interest in 1993, after Joel Dovenbarger, DAN Director of Medical Services, met Prosterman at a conference sponsored by the American Diabetes Association. Camp DAVI is DAN's first opportunity to observe divers with insulin-dependent diabetes in a diving environment. This experience — and others like it — will serve to help design a pilot field study for DAN to observe persons with diabetes who are currently certified to dive. It will also assist Prosterman, Winsett and Fredrickson in evaluating the effectiveness of blood glucose monitoring while scuba diving.

The data collected from the 1995 camp [is stored] in a database at DAN; Prosterman and his colleagues can then use the data in their ongoing research. The blood glucose monitoring schedule developed by the DAVI staff will provide a systematic way to collect information about the safety of diving in this group. Plus, a database designed by DAN researchers will be available to Prosterman for use with future camps. In turn, DAN will use the database itself to expand on future studies to help provide statistical information on divers with diabetes in the field.

The preliminary results from Camp DAVI suggest that diving is permissible — in very controlled settings where the diver with diabetes has good control, is monitored closely and is aware of blood sugar "highs" and "lows." In Camp DAVI's five years, two hypoglycemic reactions during diving have occurred. Both, however, were handled successfully by using established hand signals and rescue procedures. The risk of a hypoglycemic reaction is small in this group, but it is not zero.

Guidelines for the Present — and Future Possibilities

The future of diving safely for persons with diabetes will depend upon continued research. The success of Camp DAVI and other organized field studies involving divers with diabetes will provide the much-needed baseline of information. These projects will help define the necessary questions, future goals and help quantify the risk of diving for divers with insulin-dependent diabetes.

There are current working guidelines proposed by the Diabetes and Diving Committee of the Council on Exercise of the American Diabetes Association. This committee has acknowledged that there are individuals with diabetes mellitus now diving. Because of this, there is a need to establish safety guidelines, not only for divers with diabetes, but also for the diving community in general, who may be diving with divers with diabetes.

The current recommendations of this committee state that divers who are in control of their blood glucose levels, understand the disease and its associated episodes of hyper- and hypoglycemic episodes, and are free of severe secondary complications may participate in scuba diving. To be a safe diver with diabetes, the committee recommends following blood glucose management procedures and knowing that diving safely with diabetes depends on understanding how to prevent underwater hypoglycemia.

Excluded from diving in these guidelines are divers with diabetes with a recent severe hypoglycemic episode (within the past 12 months) or advanced secondary complications. Also excluded are divers with diabetes unaware of hypoglycemic episodes, those with poor control of blood sugar levels and those who do not possess a good understanding of the relationship between diabetes and exercise. Identifying divers in the second group is a tough call for diving medicine doctors, but it is essential for diving safety.

Conclusions

From the DAN survey and other field research, it appears that some persons with diabetes can and do dive safely. Additionally, hypoglycemic episodes are common with exercise and with diving. The reason most diving physicians see diabetes as a contraindication to diving is twofold: low blood sugar risks and associated complications with diabetes. A low blood sugar episode underwater can have adverse effects on the diver and the diver's buddy, and the associated complications of the disease — such as neurological, cardiovascular or renal disease — can add to the risks associated with diving.

DAN continues to collect diabetes survey data through observing randomly selected certified divers with diabetes from the DAN database.

— *With reports from Rebecca Winsett, Family Nurse Practitioner (FNP)*
— *From January/February 1996*

Diving Dilemma

Improved control of diabetes versus the consequences of the disease itself make a tough choice

Diabetes mellitus, affecting approximately 5 percent of the U.S. population, is a lifelong disease of the insulin-producing cells of the pancreas, characterized by the body's inability to regulate blood glucose levels. Diabetes has two faces: With Type 1 diabetes, the pancreas no longer produces insulin; the body must be supplied with insulin through injections. With Type 2, the body either does not make enough insulin, or the body cannot use the insulin that is produced.

Both conditions require vigilance in dietary management and medication.

In general, persons with diabetes suffer no impairment of their physical or mental abilities, although the disease can cause changes in some of the body's systems, causing physical limitations in severe cases or sometimes later in life. The majority control their diabetes through diet and exercise — and with medication, when it's needed. This medication can be administered either orally or as insulin injections.

The medical management of diabetes has improved over the years. Persons with diabetes have benefited from new and better types of insulin and the ability to monitor blood glucose quickly and easily. This has given persons with diabetes better overall control of their disease and can even prevent some of the long-term complications. Today, many individuals involved in diving medicine and the treatment of diabetes feel that insulin-dependent diabetes should no longer be a contraindication to scuba diving.

The major concern for a diver with diabetes is hypoglycemia. An abnormal decrease in blood sugar, hypoglycemia has a range of symptoms, from mild to severe. Untreated or unrecognized, it can precipitate a cascade of events that lead to seizures, unconsciousness and subsequent drowning if it occurs in a submerged diver. It is for this reason that hypoglycemia can be a threat underwater and why there have been obstacles to certifying divers with diabetes.

Some divers with diabetes feel they can prevent this situation by glucose — or carbohydrate — loading before entering the water. A high ingestion level of either may produce a high blood glucose level, they say, and help prevent a deficit underwater. This may work well for some individuals, but it's not fail-safe. Hypoglycemia can occur suddenly and unexpectedly, even in diabetics who have good "control" of their disease.

The dilemma created here is one of improved knowledge and technique for control of the disease versus the known consequences of the disease. Some doctors have signed medical consents so their patients with insulin-dependent diabetes can dive. This usually occurs on a case-by-case basis, taking into consideration the positive and negative aspects of each individual's history. Other physicians have simply given a blunt "no diving" recommendation. In some cases, divers have been certified and never mentioned the insulin-dependent diabetes issue.

Although there are different approaches to this issue, diving has now reached a point where the true risk for persons with insulin-dependent diabetes should be quantified if possible. This is why DAN has launched its study.

Much more information is needed, however. At present, we do not have the quality or quantity of general information to establish the relative safety of insulin-dependent diabetes and recreational scuba diving.

But we're getting closer.

— *Donna Uguccioni and Joel Dovenbarger*
— *From January/February 1996*

The DAN Diabetes Survey

Preliminary Findings

In 1993 Joel Dovenbarger, DAN's Director of Medical Services, and Dr. Guy Dear, DAN's Assistant Medical Director, published a diabetes survey in *Alert Diver* (May/June 1993). At that time, 110 individuals had been included in data analysis. Of the 110 divers with diabetes analyzed, 79 (72 percent) had insulin-dependent diabetes mellitus (IDDM). The remainder controlled their diabetes with oral agents, diet or exercise.

The average age of this survey group was 41 years old. The length of diving experience ranged from one month to 37 years, and there was a mean of 349 dives with a median of 100 dives per diver. Surprisingly, over 50 percent of these divers were diagnosed with diabetes prior to certification to dive.

Many respondents had at some time in their lives suffered a hypoglycemic episode (temporary weakness due to low blood sugar). Over half (55 percent) of the divers with IDDM had experienced hypoglycemia while exercising, while only 15 percent had experienced it while diving. Twenty percent of the divers with IDDM reported a post-dive low. In the combined group (both insulin-dependent and non-insulin-dependent divers with diabetes), 43 per-

---

cent suffered a hypoglycemic episode during exercise, while 12 percent experienced a low blood sugar episode during diving.

A larger percentage of the divers with IDDM checked their blood sugar daily (79 percent versus 64 percent in the combined group). Eighty-four percent of divers with IDDM and 42 percent of all diabetics checked their blood sugar level prior to diving, while only 66 percent of insulin-dependent and 51 percent of all check blood sugar prior to and after diving.

Only one individual reported having suffered a previous decompression illness injury — an air embolism — while no one reported suffering from decompression sickness.

The Survey Continues

Editor's note: One of the hottest topics in dive medicine in the 1990s has been diving with diabetes. Although diabetes has been traditionally considered a contraindication to diving, DAN is discovering that people with diabetes are diving and are assertive about their ability to do so.

In 1997, Divers Alert Network launched a study to analyze current guidelines. "This is an observational research project," notes Donna Uguccioni of DAN Research. "We learned a lot through a preliminary survey to DAN members initiated in June of 1993, and an additional request for information in the January/February issue of *Alert Diver* (see "The Diabetes Question"). "Divers with diabetes have given us a very positive response to our project."

Historically DAN has advised divers with insulin-dependent diabetes against diving because of the threat of a hypoglycemic episode underwater.

Keep track of DAN's progress with its study of diving with diabetes in *Alert Diver.*

— From *January/February 1996 & 1997*
— *Edited for inclusion in* The Best of Alert Diver

Asthma & Diving

BY GUY DELISLE DEAR, M.B., FRCA,
DAN ASSISTANT MEDICAL DIRECTOR

One of the most frequently asked questions DAN's medical department tackles each week involves asthma and diving. Specifically, DAN medics are often asked to explain why there may be problems for a person with asthma who wishes to dive.

In this short article, DAN describes the nature of asthma and some aspects of its treatment as well as a review of current thinking on this issue in the dive medicine community. Keep in mind, however, this is still a hot topic — with a substantial amount of controversy — even among diving medical specialists.

Whether you have asthma or another medical condition, the consideration and acceptance of the risks involved in scuba diving should be an informed decision. This article provides basic information on where you can obtain additional guidance on asthma — for yourself, for prospective divers and for personal physicians.

— Joel Dovenbarger, DAN Director of Medical Services

Overview

The topic of asthma and diving has long been a controversial subject in the recreational diving community. Traditionally, divers with asthma have been excluded from diving.

Asthma is a disease characterized by narrowing of the breathing tubes (bronchi) in response to a variety of stimuli. It is not a fixed response, and a patient can have a sudden worsening in lung function, called an "attack." An asthma attack can be triggered by pollen and other so-called "allergens," cold air, irritants in the atmosphere, colds or flu.

The bronchial narrowing in asthma has two effects: one is to decrease the amount of air that can be moved in and out of the lungs. This can reduce exercise capacity — especially for a diver, who already has reduced breathing capacity due to the external resistance of his breathing apparatus and the increased internal resistance due to higher breathing gas density at depth. Secondly, reduced airway caliber could cause trapping of gas in the lung during ascent. If trapped gas expands at a rate greater than it can be exhaled through the narrowed airways, lung rupture can result, causing arterial gas embolism or pneumothorax (collapsed lung).

Another related concern with asthma and diving has been the increased propensity of airways in asthmatics to narrow when exposed to the conditions implicit in diving: inhalation of cold, dry air and/or sea water (the latter by losing the mouthpiece or from a leaky regulator). Dr. Mark Harries from the British Medical Olympic Center has pointed out that asthmatics who dive are at risk from exercise limitation, not just peripheral gas-trapping. While exercising on land it is easy enough to stop, rest and catch one's breath; this may not be possible underwater.

Discussions on Diving With Asthma

What do dive physicians think about diving with asthma? This subject has generated much discussion worldwide, and many physicians hold opposing viewpoints.

Perhaps the most liberal guidelines are from the United Kingdom, which states that well-controlled asthmatics may dive — within two guidelines:

• Provided they have not needed a bronchodilator within 48 hours; and
• If they do not have cold-, exercise- or emotion-induced asthma.

In Australia, the most conservative country in this respect, all divers are expected to pass a spirometry (lung function) test, to exclude asthma, prior to certification.

As a general overview, DAN statistics show that several divers with asthma have died. It is unclear, though, from examination of their accident reports whether asthma was actually the cause of death or merely an unrelated finding. Data from the British Sub Aqua Club (BSAC) indicate that few divers die with asthma or as a result of asthma.

In addition to DAN's own research, the issue of diving with asthma was discussed at the 1995 annual meeting of the Undersea and Hyperbaric Medical Society (UHMS), the international organization comprised of diving physicians from around the world. The symposium "Are Asthmatics Fit to Dive?" was an important agenda item at that meeting.

On the general assessment of the risks of diving with asthma, the South Pacific Underwater Medical Society (SPUMS) has stated that diving may precipitate an asthma attack. Asthmatics are at risk of shortness of breath, panic and drowning on the surface.

Information from the DAN database on divers with asthma suggests that there may be a slight increase in the risk of decompression illness, but there are insufficient numbers as yet to assess the risk accurately.

The incidence of asthma in the general population is approximately 4-5 percent. Records indicate that about the same percentage of the diving population has asthma, whether or not they admit so on their diving medical forms. It appears, then, that a percentage of divers with asthma are diving safely. Bear in mind that this only represents divers who took up diving against medical advice, and who probably have mild asthma only. The true risk for all asthmatics may well be significantly higher than is currently appreciated by the statistics.

The treatment of the four forms of asthma is relevant in determining its severity (see below) and therefore the associated risk of diving. According to UHMS discussions, the first three types of asthma, mild intermittent and mild to moderate persistent asthma, if well-controlled, may allow carefully selected divers to continue diving.

Categorizing Risks

The next question involves assessing a diver with asthma, with these two qualifications:

• Is the asthma of a mild nature; or

• Is the treatment working sufficiently to prevent an acute asthmatic attack while underwater or on the surface?

If the treatment regimen can return the pulmonary function tests to normal, especially those taken post-exercise, divers may be safe to dive and undergo the severe exercise they may need to perform while diving. Potential divers with asthma should undergo both an assessment of lung function and an exercise test to gauge asthma severity. A physician knowledgeable in diving as well as the treatment of asthma might be in a position to offer the best advice.

One consistent theme from all the medical agencies involved was the lack of good information about asthma and diving. DAN is presently working on an assessment of the whole issue. We hope to develop guidelines as to whether individuals with asthma can dive safely and under what circumstances. The best source to help you decide on the issue of diving and asthma for yourself is your physician.

Classifications of Asthma

Some new classifications have come from the Global Guidelines on Asthma, which are a joint effort of the WHO (World Health Organization) and the NIH (National Institutes of Health) on the diagnosis and treatment of asthma. Originally presented by Dr. A.J. Torre, a member of the National Faculty of the National Asthma Education Program (a NIH program) to the UHMS, the NIH classifications include these four categories.

• *Mild intermittent asthma*

Signs & symptoms: Clinical features occur less than once a week and are associated with less than a 20 percent decrease in peak flow (the maximum rate of air flow during expiration). This type of asthma shows brief increases in the severity of symptoms (called exacerbation), lasting a few hours to a few days. Nocturnal symptoms occur less than twice monthly, and between acute attacks the patient should be asymptomatic, with normal lung function.

Treatment: Intermittent use of short-acting bronchodilators on an as-required basis.

• **Mild persistent asthma**

Signs & symptoms: Peak flow should be near normal, with less than 20 percent variation. Symptoms occur more than once weekly but less than once a day. Exacerbation affects sleep, with nighttime symptoms often appearing more than twice monthly.

Treatment: Daily anti-inflammatory controller medications such as inhaled steroids, Intal (cromolyn), Tilade (nedocromil), or, more recently, Accolate (zafirlukast), may be required. Short-acting bronchodilators may be used on an as-needed basis, and a long-acting bronchodilator may be used at night to prevent nocturnal symptoms.

• **Moderate persistent asthma**

Signs & symptoms: Symptoms, even a cough, can occur daily and often interfere with activities or sleep. Persons with moderate persistent asthma may require a short-acting bronchodilator. Peak flow is generally between 60 and 80 percent. Ironically, many patients with these symptoms do not believe they have asthma. Coughing with exercise or at night is an important symptom and a very likely indicator of this type of asthma.

Treatment: Daily medication, usually inhaled steroids, is required and may require short-acting bronchodilators for acute episodes.

• **Severe persistent asthma**

Signs & symptoms: Persons with this type of asthma have continuous symptoms and peak flows of 60 percent of normal or less. An increase in symptom severity occurs frequently, limiting physical activity, and nocturnal symptoms occur frequently.

Treatment: Long-acting bronchodilators, oral steroids are required as well as bronchodilators in the acute episodes.

Adds Dr. Torre: Any asthmatic with symptoms more than one to two times a week must be on an anti-inflammatory medication according to the Consensus Guidelines. Environmental control and avoidance of allergic triggers are also important, he notes.

— *From January/February 1997*

"Classifications of Asthma" section edited for inclusion in *The Best Of Alert Diver*

References

Obtain additional information from:

UHMS "Are Asthmatics Fit to Dive?" Workshop Report April 1996; UHMS 10531 Metropolitan Ave., Kensington, MD

UK Sports Diving Medical Committee Report 1995 British Sub-Aqua Club (BSAC), Telford's Quay, Ellesmere Port, South Wirral, Cheshire L65 4FY

South Pacific Undersea Medical Society Workshop Report (SPUMS) 1995; SPUMS c/o Australian and New Zealand College of Anaesthestists, 630 Saint Kilda, Melbourne, Victoria 3004 Australia

Global Initiative for Asthma 1995 Report (NIH 95-3659)

Diving, Hyperbarics, and Pregnancy

BY MAIDA BETH TAYLOR, M.D.

The short-term pleasure of diving must be balanced against the potential long-term effects on the fetus as a passive passenger at depth. Most workers investigating DCS and fetal risk agree that the fetus is at no increased risk of bubble formation during decompression. In fact, three researchers demonstrated that the fetus is more resistant to bubble formation than is the mother.

Studies of DCS have also measured rates of birth defects after induced DCS in animals. Most of the experiments have been done at pressures (6.4 to 7.1 ata) in excess of those encountered in sport diving. Despite the high pressures and high rates of DCS imposed on the study animals, only one of three studies in the literature demonstrates an increased rate of malformation after DCS.

Of more importance perhaps than birth defects is a very high rate of fetal death in utero found by animal researchers. Studies of dogs and rats show no increased rates of fetal death, but virtually all sheep studies show high fetal loss rates. The impression is that the closer to term, the greater the risk. The fetal circulation depends on the large patent foramen ovale and ductus arteriosus for the delivery of the most well-oxygenated blood from the umbilical vein directly to critical tissues, bypassing the systemic and pulmonary circulation.

The fetal cardiovascular system lacks an effective filter; thus any bubbles formed are likely to be directed to the brain and coronary arteries. This selective perfusion scheme probably accounts for the lethality of DCS in animals. Thus, researchers in the field concur that any bubbles in the fetus are more ominous than many bubbles in the mother. No data, reports or discussions of air embolism and its effects on mother and fetus in pregnancy appear in the diving literature. Since the volume of gas lethal to the fetus has not been measured and is probably very small, and since bubbles would be preferentially delivered to the heart and brain, even shallow diving presents grave fetal risks. The hazard of diving during pregnancy extends beyond DCS and air embolism. Since both of these injuries usually dictate hyperbaric oxygen therapy, the safety of treatment merits examination.

The medical literature offers no evidence of adverse fetal outcomes from controlled hyperbarism. The classic paper on material and fetal effects of hyperbaric states (by Assali in 1968) detailed changes in uterine and fetal blood flow during administration of hyperbaric oxygen.

Placental and umbilical flow rates decreased slightly during hyperbaric oxygen administration. The major finding was alterations in fetal blood flow pattern. Apparently the fetal pulmonary bed is exquisitely sensitive to oxygen tension and responds with vasodilation as oxygen tension rises. Thus, hyperbaric oxygen causes a shift from a fetal blood flow pattern to a neonatal pattern. The shift reverses when oxygen tension returns to normal. One can only speculate on the long-term effects of prolonged exposure of the fetus to high oxygen *in utero* due to neonatalization of the fetal circulation.

A more immediate problem, though still speculative, is concern that basic physiological changes in pregnancy may compound diving risks. During pregnancy, maternal body fluid distribution is altered, with increased interstitial fluid and edema. These so-called third-space fluids have diminished exchange of dissolved gases in the central circulation. Though not addressed in any of the literature, maternal third-space fluid might offer a reservoir for nitrogen retention. The potential sites for nitrogen sequestration include the increased deposits of body fat found during pregnancy.

Combining third-space and fat stores as harbors for nitrogen, offgassing time for pregnant women may not correspond to the limits established in the standard repetitive dive tables. Fluid retention during pregnancy also causes nasopharyngeal swelling. Women with no prior allergic symptoms often complain of nose and ear stuffiness in pregnancy. Obviously, the risk of ear and sinus squeeze will be increased.

During the early months of gestation, approximately two-thirds of pregnant women experience some degree of gastrointestinal dysfunction, including increased nausea, vomiting, increased gastric acidity and gastric reflux. Later in pregnancy, as the uterus enlarges, reflux increases.

Gastric emptying time is delayed. Obstetricians and anesthesiologists have come to regard all pregnant women as having full stomachs regardless of the timing of the last meal.

If motion sickness on the dive boat adds to morning sickness, the pregnant diver is in for difficult diving. Consequently, the pregnant diver clearly is at high risk of vomiting into her regulator, an accident few sport divers are prepared to handle safely.

The safe location and placement of the weight belt under, over or around the gravid belly may create an unforeseen inability to ditch it during an emergency. Any diving hazard has the potential to harm the fetus.

In a litigious society such as ours, diving and pregnancy seem incompatible.

The woman who wants to dive may not drink coffee in order to protect her fetus from unknown risk, although caffeine is not a teratogen (an agent that causes abnormal development). She may take vitamins and avoid paint fumes but will ask if diving is safe during pregnancy. In view of the elective nature of diving, even though pregnancy does not clearly increase maternal incidence of DCS or air embolism, the unborn may be at severe risk if a diving accident occurs. Summarizing an axiom that has been cited and said, **pregnant women should not dive.**

— *From May/June 1990*

EDITOR'S NOTE: Excerpted from Diving Medicine, ed. Bove A.A. and Davis J.C., 1990. W.B. Saunders Co.. Philadelphia.

Motion Sickness

Some salty & sage advice on an age-old problem

BY G. YANCEY MEBANE, M.D., DAN ASSOCIATE MEDICAL DIRECTOR & DIRECTOR, EMS TRAINING

MEMBER, ED,
T THROUGH THE
ULATOR BIGGER
UR ELBOW

YOU GUNNA BE
TING THAT
A FISH ?

D. JACKSON

My experience with seasickness is that at first you are afraid you will die, then after a few hours you are afraid you will not.

Seasickness, or motion sickness, ruins diving trips, vacations and travel for many. Everyone is susceptible, and motion sickness can be produced in anyone if the circumstances are right. A lot is known about motion sickness, but total understanding of the cause is not clear. There are individuals who are resistant to motion sickness, but sufficient angular acceleration will induce motion sickness in anyone.

Even astronauts are annoyed by this problem. Approximately 70 percent of all crew members experience motion sickness of some degree during the first 72 hours of orbital flight on the space shuttle.

Cause

If you have experienced motion sickness, you probably think of it as primarily nausea. One theory says that this symptom is the result of your brain's inability to resolve the conflicting signals that it is receiving from the ears, eyes and body.

The vestibular balance apparatus of the ears detects motion and is stimulated by the repeated angular acceleration of the dive boat. If you are in a compartment or have lost visual contact with the horizon, your eyes signal the brain that there is no motion. The sensors of body position are sending still another signal, and your brain is unable to resolve the conflict.

Anxiety, confusion and dismay result, leading to the first symptoms of yawning, pallor (paleness) and headache. They are followed by nausea and vomiting, and frequently a "fear" response. That is the time you are afraid you will not die.

There is more to the cause than mismatching of sensory inputs. Other hypotheses under intense study include the role of Coriolis forces (forces due to the earth's rotation), other nonphysiological stimuli, the cerebrospinal fluid and the cerebellum.

A ship moves in a complex fashion depending on the size and construction of the vessel and the condition of the sea it is sailing. Among the hundreds of research studies on the cause of motion sickness, an interesting study from 1988 reports on sophisticated measurements of vessel motion and consequent seasickness among passengers on six ships, two hovercraft and a hydrofoil. This study showed that the occurrence of motion sickness was closely related to the magnitude of the vertical acceleration experienced. There was low correlation between roll and pitch acceleration magnitude and vomiting.

This information won't cure seasickness, but it does tell us to find the part of the vessel with the least vertical acceleration and stay there. Usually that will be in the center of the vessel, and we want to stay as low as possible while maintaining eye contact slightly above the horizon. If visual contact is not possible, keep your eyes closed. It is prudent to stay away from individuals who are actively ill, though psychological support and reassurance from companions are helpful for the individual and the group.

Have you ever advised a seasick diver: "Get in the water — you'll feel better"? That may not be good advice. Motion sickness underwater occurs for the same reason as above water. When underwater, spatial disorientation occurs because of the interference with the normal clues. Poor visibility and the visual field restrictions imposed by the mask distort or eliminate visual clues. Neutral buoyancy distorts the clues provided by gravity. Motion from surge which may be encountered during entry causes potent acceleration forces. The brain is unable to reconcile the abnormal sensory input, and motion sickness develops. Anxiety of some degree is inevitable no matter how laid-back the individual, and a panic reaction can easily occur.

Vomiting underwater is not easy. Do you vomit through your regulator or take your regulator out of your mouth? There are valid arguments for both techniques, and I have seen both done successfully. There is no doubt that safety is seriously impaired under either condition.

As an experienced diver, you will be able to recognize clues available during a dive which provide spatial orientation. It is important to enter and exit along a line if visibility is poor and the bottom cannot be seen. Gravitation pull on weight belts provides the "down" sensation, while buoyancy effects will cause the chest to rise. The feet will tend to sink when not swimming. Bubbles, of course, rise. An inexperienced diver may not respond to these clues, especially in a panic situation. And what about the reverse: sickness on land? It does happen. After you have finished that 10-day "trip of a lifetime" aboard a live-aboard and have stepped onto solid ground, you may suddenly feel funny and maybe even sick. What happened? "Land sickness," or *mal de débarquement*, occurs when you return to dry land after becoming adapted to an environment in constant motion. Your brain has become accustomed to the new input from increased motion. Suddenly, the motion stops. The abrupt change will promptly produce the same symptoms as originally felt upon going to sea.

Motion is most of the story, but not all. Emotional factors (fear, anxiety, fatigue) act in concert with motion to precipitate an attack. Alcoholic or dietary excesses before or during the trip increase the likelihood of motion sickness. Jet lag, which results from rapid transition of time zones, places you out of synchrony with the local social and time cues, producing fatigue, loss of appetite, gastrointestinal duress and other symptoms. If you feel that way before the dive boat leaves the dock, guess what's going to happen on the way to the dive site!

PREVENTION

Now that you know that we don't fully understand the causes of motion sickness, you may not be surprised that we also don't really know how to prevent it. There are literally hundreds of gadgets, procedures, medicines, herbs, foods, etc., all touted as good for motion sickness — that in itself should tell you that none of these choices are completely effective. Perhaps you have already discovered a system that works for you. If so, congratulations. Be sure that your system is safe and stay with it.

MEDICATIONS

The use of medications to prevent motion sickness may be helpful, but none of the medications are free of side effects. As most of the side effects affect performance, there are serious questions concerning their use by divers — who must be alert at all times. You must be cautious in their use, and your best plan is to avoid them entirely. If you choose a medication, give it a trial many days before diving in order to determine the response and side effects for you.

Antihistamines

The most commonly used medications are antihistamines, available without a prescription, and similar in their side effect profile. The medications include Dramamine® (dimenhydrinate), Bonine® (meclizine),

Benadryl® (diphenhydramine) and Marezine® (cyclizine). The common feature of this group is drowsiness, which could seriously impair a diver's ability to perform safely. There are other side effects — you should study all the information which comes with the medication before using it.

Phenergan® (promethazine) is a prescription drug chemically related to the tranquilizers, and it also has antihistamine properties. Drowsiness is a prominent side effect, and it can be used as a sedative-hypnotic. The drug may impair your mental and physical abilities required to perform potentially hazardous tasks. Alcohol and similar drugs accentuate the sedative effects of promethazine. Intramuscular injection of this drug can provide great relief for severely motion-sick individuals. Of course, diving would be out of the question if intramuscular injection is needed.

Other Medications

Scopolamine-dextroamphetamine (a combination of 0.4 milligrams oral scopolamine and 5.0 milligrams oral dextroamphetamine) has been studied for use in the space program. These are very potent medications and are useful in situations for individuals performing complex tasks while being closely monitored. A recreational diver will have some difficulty in obtaining these drugs, as dextroamphetamine is a Schedule II controlled substance prescription drug and the combination has not been approved by the Food and Drug Administration (FDA) as indicated for motion sickness. A physician prescribing this combination for motion sickness will be outside the FDA indications.

Trans-Derm SCOP® (scopolamine patch) is used for motion sickness and has been used by many divers who found it beneficial and reported few problems. At present, the medication is not available pending manufacturing changes which should allow production to resume later this year.

Editor's Note: As of May 1997, Trans-Derm Scop is still in redevelopment. Its manufacturer states that it is hopeful the medication will be available in 1997.

Trans-Derm Scop does have some unwanted side effects which affect diving adversely. Dry mouth occurs in about half of the users studied (non-divers) and is probably more prevalent in divers due to the dry air in scuba cylinders. Blurred vision after about 24 hours' use is common and may persist after the patch is removed. Repeated applications will cause visual disturbance to increase. If your finger contacts the medication side of the patch and then your eye, the pupil will dilate. Wash your hands thoroughly after handling the patch.

Trans-Derm Scop occasionally causes hallucinations, confusion, agitation or disorientation. These effects are more common in children and the elderly. Therefore, children under 10 should not use the patch. The dose is fixed and cannot be altered by cutting the patch, which also disrupts the rate-limiting membrane delivering the medication. The package insert contains the following precautions: "Since drowsiness, disorientation and confusion may occur with the use of scopolamine, be careful when engaging in activities that require mental alertness, such as driving a motor vehicle or operating dangerous machinery, especially when you first start using the drug system." Studies indicate that the patch is slightly more effective than Dramamine®.

Dilantin® (phenytoin) has been shown to protect against motion sickness in several studies. However, the medication is an antiepileptic drug and has not been approved for use in the treatment of motion sickness. It is a fairly safe drug, but not free of side effects and adverse reactions. There has been one study on divers in chamber tests at 460 kilopascals (approximately 150 feet/46 meters of seawater) which did not reveal any change in susceptibility to nitrogen narcosis.

Royal Made Ping an Dan (PAD) is a royal clandestine prescription of the Qing Dynasty Imperial hospital for emperors, empresses, ministers, imperial maids and eunuchs. Experimental study has confirmed that it is effective on motion sickness. There is no information on composition or drug safety for this preparation.

NONPHARMACOLOGICAL INTERVENTION

There are many devices, herbs and procedures which are advocated for prevention and treatment of seasickness. The efficacy of both pharmacologic and nonpharmacological agents is difficult to determine in this condition, which has such a powerful emotional component. The placebo effect is very strong here. It is also complicated to determine if the agent used to prevent an event was effective or perhaps the event was not destined to occur. For instance, I keep a charmed shark tooth in my office to prevent shark attack. There hasn't been a shark in my office since I got that tooth — that's 100-percent effectiveness.

There are enthusiastic advocates of ginger for prevention of seasickness, but its efficacy has not been substantiated in controlled laboratory trials.

Seabands® (elasticized wristband devices) are sold as a means of treating seasickness. There is a stud incorporated into the device which applies pressure over the Neiguan point (located within tissue about 3 centimeters above the wrist joint). The Neiguan point is reported as being implicated in the control of nausea and vomiting, although the results of acupuncture applied to this point are contradictory. Seabands have been available for several years, although no controlled trials demonstrating their effectiveness have been published.

FINALLY...

So, how do you reduce your risk or susceptibility to motion sickness? First, you should be adequately rested, nourished and hydrated. If you are apprehensive, avoid placing anything at all in your stomach during the two hours more or less before you embark. You will be more comfortable with an empty stomach than with a full one. Adequate rest and hydration means that you have essentially recovered from jet lag, excessive food, or alcohol, and have satisfied your usual requirement for sleep.

After boarding, prepare your gear for diving before the boat reaches open water so that you can avoid working on diving equipment while looking down. Find a place on the boat where the motion is least and stay low. Avoid the bow, flying bridge or upper decks where the motion is intensified. The motion at the stern is not unpleasant, but exhaust fumes may be present. Maintain eye contact with the horizon or slightly above.

If you are using a medication or device to prevent sickness, have faith and it will probably work. Remember that all medications have side effects, and you should have tried the one you will be using long before exposing yourself to motion. The nonpharmacological agents are usually harmless, but you must be certain about your choices.

Adaptation to motion does occur with most individuals, so that motion sickness frequently ceases after a few hours. Motivation and willpower are important, as are sounds, sights and smells; individual tolerance to motion is also a factor. Seasickness is an unpleasant acquaintance, testified to by armadas of past, present and future sufferers.

— From March/April 1995

Diving and Menstruation

BY KENNETH W. KIZER, M.D., MPH

Each woman responds individually to exercising during her period. Some say that cramps and other unpleasant symptoms are lessened. Other women notice no effect. Still others report that exercising aggravates menstrual cramps and that they have a decreased exercise tolerance.

With respect to diving during the menses, the best rule seems to be that if other types of vigorous exercise do not increase menstrual symptoms, then there is no reason that diving *per se* will be a problem. However, if anything stronger than aspirin is needed to allay a woman's cramps or other symptoms, then she should not dive while she is so symptomatic.

There are several concerns about possible effects of menstruation on the safety of diving.

One is whether there is an increased risk of developing decompression sickness (DCS) during the later part of the menstrual cycle when many women retain fluid. Although it is theoretically possible that the tissue swelling that accompanies this fluid retention could impair one's ability to get rid of dissolved nitrogen so much so that there was a higher risk of getting the bends, there is no scientific data to show that this really happens.

Another possible negative influence is related to the premenstrual syndrome (PMS). This condition occurs to some degree in 25 percent to 50 percent of all women. The PMS is characterized by varying degrees of irritability, emotional lability [instability], depression, lethargy, decreased mental alertness, slowed reaction time, and other symptoms at the end of the menstrual cycle just prior to the onset of menstrual flow. Since studies have shown that accidents are more frequent among women during the general time frame of the PMS it seems prudent for those women who are bothered by these types of symptoms to dive conservatively during this time of the month, if they dive at all.

One frequent topic of concern among women divers is whether there is an increased risk of shark attack during menstruation. There are very few reports of shark attacks on women in general, and there is no objective data to support the belief that there is an increased risk of attack on the menstruating woman diver. The average blood loss during menstruation is small and spread out over several days. Obviously, the amount of blood and other cellular debris that might be released into the water during a single 30- to 60-minute dive is very, very small. This is reduced to essentially nothing if the menstruating woman uses a tampon.

In addition, it is known that at least some species of sharks are not attracted to the blood and other material found in menstrual flow. Thus, at the present time, there is no reason to believe that the menstruating woman diver who uses a tampon is at increased risk of shark attack.

Each female diver should be aware of how she responds to the phases of her menstrual cycle, and she should understand how her internal changes might affect her ability to respond to an emergency situation. In general, though, there is no reason why a menstruating woman cannot dive.

— From May/June 1990

DECOMPRESSION ILLNESS

Bubble Quest

Developing dive tables & computers is still not an exact science

BY BRUCE R. WIENKE, PH.D.

Divers often view the numbers on their dive tables or dive computer as holy writ. These tiny black figures define the limits of what divers see as acceptable and unacceptable risk.

Many divers now realize, however, that data presented by dive tables and computers do not equal absolute safety. If you ask them why, they'll often respond with an answer about how everyone's physiological makeup is different.

But that answer only addresses half the question. Of equal importance are general questions about the mathematical formulas and physiological theories used to construct modern tables and computers.

Biophysical models of inert gas transport and bubble formation all try to prevent decompression sickness. Basically, these mathematical formulas try to predict the time/pressure schedules that are required for nitrogen gas to leave a person's body through normal respiration — instead of leading to decompression sickness (DCS). Developed over years of diving application, these models differ on a number of basic issues, most of which are still unresolved.

For every answer a modeler and table designer finds, others arise, refuting the first. The substance of these questions ultimately links to bubbles — that is, how they are formed, where they grow, when they move, and how they are eliminated. The dilemmas are formidable.

Put simply: Dive physicists' nightmares are full of bubbles.

Why bubbles form

We do not really know where bubbles form or lodge, their migration patterns, their birth and dissolution mechanisms, or the exact role they play in the chemical reactions that lead to decompression sickness. If it sounds like we don't know a lot, that's right.

But we do have theories. At present, the predominant bubble theory is a combination of two ideas.

Idea number one says that bubbles might form directly (de novo) in supersaturated body tissues as the surrounding pressure is reduced. An oversimplified rendition of this theory accounts for the "soda pop analogy" that some use to describe how decompression sickness happens. Idea number two states that bubbles grow from pre-existing bubble "seeds" or "nuclei" as the surrounding pressure increases and decreases. There is no proof that these nuclei exist in human tissue and blood. But since preformed nuclei are found in virtually every aqueous substance known, their preclusion from the body would be a surprise. Plus, decompression studies on salmon, rats and even humans seem to back up the nucleation theory.

Where bubbles form

Presently, most researchers work under the assumption that bubbles form in the blood (intravascular) and / or outside the blood in the different tissues of the body (extravascular).

Once the bubbles are formed, a number of things may happen. Intravascular bubbles may leave the circulatory system and take up residence in body tissue sites as extravascular bubbles. They may also induce blood sludging and chemistry degradations (ischemia), or mechanical nerve deformation. Ischemia resulting from bubbles caught in the arterial network has long been implied as a cause of decompression sickness.

Extravascular bubbles may form in aqueous (watery) or lipid (fatty) tissues. They are seldom observed in heart, liver and skeletal muscle. Extravascular bubbles may remain locally in some tissue sites, assimilating more gas by diffusion from adjacent supersaturated tissue and growing until they press on nerve endings — which we feel as pain. Or extravascular bubbles might enter the circulation system, at which point they become intravascular bubbles.

The fatty tissues act as a storage center for most of the extravascular nitrogen bubbles. This is because fatty tissue has a five-fold higher solubility of nitrogen than watery tissue. Since fatty tissue has fewer nerve endings, bubbles aren't likely to push on nerves and cause local pain. On the other hand, a large amount of nitrogen gas in fatty tissues could induce vascular hemorrhage, depositing both fat and bubbles into the circulation. This type of hemorrhage has been observed in animal experiments.

Tissues like tendons and the spinal cord are primarily watery tissues. There is also a smattering of fatty tissues which may reflect the individual's total body fat. Since these areas have a high nerve density combined with some fatty tissue which can support formation and growth, this may explain why joints and the spinal cord are areas that can suffer severely from a decompression injury.

Intravascular bubbles have been seen in both arterial and venous circulation, with vastly greater numbers detected in venous flows (called venous gas emboli). Since the lungs are effective filters of venous bubbles, arterial bubbles would then more likely originate in the arteries or adjacent tissue beds. The most numerous venous bubbles, however, are suspected to form first in lipid (fatty) tissues sites draining the vein. Veins, thinner than arteries, appear more susceptible to extravascular gas penetration.

From theory to computer

Using the theories of bubble formation that we've just discussed, researchers are faced with the challenge of creating a mathematical model that will predict when bubbles will occur. The most effective way of doing this is by creating a computer algorithm.

The ultimate computational algorithm — which would combine nucleation (clustering of bubbles), dissolved gas absorption and elimination, bubble growth and collisional coalescence (the meeting and joining of smaller bubbles into larger ones), and critical sites — would be very complicated, requiring the use of expensive super computers.

Similar computations for nondiving problems are being done at the Los Alamos (New Mexico) and Livermore National Laboratories (California), on lightning-fast super computers with near-gigaflop speed (one billion floating point operations per second). Even at these speeds it takes 16 to 32 hours to find a solution to the problem. While dive computers have revolutionized diving and decompression calculations, it will be some time before the ultimate computational algorithm fits into a wrist computer.

Venous gas emboli

One way researchers can learn more about the validity of modern decompression theory is by conducting experiments and collecting data. Enter Doppler bubble detection.

Sound reflected off a moving object undergoes a shift in acoustical frequency — the so-called Doppler shift. The shift is directly proportional to the speed of the moving surface and the acoustical frequency of the wave, and inversely proportional to the sound speed. Translation: Something coming at you sounds different than when it goes away — it doesn't matter if it's an airplane or tiny nitrogen bubble in someone's bloodstream.

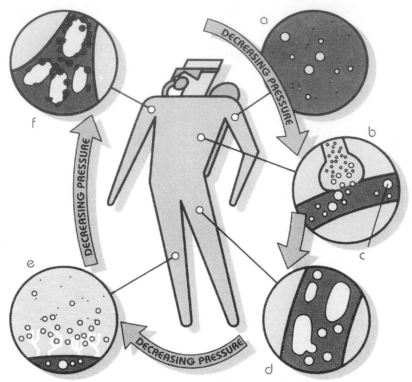

Bubble Formation in Divers — Although bubbles do not necessarily form on every dive, this is a graphic theoretical representation of a diver with symptoms of DCS. For additional information, see the sidebar on the next page.

In the case of bubbles, modern researchers use special monitoring equipment to detect Doppler shifts in the circulatory system caused by bubbles. The audible chirps, snaps, whistles, and pops produced by the bubbles are noted and recorded. Unfortunately it's more difficult — sometimes impossible — to "hear" fatty tissue, "sludged" blood cells, or bubbles with diameters of less than one-ten-thousandth of a centimeter travel through the circulatory system.

Ultrasonic techniques for monitoring moving gas emboli in the pulmonary circulation are partially responsible for the discovery of "silent bubbles" — tiny bubbles that form in the circulatory system but don't result in any symptoms. Using Doppler detection, researchers revised the exposure ranges and non-stop limits of their tables and algorithms, so these new limits were more in line with "acceptable" levels of bubble formation.

An Overview of
One Theory of DCS Physiology

a. As a diver ascends, nitrogen diffuses into microbubbles. Some of these microbubbles are transported through the heart and into the capillary beds of the lungs.

b. Once in the capillary beds, these bubbles are trapped. The gasses in these bubbles expand and leave the body through normal respiration. If the bubbles are not numerous, the lungs will clear them out sufficiently to prevent any occurrence of DCS.

c. Bubbles will form if there is too much nitrogen in a scuba diver's tissues — or if the diver ascends too rapidly. Too many bubbles may not be absorbed and could remain in the circulatory system.

d. As bubbles grow, they become elongated, and smaller bubbles begin diffusing into larger bubbles.

e. In the meantime microscopic bubbles of gas in ligaments and tendons can attract escaping nitrogen, which results in extravascular bubbles. If large enough, this type of bubble can crowd and pinch nerves, giving the classic joint pain so typical of DCS.

f. Back in the circulatory system, nitrogen bubbles grow and attract blood platelets, constricting blood vessels. Protein is released which causes the blood to "sludge," or thicken, and blood volume drops.

Keep in mind that symptomatic bubbles do not necessarily form on every dive. This illustration represents what could happen to a diver who has either stayed at depth too long, ascended too rapidly, or incurred DCS for a more subtle physiological reason.

However, fundamental issues are not necessarily resolved by listening for bubbles. First of all, venous gas emboli are probably not the direct cause of bends per se, unless they block the pulmonary or arterial circulation. Second, since blood constitutes no more than 8 percent of the total body capacity for dissolved gas, listening to bubbles in the bloodstream only gives us a peek at what's really happening in other parts of the body. Third, there has not been any substantive proof of a link between gas micronuclei, vascular bubbles and extravascular bubbles in various body tissues. While some believe that bubbles detected in the bloodstream correlate with bubbles in places like tendons and ligaments, that concept does not hold water when compared to data from repetitive and saturation diving or more severe forms of decompression sickness, such as chokes and central nervous system (CNS) hits.

Still, whatever the origin of bubbles in a diver's bloodstream — or anywhere else in the body, for that matter — procedures which reduce bubbling deserve attention. The moving Doppler bubble may not be the bends bubble, but perhaps the difference may just be a matter of its location. Or the venous bubbles may be the "canary in the coal mine" that lets us know when the rest of the body has reached the critical state where DCS is imminent. And so, until we know more, studies and tests based on Doppler detection of venous gas emboli are still the only viable means of monitoring bubbles in the body.

— *From March/April 1994*

Decompression Theory in Plain English

BY JOLIE BOOKSPAN, PH.D.

How can you make decisions about tissue tensions and nitrogen uptake when you don't know what that means?

Getting understandable information about diving physiology is like trying to learn what really happens when you exercise: the truth lies concealed in research jargon, but you just want it in plain English.

Many divers want more bottom time. There are plenty of new computers and tables with complicated vocabularies and concepts to help you get it. But do you have to understand what they're talking about to use them wisely? Yes!

What is a Multi-Tissue Model?

Almost every known substance absorbs gas when placed under pressure, and releases it when pressure is reduced.

You already know that your entire body absorbs nitrogen under pressure, but different areas of your body absorb gases at different rates. The areas are commonly called tissues, but are more properly called compartments since no one tissue corresponds to any one rate of nitrogen uptake.

In fact, there are actually only four basic kinds of tissue in the human body: muscle, connective, epithelial, and nervous tissue. An organ like your heart or lungs is made up of several tissues which each contribute their specific properties.

The idea of a number of different "tissues" representing the different areas of your body that absorb inert gas at a certain rate is just a mathematical convention. You couldn't take someone's liver, for example, and say it absorbs nitrogen at one such rate. But this convention is crucial for calculating decompression tables. This is called a multi-tissue model.

What is Uptake?

If you inhale, take up or absorb gases, a portion of each of the gases you breathe dissolves into your blood through your alveoli (tiny air sacs in your lungs) and moves into your tissues by diffusion from areas of higher pressure to areas of lower pressure.

The entrance and dissolving of gas in your tissues is called uptake. Uptake increases with both increasing depth and time at depth. The elimination of absorbed gas is called offgassing or outgassing.

Your body uses oxygen for metabolism. But, nitrogen accumulates under pressure because it doesn't enter into any chemical reactions in the body — it is metabolically inert.

Any inert gas you breathe at pressure is taken up, but each has different properties of solubility and diffusivity which affect uptake.

Helium, for example, is much less soluble in tissues than is nitrogen but diffuses faster. The lower solubility decreases the total amount taken up, and so decreases decompression time after long deep dives. But helium's increased diffusivity requires deeper stops to keep from coming out of solution too fast and causing bubbles. (More on bubbles later.)

Uptake and outgassing takes place primarily through the lungs.

What is Nitrogen Tension?

Nitrogen tension is a measure of how much nitrogen you take up. Nitrogen tension is measured by pressure, not volume. These pressure units are commonly measured in feet (fsw) or meters (msw) of sea water.

When you dive, you suddenly increase your ambient pressure, but it takes time for you to absorb enough nitrogen for your tissue tensions to catch up. Longer bottom time increases tissue nitrogen tension. Longer surface intervals decrease tissue nitrogen tension.

That's why it's desirable to have shorter bottom time and longer surface intervals.

You may remember that at sea level the pressure of the six-mile-high air column is equivalent to the pressure of 33 fsw / 10 msw (note: absolute pressure equals the pressure of this six-mile-high air column plus the water pressure while diving). You should also know that at sea level, 100 percent of the air is pressing on you. But nitrogen only makes up 79 percent of the air, so only 79 percent of that 33 fsw of pressure is exerted by nitrogen. That's why nitrogen pressure is called a partial pressure. The other 21 percent of the pressure on you is exerted by oxygen and small amounts of other gases.

When you dive, you don't increase the percentages of oxygen or nitrogen, you increase partial pressures. At two atmospheres, you have twice the partial pressures of gases at one atmosphere.

The partial pressures of the various atmospheric gases drive the uptake of tissue gases. That means that the nitrogen partial pressure (PPN2) in the air you breathe drives the uptake of tissue nitrogen, and the partial pressure of oxygen (PPO2) is responsible for your oxygen uptake. You may recall that from Dalton's Law.

This is one of the reasons oxygen administration is so important in treating decompression sickness. Less nitrogen in the breathing mixture increases the driving force (gradient) for offgassing tissue nitrogen.

Since you've been living on land for a while, all your tissues have absorbed all the nitrogen they'll hold at your elevation because your tissue tensions have had time to become equal to ambient pressure (equilibrate). For example, at sea level, 79 percent of 33 is 6.07. So, the nitrogen tension in all the tissues of your body is 26.07 fsw / 7.94 msw.

However, if you lived all your life in Vail, Colorado, or La Paz, Bolivia, your tissue nitrogen tension would be less because there is less ambient pressure to drive nitrogen uptake, but there would be the same lower tension in all your tissues. It's when you travel quickly from one pressure to another (either direction) that tissue tensions become different from each other. Half-times tell you why.

What is a Half-Time?

It takes time to change your tissue nitrogen tension. Tissue tensions increase gradually according to the rate that each can take up nitrogen. Your different tissues are made of different materials and have varying blood supplies, so they absorb nitrogen at different rates. The different rates are called half-times (also written T 1/2).

A half-time is the same as a half-life when talking about radiation. A half-life is the time for a radioactive sample to decay to half its original value. Half-time tissues are named for the time in minutes it takes to fill (saturate) half the tissue with nitrogen. Then, it takes the same amount of time to absorb enough nitrogen for the other half to become half saturated. Then, it takes the same amount of time for the quarter that's left to become 50 percent saturated, then, the same time to absorb enough for the eighth that's left to become half saturated, and so on.

It's like trying to stuff more things into a gear bag. The fuller it gets, the harder (and slower) it is to pack more stuff in. The slowing of uptake, as total saturation approaches, follows a mathematical curve that is exponential.

To understand how a half-time is calculated, picture a 60-minute tissue. A 60-minute tissue will become half saturated with nitrogen in 60 minutes. The tissue will be 3/4 or 75 percent full after another 60 minutes, or two hours total. It will take another 60 minutes for the remaining 1/4 to "fill up" halfway, making the tissue 7/8 saturated (1/2 + 1/4 + 1/8 = 7/8 or 87.5 percent) in three total hours.

Nitrogen uptake rate falls along a continuous spectrum. That means some of your tissues absorb gases with half-times ranging from seconds and minutes on up to several hours. To represent the various tissue uptake rates mathematically and conceptually, they are grouped into convenient multiples of minutes. So there can be a five-minute tissue, a 10-minute, a 20-minute, and so on.

Different models use different half-time tissues. How many and which ones are up to the modeler.

A factor that complicates calculations is that not all gas diffuses directly back into your blood stream for direct offgassing by exhalation. Since adjacent tissues may be of different half-times, higher tension in one than another produces a tissue-to-tissue gradient, causing off-gassing of one tissue to another.

What is a Fast Tissue, What is a Slow Tissue?

A fast tissue takes up gases and offgasses in a shorter half-time. Fast tissues generally have higher tensions after a dive than slower ones because they absorbed more in a given time.

Safety stops greatly lower tensions in the very fast tissues because they also offgas quickly. Where it becomes really interesting is after repetitive dives. The slower tissues have not had enough time to offgas much before the next dive adds more nitrogen tension. The staircase effect raises nitrogen levels in these tissues, sometimes too high.

What makes one tissue faster than another? Both the capacity of the tissue to hold nitrogen and the amount of tissue blood flow (perfusion) are factors. Fatty tissues can hold more nitrogen than watery tissues which increases the time to absorb and offgas. This is a property of fat and is true even for fatty areas with the same degree of blood supply as leaner tissue.

As a generality, your body areas well supplied (perfused) by blood, like lungs and abdominal organs, absorb nitrogen faster than other tissues. Fat, bone, and scar tissue which are less vascular, and the avascular cartilage and synovial fluids are slower tissues. The greater distance between capillaries in these slow tissues means that diffusion, along with perfusion, plays a role in uptake.

The half-time of these tissues is affected by the diffusivity of the inert gas used and the geometry of the tissue, and it is rather involved. These tissues are controlled by both perfusion and diffusion.

In diffusion-limited tissues there must be higher pressure gradients to drive uptake and offgassing than for perfusion-limited tissues. During decompression, these tissues will have substantially higher nitrogen tensions than vascular tissues.

These slow tissues create a reservoir of gas that can contribute to bubble growth long after leaving the water.

Tissue perfusion varies greatly with exercise, PPO2, temperature, your physical condition and nutritional state, and descent rate.

Exercise causes blood vessel expansion (vasodilation) and increased blood flow in working muscles, which brings in more nitrogen. It also causes vasoconstriction and decreased blood flow in non-exercising tissues, like the viscera and skin, which slows offgassing of nitrogen. Increasing PPO2 with depth decreases blood flow in almost all tissues. Cold has little effect on central blood flow but causes peripheral vasoconstriction and reduced blood flow. A rapid descent rate can greatly reduce perfusion in bone and peripheral tissues. Finally, factors like cigarette smoking, dehydration, and common medications also cause selective vasoconstriction. Many varying influences complicate mathematical calculation of nitrogen uptake and offgassing.

What is Saturation?

When a tissue has absorbed all the nitrogen it can at any particular depth, it is called saturated for that depth.

It takes six half-times for any tissue to become 99 percent saturated or desaturated. For practical purposes, 99 percent is considered saturated or desaturated. So a 60-minute tissue is considered saturated in 6 hours (6 x 60 minutes). The slower 120-minute tissue saturates in 12 hours (12 x 60 minutes). A fast tissue like a five-minute tissue saturates in only 30 minutes.

For practical applications, desaturation is considered to proceed at the same half-time rate as saturation, although there are many complicated factors that slow desaturation. The longest tissue considered by the U. S. Navy Decompression Tables is the 120-minute tissue. All of your tissues are considered desaturated 12 hours after a dive, since it takes 12 hours for the 120-minute tissue to be considered desaturated, and all faster tissues will desaturate more quickly. That's why there's a 12-hour minimum between dives to end the repetitive dive category when using Navy tables.

The amount of dissolved gas a tissue can hold changes with pressure. You may remember that from Henry's Law. It takes 12 hours at depth to be saturated according to U.S. Navy calculations. Regardless of how much longer you remain at that depth, you cannot absorb any more nitrogen. If you go deeper, you increase the pressure that drives uptake so you can absorb more. Given enough time, you will become saturated at the new depth.

Of course, this is completely outside no-decompression recreational diving, and there is a large decompression obligation to remove the nitrogen safely. Rather than spend time in decompression after each task, saturation divers remain at depth for days or even weeks until project completion. They still incur only the same decompression obligation required after first reaching saturation for their depth. That is the principle behind saturation diving.

Saturation diving requires extensive life support, and is only for professional tasks. Many saturation tables use tissues longer than 120 minutes. One researcher used a 240-minute half-time that is saturated (to one percent) after 24 hours (6 x 240 minutes). Recent research indicates there may be half-times of 500 minutes which take 48 hours to saturate and desaturate.

What is Supersaturation, and What are Supersaturation Ratios?

In recreational diving, a one-hour dive will saturate all tissues with half-times of 10-minutes or less and raise tensions in others to levels where they will reach or exceed saturation when you reduce pressure by surfacing. When pressure drops on ascent, these tissues will temporarily increase to a higher tension than they can contain in equilibrium, or become supersaturated.

Whether that's dangerous depends on how much supersaturation exists, and for how long. Each half-time tissue can tolerate a different amount of supersaturation before bubbles are thought to form.

When a gas is dissolved, it isn't in a gaseous state anymore. It is, rather, individual molecules squeezed between and in the cells of your tissues. When ambient pressure drops, dissolved gas tension in your tissues rises. The molecules begin to become a gas again (return to a gas phase).

The whole ball game is how much you can decrease your ambient pressure and keep supersaturation from being high enough to produce a gas phase before you eliminate the excess inert gas. When enough tissue supersaturation exists, the gas phases may grow into bubbles.

Recreational diving is based on being able to ascend directly to the surface from depth. No-decompression calculations involve the supersaturation ratio of tissue tensions produced after a dive profile to the pressure at the surface.

Haldane originally thought the ratio of tissue tension to ambient could be 2:1 without forming bubbles. That was back in 1908. There have been many modifications since then.

Now we know that fast tissues tolerate higher supersaturation ratios than slow tissues. For example, the ratio of a five-minute tissue is more than 3:1. The supersaturation ratio of a 120-minute tissue is less than 2:1. But don't forget about your slow tissue reservoirs. Given a large enough reservoir, the fast tissues can be continuously "overfed" by adjacent slow tissue offgassing, producing a decompression problem while still inside the tables. The reservoir is increased by large amounts of fat or poorly perfused scar tissue.

Divers aren't the only ones who have to know about supersaturation ratios. Recompression chambers are used in the aerospace industry too. When you ascend from the earth into space, ambient pressure drops, too. Luckily, air is plenty lighter than water, and you have to go to about 18,000 feet / 5,486 meters before pressure drops to half that of sea level. However, there have been documented cases of embolism and ear equalization trauma in flight crews who experienced rapid cabin depressurization during a flight emergency, and decompression sickness is a concern in extravehicular activity during space flight.

What is an M-Value?

M stands for Maximum. M-Values are maximum allowable tissue tensions. In the early development of decompression theory, it was thought that gas wouldn't separate appreciably from solution to form bubbles if a specific maximum amount of supersaturation wasn't exceeded. The specific maximum value (M-value) was calculated for each half-time tissue. M-values are pressures (tensions), and so are expressed in feet (fsw) or meters (msw) of sea water.

Each half-time tissue has a different M-value. To return to the surface, no tissue may exceed its defined surface M-value of nitrogen tension. A higher tension indicates pressure in that tissue is sufficient to begin bubble growth. A prior decompression stop must be made for sufficient outgassing to lower the gas tension to less than the tissue's M-value for the surface.

In a no-decompression dive, no tissue must exceed its surfacing M-value. If nitrogen tensions for no-decompression diving would be exceeded at the surface, there is a depth where the tension does not exceed the maximum allowed for the involved tissues. That is the depth where you must make your first decompression stop. The M-values for various depths are calculated for each tissue and enter into construction of decompression computers.

Can we regard M-values as absolute limits where bubbles will not form if not exceeded? No. Many variables interfere with strict use of M-values as a threshold. It's now recognized that most tissues always contain microscopic gas phases called micronuclei. And each person's tissue makeup is different. In view of the variability of decompression results, M-values should not be approached as absolute threshold limits. M-values have also been defined as the inert gas partial pressure where the rate of gas phase formation is very slow with respect to gas elimination time via the capillaries.

There are various recreational diving tables and computers with varying M-values, meaning tissues may have different inert gas tensions upon surfacing than the maximum allowed by the Navy tables. In considering them, the bottom line is that less time spent at depth equals less nitrogen uptake.

Now you know a lot about decompression theory. When someone thanks you for explaining it to them, just tell them that "the pressure was all yours."

— *From May/June 1991*

Reprinted courtesy NAUI *Sources* magazine.

Unfortunately, DCS is a Lot More Complicated than Just Simply Blowing Bubbles

BY RICHARD D. VANN, PH.D., DAN RESEARCH DIRECTOR

In 1900, a Royal Navy diver surfaced in a cheerful mood following a 60-minute dive to 150 feet of sea water (fsw) / 45.7 meters of sea water (msw), with an ascent to the surface in 20 minutes. Ten minutes after the dive, he complained of stomach pain and collapsed. His skin was cyanotic (blue) and his breathing labored. He died five minutes later.

The Scottish physiologist J.S. Haldane reported this story in his 1907 report to the British Admiralty. This story illustrates that decompression sickness (DCS) today is generally a minor problem compared to diving performed before the turn of the century.

There is overwhelming evidence from studies that bubbles form on decompression. From the first experiments in the 1870s by the French physiologist Paul Bert, it was found that a rapid ascent after a severe exposure resulted in a massive influx of venous bubbles into the heart and lungs, which displaced the blood and caused cardiopulmonary collapse followed by asphyxia (unconsciousness from suffocation) and death.

Ironically, the etiologies, or causes, of the less severe manifestations of DCS are not as well understood as in more severe DCS.

Some symptoms are attributed to extravascular (outside blood vessels) bubbles and others to intravascular (inside blood vessels) bubbles which may originate at remote sites. Bubbles may also have both mechanical and biochemical effects.

Further contributing to this uncertainty is that the signs and symptoms of air embolism (AGE) and DCS can be similar and may have common causes. Thus, a diagnosis of DCS is often subjective and speculative.

For these reasons, the term "decompression illness" (or DCI) has been introduced to describe the frequently ambiguous clinical presentation.

Pulmonary DCI

Pulmonary decompression illness, or chokes, is presented as a sore throat with a cough upon deep inspiration (inhalation). Coughing can become paroxysmal and may be accompanied by severe chest pain, difficult respiration and unconsciousness.

In the nineteenth century, an attack of severe chokes often forecast a grave clinical outcome. While chokes is usually reversed by prompt recompression, untreated chokes can lead to edema (swelling), pulmonary hypertension, respiratory failure and death.

Pulmonary DCI has contributed to a number of deaths following severe altitude exposure but is infrequently seen today, probably because exposures are less severe than before, and treatment is more effective.

Neurological DCI

Four mechanisms are proposed for the initiation of neurological DCI: arterial gas embolism; arterialized venous gas emboli; extravascular or autochthonous (originating in the place where found) bubbles; and vascular obstruction by venous bubbles.

The pathological consequences of arterial gas embolism arising from lung overexpansion are well recognized, but decompression sickness also may occur if arterial emboli seed regions of the systemic circulation, such as the brain, spinal cord, or heart which are supersaturated with nitrogen (the concentration of dissolved nitrogen is greater than can be maintained in solution) from previous diving. This may be relevant in severe cerebral and spinal DCI which occurs after relatively safe dives that end with pulmonary barotrauma.

A recent case treated by DAN appeared to be of this nature. A 41-year-old male diver had chest discomfort during a normal ascent from 100 fsw / 30 msw after a 20-minute dive. He was semiconscious and paralyzed upon reaching the surface.

Such cases are probably the most serious diving accidents which occur today and reinforce the importance of normal breathing during carefully controlled ascent.

Except during rare cases of blow-up, or missed decompression, cardiopulmonary collapse from massive venous gas embolism is avoided today by restricting dive depth and bottom time and by decompression stops which allow inert gas (a gas, for example nitrogen, which takes no part in metabolism) to be eliminated before bubble growth becomes excessive.

Nonetheless, bubbles are routinely detected by Doppler ultrasound in the venous blood and right side of the heart even after

MIKE WEBSTER ILLUSTRATIO

dives not considered severe. Studies have demonstrated that these bubbles enter the arterial circulation through a defect in the wall separating the atria (upper chambers) of the heart, which is commonly known as a patent foramen ovale (PFO).

Retrospective studies have indicated a greater incidence of PFO in divers who have had cerebral or spinal DCI symptoms than in a control population or in divers who have had pain-only symptoms. Definitive evidence for PFO as an active mechanism in decompression illness awaits a prospective study.

In the absence of PFO or pulmonary barotrauma, arterial bubbles are rare because the lungs are a reasonably good filter for gaseous emboli. Arterial emboli can occur, however, if the bubble volume exceeds the filtering capacity of the lungs, if pulmonary disease is present, or if the pulmonary arterial pressure increases as a result of gaseous obstruction.

The arterial bubble theory cannot account for all neurological DCI. Both solid and gaseous emboli seek the brain as their principal target organ, but cerebral injury after decompression is less common than spinal injury.

Bubbles in the white matter of the spinal cord are called "autochthonous" and are believed to be extravascular and to expand when a threshold supersaturation of perhaps 80 fsw / 24.3 msw is exceeded.

The obstruction of the venous drainage of the spinal cord by bubbles has been observed and also proposed as a mechanism for spinal injury. This mechanism depends, in particular, upon bubble-induced biochemical tissue damage. There appears to be no reason why arterial, autochthonous, and venous bubbles could not contribute separately or together to decompression induced cerebral and spinal cord injury by both mechanical and biochemical mechanisms.

Joint Pain

The most common DCI symptom among Navy divers is joint pain, which has at least three possible origins: neurogenic (from the nervous system), medullary (from the bone marrow) and articular (from the joint).

Neurogenic pain originating at a remote site appears rare, and goats affected only by limb pain had no apparent cerebral or spinal lesions.

Bubbles in the bone have been proposed as a cause of both dull, aching pain and bone necrosis (localized death of living tissue) which is considered a long-term consequence of diving deeper than 165 feet / 49.2 meters. Bone necrosis is statistically associated with decompression illness in saturation divers and caisson (tunnel) workers but is rarely found among recreational divers.

At least some decompression pain would appear to be of extravascular rather than intravascular origin as:

1— there is no local cyanosis;

2 — anoxic pain is usually maximal during the reactive hyperemia (blood congestion) of recovery;

3 — local recompression sufficient to obstruct blood flow relieves rather than intensifies pain;

4 — bubbles associated with pain on X-ray have an articular, not vascular, distribution; and

5 — pain relieved by recompression recurs at the same site upon decompression four to six hours later.

Expanding extravascular bubbles might cause pain by mechanically distorting sensory nerve endings. Thus, delayed symptom onset after diving could be due to gradual bubble growth, and immediate relief upon recompression could be due to rapid bubble shrinkage. This mechanism might explain many DCI incidents but not unresponsive cases to recompression therapy or the occurrence of symptoms hours after descent from altitude when bubbles should be resolving. These observations are inconsistent with simple mechanical effects and may reflect biochemical damage which might accumulate as long as bubbles were present.

Skin Bends & Counterdiffusion

Itching and rash, commonly known as "skin bends," often occur following decompression. Less frequently, skin bends is manifested as a sense of heat. Skin bends usually disappears within an hour and, by itself, does not warrant recompression, but affected areas can be painful for a day or more.

A more severe form of skin bends, blotchy purple markings known as "marbling" or "mottling," is sometimes felt to precede serious DCI including chokes.

Subcutaneous (under the skin) bubbles are the common explanation for skin bends, but there are only rare reports of visible bubbles under the skin at altitude and in tunnel workers.

In human exposures at high pressure, intense itching was accompanied by hard, raised, bloodless lesions and severe dizziness.

— From January/February 1993

Understanding How to Decrease Your Risk of the Bends

Your biggest challenge underwater won't come with teeth or fins.

BY RICHARD DUNFORD, M.S., DAN NORTHWEST REGIONAL COORDINATOR

"It ain't the things you don't know that makes you ignorant, it's the things you know that ain't so."

— *American Proverb*

In the diving world there are a lot of things that are thought of as true beyond question. The fact is, some of the truths just ain't so. Take, for example, "I followed the tables: I can't be bent." Well it just ain't so. You *can* be bent. It's a matter of gas-loading and bubble formation.

First, you dive and load up on nitrogen in your tissues. Then you surface and unload nitrogen out of the tissues. And you make bubbles. And as far as we know, where there are bubbles there can be bends. No decompression table exists today that can prevent bubble formation following diving. Mother Nature, it appears, doesn't care one whit whose table you use.

It is biology we are dealing with here. And there is one biological fact that divers should never forget. Dives to 12 feet / 3.6 meters have produced bubbles in divers. They were long dives (48 hours), but the results indicate that the threshold for bubble formation is very low. We are also finding that bubbling is a part of diving. On a DAN Doppler study trip, 74 percent of all exposures and 95 percent of divers tested showed bubbles following a dive. The conditions for detecting bubbles were not the best, and it is probably true that all divers bubbled during the trip.

It is also true at our facility at Virginia Mason Research Center — and for the DAN diving accident database as well — that many divers are reporting decompression sickness symptoms who claim that their dives are within the table limits or who were following their computer faithfully.

Historically, these claims would be considered spurious or a result of some risk factor present for the diver. While those possibilities can never be discounted, there is increasing awareness that "safe" decompression is not a risk-free exercise. My advice to divers is: "There is no such thing as 100 percent safe decompression, so, if you want zero risk, then don't dive, or don't leave the bottom. Every one else assumes some risk." Some experts argue this view point is either too extreme or not true at all.

Perhaps. But a review of the data from the U.S. Navy No-D limits indicates two bends in 100 exposures for those tables dived to their limits. That's a specific risk for a recreational diver in a remote location where evacuation may be difficult. But where does true risk start? Risk that is small, though real. We don't know.

It is certainly true that a dive in a swimming pool is not deep enough to cause gas bubble formation. But what of a dive to 40 feet / 12 meters for 30 minutes? Or 60 feet / 18.2 meters for 20 minutes? People have been treated in chambers in the United States for these dives. Are they spurious? That's possible — even probable — but it's also possible that bends is actually present. It is that remote possibility which causes physicians to provide chamber treatment.

This is difficult business to sort out. To manage the uncertainty, the U.S. Navy and other major centers of table development (Duke University and the University of Pennsylvania) are adopting a different approach to table development. Bends is assumed to be a probabilistic event. Tables are designed for a chosen risk level. Currently the U.S. Navy is producing a table for which a 2.2 percent risk level has been chosen to as high as 5 percent in certain cases (See note, page 144).

By now, most diving researchers have agreed that the concept of a 100 percent risk-free table has been formally discarded. The U.S. Navy knowingly accepts 2.2 cases of bends for every 100 exposures taken to the limits of the tables. Is the assumed risk greater than that in the recreational diving community? They don't think so. By their calculations, some commonly used recreational dive tables assume an average 5 percent risk.

The general population applies this type of probabilistic thinking in their daily lives all the time. For example, if you were crossing a railroad track and a train was coming, you would make a decision based on the speed of the train, how close it was, and how quickly you could get across. Then you would apply a safety factor since it is not good practice to miss a collision with a speeding train by one foot or one second. Based on this information and your personal comfort safety level, you would make your decision on whether to cross. In general, you would try to keep the risk of the collision low.

Divers need to apply probabilistic thinking to their decompression as well. Pushing the table involves risk. We can decrease the risk by shortening the bottom time, diving shallower, and, we think, using safety stops. It's also possible to decrease the risk to the point that the dive simply isn't worth doing. Between these extremes, divers have a choice of the risk they will accept.

Perhaps the concept that there is no such thing as 100 percent safe decompression is unrealistic: it is possible to do a dive where gas loading is so limited that bubbles cannot form. A better rule is: "Zero risk, zero fun, but nobody else dives risk-free."

The Navy concept of accepted risk has some significant advantages. Tables could be designed with the acceptable risk stated up front — on the label, as it were. In the future, you could choose a 2 percent risk table, say, for general diving; a 5 percent risk table if near a chamber; and a .5 percent risk table if you are diving at a remote location that doesn't have evacuation facilities or communications. In addition, since the risk is stated right on the label, we won't have to hear ever again: "I followed the tables, so I can't be bent." The moral of the story? It's an old one. Be prepared.

The Lonely Decision

The dive was within the limits of the tables, there were no problems on the dive, and no obvious risk factors. But something is wrong: The diver is complaining about some troublesome symptoms. These aren't obvious symptoms of DCS, yet to the injured diver they seem real. Is it bends?

If the dive was outside the limits, and the symptoms were obviously consistent with DCS, the answer is easy: Do what you can with what you have, and get to a hospital fast. But when things aren't so obvious, aren't what they should be, or aren't by the book, then the decision is more difficult. What you do may affect others. You're probably not a dive medicine expert. Making this decision can be a lonely experience. Before deciding what to do, ask yourself these three questions:

1 - Is it unusual for this diver to have these symptoms?

Everyone has his own batch of "normal" aches and pains. These are less worrisome, because bends symptoms usually have a different character — even in areas of old injury. To someone who's been bent, the symptoms are different and unmistakable.

2 - Are the symptoms unexplained by recent activity?

Be careful here. A pain in the shoulder or arm may be the result of a strain while moving tanks, but it is also a significant bends symptom. If the diver didn't notice the strain while moving the tanks, then bends remains a real possibility.

3 -Are the symptoms persistent — i.e., two hours or more?

If your answer to all these questions is yes (or even a qualified yes), you have all the information you need to take positive action. This doesn't necessarily mean calling the helicopter. After contacting the local EMS, calling DAN is your next logical step. You'll have help with any other decisions you may need to make, and life won't seem so lonely.

— From July/August 1993

Special thanks to Dr. Fred Bove of Temple University for his ideas and suggestions.

Note: The U.S. Navy Tables mentioned have not been released as of June 1997. The reason has nothing to do with table safety but rather the operational impact of shorter no-decompression limits at depths 40 fsw / 12 msw and shallower and the increased decompression time in other schedules.

— E.D. Thalmann, Captain, MC, USN (retired),
DAN Assistant Medical Director.

The Oxygen Window

BY RICHARD D. VANN, PH.D., DAN RESEARCH DIRECTOR

The reasons for the positive effects of oxygen on injured divers are subtle, and neither the process of bubble formation nor how oxygen works on these bubbles are well understood.

Inert gas exchange and bubble growth are strongly influenced by the metabolic consumption of oxygen. The conversion of oxygen into carbon dioxide reduces the tissue oxygen tension to below its level in the lungs, but the carbon dioxide tension rises only slightly because carbon dioxide is some 20 times more soluble than oxygen.

This is illustrated in Figure 1, where the bar on the left represents gases in a diver's lungs at sea level. Dalton's law of partial pressures requires that the sum of these gases be 1 ATA. The bar on the right shows the gases in the diver's tissues. Their sum is less than 1 atmosphere absolute (ATA) because oxygen is converted into carbon dioxide.

Figure 1

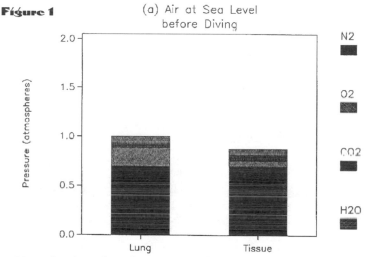

(a) Air at Sea Level before Diving

Now, the diver breathes air at 33 feet of sea water (fsw) / 10 meters of sea water (msw). In Figure 2 the bars on the left show the gases in his lungs and tissue upon arrival at depth. The oxygen and nitrogen partial pressures in his lungs have increased to make the sum of all gases equal to the absolute pressure of 2 ATA, but his tissues have absorbed no additional nitrogen.

The bars on the right show the lungs and tissues after nitrogen equilibration.

Figure 2

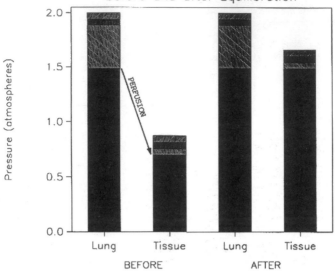

(b) Air at 33 fsw
before and after Equilibration

Figure 3

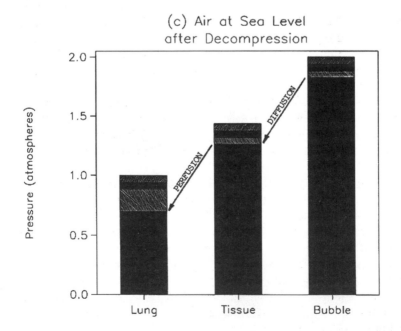

(c) Air at Sea Level
after Decompression

Figure 4 (d) Oxygen Breathing at Sea Level and 20 fsw

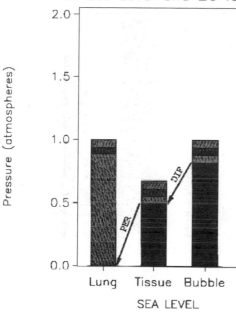

Lung   Tissue   Bubble

SEA LEVEL

The tissue nitrogen tension now equals the alveolar nitrogen partial pressure.

Upon returning to sea level, a bubble forms in the diver's tissues (Figure 3). By Dalton's law, the sum of the partial pressures in the bubble is 1 ATA.

The water vapor pressure is constant and the oxygen and carbon dioxide partial pressures are controlled to tissue levels. Since the nitrogen tension in tissue is elevated, nitrogen diffuses both into the bubble and into the blood. Nitrogen diffusing into the blood and remaining dissolved is carried to the lungs and eliminated harmlessly, but nitrogen diffusing into the bubble causes it to expand.

Bubble growth by diffusion can be a slow process which delays the onset of DCS symptoms and the appearance of precordial bubbles. It is probably slow bubble growth which makes surface decompression possible.

Diffusion slows bubble resolution as well as bubble growth. Note that gas in a bubble must diffuse back into tissue before it can be carried to the lungs by the circulation (Figure 3). Thus, the effective half time for the elimination of gas in a bubble is greater than for the elimination of dissolved gas.

In repetitive diving, this might lead to an accumulation of inert gas not expected by a Haldane decompression model, which assumes gas to remain dissolved.

Figure 4 shows that nitrogen elimination is accelerated by breathing 100 percent oxygen at sea level. Oxygen increases the nitrogen gradient between lungs and tissue, which makes perfusion more efficient in removing dissolved nitrogen. The reduced tissue nitrogen tension also increases the gradient for the diffusion of nitrogen from the bubble back into tissue. This gradient between nitrogen in the bubble and in tissue is known as the oxygen window.

For repetitive diving, a diver breathing oxygen between dives has the potential benefit of reducing surface intervals and increasing repetitive dive times (Figure 4).

This advantage is also useful for helping an injured diver if he is breathing 100 percent oxygen following a diving accident.

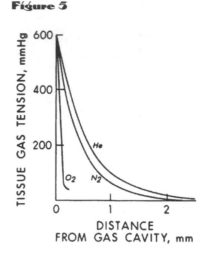

Figure 5

Nitrogen Exchange between Bubbles and Tissue

As diffusion and perfusion are in series when a bubble is present (Figure 4), nitrogen in a bubble must diffuse back into tissue before it can be removed by blood flow.

Figure 5 shows simulations of the concentration gradients of oxygen, helium and nitrogen around a dissolving bubble.

Oxygen has the steepest gradient because it is consumed metabolically. The helium and nitrogen gradients extend further into tissue because they are eliminated only by perfusion. Nitrogen has a steeper gradient than helium because nitrogen is less diffusible than helium.

Nitrogen Exchange Between Blood and Tissue

Diffusion gradients disappear several millimeters away from a bubble (Figure 5), and the diffusion distances between capillaries are so short in most tissues that the intercapillary domains are essentially well-stirred.

Nitrogen exchange in these domains can be considered to be perfusion-limited as in a Haldane tissue compartment. Indeed, gases diffuse so rapidly that they can diffuse directly between adjacent arterial and venous vessels. Arteriovenous shunting in this manner allows nitrogen to bypass a tissue in which the intercapillary domains are otherwise perfusion-limited.

Nitrogen exchange in such a tissue would be slower than expected on basis of perfusion alone. This may partially explain the long nitrogen exchange halftimes required by decompression models.

Research is continuing in a number of laboratories on the roles of bubbles and oxygen in decompression sickness.

— *From January/February 1993*

Cracking the DCS code

Hyperbaric researchers shed new light on the risks of flying after diving

BY ANTHONY K. ALMON, CHT, F.G. HALL HYPO/HYPERBARIC CENTER

It's been a wonderful week — probably the best dive vacation you've ever taken. The fish have been plentiful, and the reefs are teeming with activity. There's a dive this afternoon at 5 p.m., and you really wanted to have one last look at that enormous school of jacks out on the reef. There's just one minor problem. Your flight back home is at 7 a.m. tomorrow morning, and you don't want to suffer decompression sickness (DCS) because you flew too soon after diving. . . .

Should you go on the dive? The U.S. Navy tables recommend that you wait at least two hours before you board a plane after diving; the U.S. Air Force says you should wait 24 hours; DAN recommends a 12-hour minimum surface interval before flying.

Which guideline should you follow? If you fly after diving, what you really want to know is:

• What are my chances (or probability) of experiencing a decompression injury; and

• If I do get hit, how severe might this injury be?

These two factors, the probability and the severity of injury, help determine the risk you are willing to take.

So your next question might be: How much risk is right for you? You need to consider many factors before making your decision. The number of previous dives you've made on this dive trip, your general health and your age are but a few points to ponder.

What if you were returning to a location like Raleigh-Durham, N.C., where a chamber is available? Would you be willing to take more of a chance? The risk that some divers are willing to accept may be absolutely unacceptable to you.

The information you act upon is very important, so it's worth looking into. Unfortunately, in many cases little or no information is available, and we act on nothing more than speculation and hearsay. What do we really know about the flying after diving question? Because so little data is available to support the current guidelines, DAN is conducting an experimental research study at the F.G. Hall Hypo/Hyperbaric Center of Duke University Medical Center to help answer this question. Although the study is far from complete, we will use the preliminary results here to discuss safety and the practical application of the data.

What we want to know is how the probability of DCS changes as we increase the length of the preflight surface interval. Our first series of experiments consisted of one dive followed by a flight. Figure 1 shows this profile. The x-axis (horizontal) represents time; the y-axis (vertical) shows depth or altitude. A dive to 60 feet sea water (fsw)/18 meters for 55 minutes was performed, followed by a predetermined surface interval. The surface interval is represented by a dotted line and is the experimental variable. The altitude exposure of the flight was

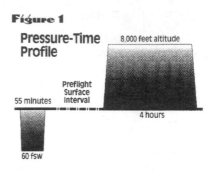

Figure 1

Pressure-Time Profile

8,000 feet altitude

Preflight Surface Interval

55 minutes

4 hours

60 fsw

8,000 feet/2,440 meters for four hours. Eight thousand feet is the maximum cabin altitude allowed in a commercial aircraft.

To produce meaningful information about DCS and the preflight surface interval, some DCS must occur. This information is used to estimate the probability of decompression sickness. Note that we cannot actually measure probability — we can only estimate it statistically from experimental data.

Decompression sickness that occurs in laboratory experiments is generally mild and easily treated, but we have a responsibility not to expose our volunteer research subjects — who are recreational divers — to experiments that are likely to produce DCS that does not resolve completely. The only way we could completely eliminate risk is not to conduct the experiments at all, but this leaves us where we started — with uncertain information about flying after diving. And without research, thousands of people would continue to experiment on themselves by flying home from vacation without the benefit of medical supervision provided in a laboratory study.

The protection of volunteer divers is a very important issue. We subject people to experimental protocols that we know will produce some DCS, so what do we do to protect these volunteers?

First, before anyone can participate in one of our studies, a comprehensive medical history and physical are performed by a hyperbaric physician. Anyone with severe medical problems is not allowed to participate. Some of the problems which may disqualify a diver are neurological problems, chronic injuries and lung conditions that may cause gas trapping. Additionally, because diving is a hazard to an unborn child, pregnant divers are not permitted, and all women of childbearing potential must undergo a pregnancy test.

The next issue is to decide when DCS has occurred. Since there is no lab test for DCS, we must diagnose it by the presence of signs and symptoms. Unfortunately, the milder forms of DCS may have signs and symptoms that are the same as some daily-life aches and pains from which we all occasionally suffer — particularly as we get older. Because of this uncertainty, we ask divers to report any and all symptoms, no matter how mild or seemingly unrelated to the experiment. After the experiment, these are broken into three categories: "Not DCS," "Ambiguous DCS" and "Definite DCS."

"Not DCS" refers to signs or symptoms that are clearly unrelated to the experiment, such as the diver who sprained his ankle playing basketball during the preflight surface interval. (We no longer allow sports during the surface intervals.) "Ambiguous DCS" refers to signs and symptoms that may have lasted only a short time, were very mild and uncertain in the judgment of the hyperbaric physician, or may not have responded to recompression therapy. "Definite DCS" refers to clear and certain signs and symptoms that improve or resolve completely with recompression.

Within the category of Definite DCS there are two types: pain-only and neurological. We generally worry more about neurological symptoms than joint pain. Neurological signs and symptoms that have occurred in our studies have included numbness, tingling, weakness, confusion and visual disturbances, all of which resolved with recompression. Obviously, we want a lower probability of neurological DCS than either joint pain or Ambiguous DCS.

One of the most important factors in providing diver protection is the diver himself. Complete and timely reporting of any and all signs and symptoms ensures the earliest possible recompression, if needed, and the collection of good quality data.

To reduce the chances of testing a preflight surface interval that may have too high a DCS probability, we establish acceptance and rejection rules that define how many times we should test a surface interval based on the occurrence of Definite DCS in previous tests. These rules must be approved by the Duke Medical Center Institutional Review Board, which oversees all human experimentation.

The acceptance/rejection rules for a surface interval in the Flying After Diving study, based on Definite DCS, are:

Note that acceptance of a surface interval applies only within the Flying after Diving study and does not imply acceptance for actual use in recreational diving.

Figure 2 shows the results for the single-dive exposure (60 feet/55 minutes) and represents the first step in estimating how the probability of DCS for a single dive and flight changes with the preflight surface interval. The x-axis shows the surface intervals that were tested before the flight. The y-axis shows number of trials performed at each surface interval, with symptoms indicated. The Definite DCS symptoms represent both pain-only and neurological cases. Ambiguous DCS is also shown.

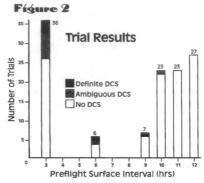

The three-hour surface interval had one pain-only and two neurological incidents of Definite DCS, and seven incidents of Ambiguous DCS. A single incident of neurological Definite DCS occurred at six and at nine hours, and one Ambiguous DCS incident occurred at six hours.

Because of neurological DCS, the surface intervals for three, six and nine hours were rejected. Ten-, 11- and 12-hour surface intervals, however, were considered acceptable according to the acceptance/rejection rules described above. The 10-hour surface interval produced one ambiguous symptom in 23 trials, but the 11- and 12-hour surface intervals had no symptoms in 23 and 27 exposures.

As with all research, proof lies in numbers. The more trials made at a given surface interval increases the confidence in the accuracy of the data. For example, if you performed 100 trials, you would be more confident in the accuracy of your results than if you performed only 10 trials.

Figure 2 illustrates this point very well.

• There were three Definite DCS incidents in 36 trials of the three-hour surface interval, for an 8.3 percent DCS occurrence.

• When the surface interval was increased to six hours, there was one neurological incident in six trials, for a DCS occurrence of 16.7 percent.

• At nine hours, there was one neurological incident in seven trials, for a 14.3 percent DCS occurrence.

The DCS occurrence was higher at six and nine hours than at three hours because the six- and nine-hour intervals had to be rejected after a single case of neurological DCS. The three-hour surface interval, on the other hand, was not rejected until 36 trials were conducted.

That may be due simply to luck, but this is a classic example of having a very low level of confidence in the data for the six- and nine-hour surface intervals because there were so few trials. It is reasonable to suppose that if we could conduct more trials at six and nine hours, the DCS percentage would be lower.

From the data in Figure 2, we are able to estimate the probability of developing DCS through statistical analysis. Figures 3 & 4 represent these findings.

Figure 3 shows the probability of developing Definite DCS, while Figure 4 indicates the probability of developing Ambiguous DCS. In each figure, the x-axis shows the surface interval, while the y-axis indicates the probability of developing DCS at a given surface interval.

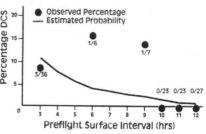

Fígure 3

Probability
of "Definite DCS"

● Observed Percentage
— Estimated Probability

Preflight Surface Interval (hrs)

The correlation between the percentage of Ambiguous DCS and the surface interval in Figure 4 was statistically significant, suggesting that the ambiguous symptoms were a mild form of DCS. At a three-hour surface interval, for example, there was a 10 percent estimated risk of Definite DCS and nearly a 20 percent estimated risk of Ambiguous DCS. The observed DCS percentage at six and nine hours does not follow the estimated trend due to the low number of studies that were conducted.

What is important about the information in Figures 3 and 4 is that it can help you decide how much risk you are willing to take. If you think a 2 percent risk of Definite DCS is acceptable, you could find the point on this curve that represents 2 percent and choose the corresponding preflight surface interval of about 10 hours.

Does 2 percent seem too high to you? No problem. You could decide to wait for 12 hours before your flight, and have an estimated 1 percent risk of Definite DCS and approximately 2 percent risk of Ambiguous DCS. If you want to keep your level of risk at zero, then don't dive or don't fly. Every time you dive, you are subjecting yourself to a risk of DCS. No tables guarantee absolute safety.

In making decisions about risk, you can look to existing guidelines and practical experience for clues, such as the 12-hour flying-after-diving guideline. The estimated DCS probability for this surface interval is about 1 percent. Another clue is the estimated probability for a 55-minute dive to 60 feet. The

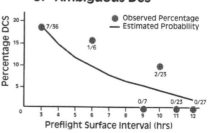

Fígure 4

Probability
of "Ambiguous DCS"

● Observed Percentage
— Estimated Probability

Preflight Surface Interval (hrs)

"Don't Try This At Home"...

Our conclusions shouldn't be tried "in the field" as gospel. All of our exposures at present are dry, resting dives under carefully monitored conditions. In no way should these results be construed as guidelines at this point. Wet, working dives may give very different results. Further testing is required before definitive guidelines can be developed.

Editor's note: The Flying After Diving studies conducted by the DAN/Duke team are ongoing, with a steady stream of volunteer diver participants from all over the United States to help gather this important data. New profiles have been added and tested since this writing, involving both single and multiple dives. Keep abreast of the latest information through Alert Diver; and to become a participant, call DAN Research at (919) 684-2948 or the F.G. Hall Hypo/Hyperbaric Center at (919) 684-6726.

estimated risk of DCS is 0.5-1.0 percent for this dive. We have far to go before we are comfortable with our estimates of DCS probability, but the information we've gathered thus far is already making decompression safety less mysterious.

If these decisions seem arbitrary to you, keep in mind that there is no "right" or "wrong" when deciding whether a profile is "safe" or "unsafe." Whatever preflight surface interval you choose, whether by guess or by probability estimate, there will be some DCS risk — there is no way to avoid it. Our goal at DAN is to develop information that can help you, the diver, make these choices as rationally as possible.

Well, we haven't succinctly answered the question of "How long should I wait after diving before I fly?" but that wasn't the real purpose of this article. We wanted to make you think about what "safety" is and how it is determined. If we had all the answers, DAN Research could close up shop and take jobs teaching diving where the water is always clear and warm and the sun is always bright.

Instead, we will continue to focus our attention on these and other issues — and teach diving when and where we can. And we've moved into new levels of flying-after-diving research, studying flying after repetitive diving. We will relay our progress on this in later articles, as well as discuss how the number of tests we conduct affects the uncertainty or confidence in our probability estimates.

— *From July/August 1995*

The Quagmire

Is in-water recompression a valid emergency procedure? It's an interesting question, but creating a sound scientific study to reach any conclusions might be logistically — and ethically — impossible.

BY RICHARD DUNFORD, M.S., DAN NORTHWEST REGIONAL COORDINATOR

Could Doppler monitor measurements of bubbles in a diver's bloodstream be used to establish safety guidelines for when a diver surfaces after violating the tables, but where no symptoms of decompression sickness (DCS) are evident?

This straightforward, thoughtful question was raised by a reader of a past *Alert Diver* article I wrote. The reader was particularly interested in the use of in-water recompression as the safety measure because he had seen it used successfully in a remote location.

I didn't have an answer, but it made me think. If I wanted to answer that question, how would I go about it? Here's how my theoretical project evolved:

The United States Navy Surface Air Decompression (Sur-D) procedures are an example of decompression tables designed to allow recompression out of the water in lieu of the USN Standard Air Decompression Tables. Sur-D procedures are normally carried out on ship deck in a chamber after the diver exits the water. Decompression risk is higher for these tables than for the Standard Air Tables, but they do work. They are primarily employed in situations where the in-water decompression is very long or where environmental conditions, such as high seas or very cold water, present significant risks to the diver and decompressing at the surface is chosen as the lesser of two evils.

I have observed the response of Doppler-detected bubbles to immediate recompression on air for profiles similar to Sur-D tables, albeit under laboratory conditions during dive experiments using goats. I can say with confidence that recompression beyond 60 fsw (feet sea water/18 meters) following a lengthy and deep exposure will repress Doppler-detected bubbles to near zero relatively quickly. These were deep recompressions, however, and to apply this observation to a recreational diver recompressing to 20-30 fsw/6-9 meters is not advisable because we do not fully understand how shallow recompressions will affect bubbles. A research study is necessary to improve our understanding.

In any test comparison, the further the test conditions depart from the real world conditions, the greater the inherent variability of result and the softer the conclusions. For research design, it's better to do a diving safety study on divers than on goats or dogs, and better on those than mice or salmon fry.

All of these animals have been used for diving research, by the way, and gelatin, too. But the purpose of those efforts was not diving safety but rather to understand some question of basic science. In the case of gelatin, for example, the researchers were not designing tables but rather trying to understand how bubbles form. Using gelatin allowed them to eliminate a whole host of problems while concentrating on just bubbles and under what conditions they form. Applying what they learned to decompression tables would come later and by others.

For our problem — the beneficial effects of shallow recompression — the strongest approach would be to use divers and compare decompression sickness of those recompressed to those not recompressed. The profile should exceed known decompression limits. This is, after all, the issue at hand, so if we do not exceed the tables, we do not test the real situation.

Undertaking the numerous exposures required to achieve a useful degree of precision would place many individuals under considerable risk of serious or permanent injury from decompression sickness. Perhaps, fortunately, such research design exceeds ethical boundaries presently acceptable to most research committees that oversee experimentation on humans.

Our next best tool to replace decompression sickness as a measure of outcome with Doppler scores as estimate DCS risk. Our design still calls for one group to prematurely surface with decompression debt. This is highly risky for decompression sickness, Doppler evaluation or no Doppler evaluation. The design also calls for a second group to exceed the tables and subsequently be recompressed to some shallow depth such as 20-30 feet/6-9 meters. This latter exercise may reduce risk compared to no recompression, but maybe not. In either case, it is very likely that both groups will be at more risk than someone observing the limits of the tables. The Human Subjects Research Review Committee is still not going to be pleased.

Our salvation is that Doppler bubbles are detected from profiles undertaken within the limits of standard tables. This is good news because it says that we don't have to place divers in high risk of DCS in order to obtain data. The down side is that Doppler systems, as we use them, detect bubbles in the veins traveling from the tissues to the lungs. Those detected bubbles are not likely to cause decompression sickness *per se* since they are normally passed out of the body upon reaching the lungs. In other words, the bubbles heard are physiologically remote from the areas of DCS. Doppler technology cannot, therefore, give us a precise estimate of DCS risk. The best we can say is that higher levels of bubbles indicate higher risk and limited estimates of DCS risk can be made from that data.

We must live in a real world, so conditions beyond our control often force compromise. This project would be no exception. In scientific terms, however, we are introducing variability because we are using a less precise measure, Doppler score, and not DCS as result, and because we cannot ethically exceed the limits of the standard decompression tables through that is precisely the condition we want to test. As a result, confidence in our conclusions will be impaired and tend toward "squishy."

Animal experiments are an alternative to improve variability. We may still rely on Doppler results or even use DCS as an outcome, and we can push animal profiles beyond standard limits. However, animal experiments always suffer from a need for verification in human trials, because extrapolating the results to the human conditions is indicative of a risk, but never conclusive. For example, the type of profile required to produce sufficient bubbles or recognizable DCS may be much different than that required for humans. If an effect of recompression is seen, little can be said regarding the appropriate recompression depth or time for human dives because the design has departed too far from the problem of people in the water. Animal rights activists would likely take a dim view of the experiment since it hardly relates to what they would see as a life or death issue.

In my opinion, the best alternative is to use humans with dive profiles within acceptable table limits. Comparing Doppler scores for divers recompressed to a selected time depth profile to those not recompressed is low risk, ethical and has the earmarks of good design in view of the problems noted above.

With this decision in hand, two issues remain troublesome. In order to overcome the notorious variability of Doppler bubble scores, many exposures are going to be required (read *expensive*). Secondly, we must assume that the decompression stresses our subjects undergo in the experimental exposures are physiologically similar, albeit to a lesser degree, to those incurred in the real life field situation.

This latter assumption seems a small point and likely to be correct, but it is important. If the stresses were physiologically dissimilar, than the effects of recompression are also likely to be different and any subsequent conclusions could be rendered useless. For example, a diver who has exceeded the tables may have bubbles in a DCS-sensitive area that are altering the local circulation, while a diver within the tables may only have bubbles in the veins. This dissimilarity may be crucial, and we may never be the wiser.

At some point you must accept these limitations and go forward with the experiment. Let us do so and assume that the results show an effect of reduced bubbles for those recompressed. Shall we then state to the diving community that in-water recompression following a premature surfacing outside the limits of the tables but without symptoms of DCS is an acceptable solution to prevent DCS onset?

I think not. The bubble counts detected by Doppler may be reduced by a recompression to 10, 20 or 30 feet/3, 6 or 9 meters by shutting off the formation of new bubbles released into the veins. The effect of that depth also will be to reduce the size of, but by no means eliminate, any existing tissue bubbles. It is the tissue bubbles that are of concern in DCS. Consequently, festering decompression sickness may still prevail upon resurfacing. Ultimately, what effect recompression will have on a missed decompression for a typical scuba dive remains unknown. We can only speculate based on soft data.

The pivotal rule of medicine is "first do no harm," and that is a good admonition to keep in mind here. Releasing a statement regarding the effect of in-water recompression as described above based on the latter proposed research design would not be wise. The tests were not conducted under realistic circumstances and any conclusions will be circumstantial at best. However, once a statement is conveyed to the diver public in the form of a recommendation, it cannot be fully retracted. Serious harm could be done if it were wrong.

We are left with needing an answer because our data is soft, wanting human trials that are too risky, and little where else to go.

But not quite. DAN is developing a study (*Project Dive Safety, now well under way. — Ed.*) that will collect data from 1 million dive profiles (recorded by dive computers) and a post-dive interview. In these one million divers, some are likely to have recompressed on air following premature surfacing with decompression debt. There are many uncontrolled variables in this type of study, and any results based on this data regarding premature surfacing with decompression depth are again soft. But if the results of our proposed Doppler study agreed with the one million divers surveyed, then the two together provide stronger support for any recommendation made.

Ever wonder why you never seem to get a straight answer out of some scientists? Well, now you have an idea why.

— *November/December 1994*

Women and DCS

Do risks for DCS differ with gender?

BY RICHARD DUNFORD, M.S., DAN NORTHWEST REGIONAL COORDINATOR

The way we view the risks of decompression in divers is changing, but what about women divers? Do they need special attention? Does a diver's sex influence the risks of decompression sickness (DCS)?

The gender-related risk of DCS is not clear.

In 1980, biochemist Dr. Susan Bangasser, reported an increased risk for DCS in women scuba divers at the National Association of Underwater Instructors International Conference on Underwater Education (ICUE). The study relied on the results of a questionnaire sent to dive instructors.

Dr. Bangasser reported that 10 suspected cases of DCS were recorded in an estimated 44,154 dives from the female group (0.023 percent). Male instructor divers reported only three suspected cases for an estimated 43,126 dives (0.007 percent). The difference is a 3.3-fold greater incidence of DCS in the female divers.

Retrospective questionnaires such as this are often the first approach to investigating large and diffuse populations where the occurrence of the problem is rare, such as the occurrence of DCS. They are relatively easy to set up and sometimes are the only legitimate investigative tool available. But questionnaires can suffer from several significant drawbacks.

First, Dr. Bangasser's study, for example, was undertaken after the potential DCS occurred — which may have been years before. In addition, the survey was unable to control for biases — such as the possible differences in the way that men and women accept or deny DCS. The respondents (instructors) were the sources of information, and their response was based on their understanding of the disease. Finally, divers incapacitated by the accident are not likely to be included in the survey. There is no way of knowing how many could be missing from the equation.

The results were the first to report a possible gender-related susceptibility and have been quoted widely as indicating an increased risk for DCS in female divers.

In other analyses, Air Force studies by Dr. Bruce Bassett in 1978 at the School of Aerospace Medicine at Brooks Air Force Base in San Antonio, Texas, reported that altitude chamber exposures to Air Force personnel were four times more risky to female participants

ALESE/MORT PECHTER PHOTO

than males for DCS. Later Air Force studies at Brooks found similar results .

This apparent increase in susceptibility to DCS is difficult to explain. Some investigators have theorized that a general higher percentage of body fat in women may be responsible. Since nitrogen is five times more soluble in fat than in muscle, the speculation is that the more nitrogen that is absorbed, the greater the risk of DCS. Women are hence more prone to DCS because of this. Is this correct? Not necessarily, but in some circles — both scientific and recreational — this speculation has risen to hard fact. It is at least being treated as such in classes taught by some instructors.

This concept, however, should remain as speculation. DCS is primarily a nerve and joint tissue problem, not one of fat. The type of fat we are talking about is in the butt and about the gut. One rarely gets bent in a love handle. There is physical distance between the target organs (nerves and joints) and our fat deposits. So how does one affect the other?

Bubbles moving in the blood is the most plausible answer. If fat has a lot of nitrogen to make bubbles, these can and do get into the venous side of the bloodstream. From there they may travel to the spinal cord or the joints, but they must pass by the lungs. The lungs are quite efficient at removing bubbles, and unless they are overloaded, few bubbles will get by. The lungs normally, will clean out all the venous bubbles.

An alternative route to the spinal cord or the joints is through a septal defect in the heart. Though affecting a relatively small percentage of the diving population, the risk is real. This hole in the septum separating the right and left sides is known as patent foramen ovale. Bubbles in the venous blood can pass through the septal defect to the arterial blood and then act as an embolic agent, increasing the risk of DCS. These defects occur in about 10 to 30 percent of the general population, and most researchers assume the same percentage for the diving population.

When applied to sport divers, the "excess fat" scenario requires that the average increase in body fat in women be sufficient to cause an increased bubble formation in 10 to 30 percent of the women with a septal defect, thereby accounting for a fourfold increase in DCS in women. This is a bit of a stretch, to say the least. Especially when we know from DAN research data that women and men bubble similarly after recreational dives.

Indeed, a 1987 U.S. Navy study of the records from the Naval Diving and Salvage Training Center in Panama City, Fla., poked some holes in this concept. They found no gender-related differences for risk of DCS where the dives occurred primarily in a wet pot (a pool-like area) of a hyperbaric chamber. At the time of the study, they had trained over 6,000 divers, 29 of whom were females. Females participated in 988 dives; males participated in 13,386. In this training, all students performed decompression in a similar manner according to strict U.S. Navy regulations. About 7.5 percent of the divers were classified as deep dives (120 to 300 feet / 36.5 to 91.4 meters of sea water on air and helium/oxygen mixes) and were performed by both genders equally.

Dr. K.M. Zwingelberg, the author, compared these results to the Air Force results, noting some important differences. Ascending in an altitude chamber is like ascending from a very long dive (saturation) where all the tissues are full (saturated) including the areas of high fat content. Tissues with high fat content are also called slow tissues, because they typically have low blood supply and take a long time to fill or empty. Slow tissues are thought to be important in decompression from dives of long bottom times or saturation because they have had time to fill and, in turn, take a long time to release nitrogen. If adipose (fatty) tissue is a risk factor for DCS, then long dives and altitude exposures are where it would be evident. Since the U.S. Navy training center undertakes relatively short bottom time dives, Dr. Zwingelberg suggested adipose tissue should not be a factor and that female divers should not be at more risk.

Dr. Zwingelberg's arguments that fat as a factor in long dives or decompression from saturation but not in dives of short duration make somewhat better sense of the fat issue. When the tissues are fully saturated, the amount of body fat can contain a large amount of nitrogen and in turn produce a large amount of bubbles on decompression. If the lung becomes overloaded with bubbles, some can get past the normal lung filter, enter the arterial blood and become embolic agents even though no septal defect is present. This would certainly increase the risk of DCS. On the other hand, for a short recreational type exposure, a slow tissue does not have time to absorb enough gas to produce a significant bubble load before the dive is over.

In yet another Air Force study at the School of Aerospace Medicine, Brooks AFB, and, again, with aviators decompressed to altitude, Frederick Rudge showed that the presence of menses was a significant factor in DCS risk. Women aviators showed the highest risk of DCS during menses; that risk dropped in a linear fashion to its lowest point at 25 to 29 days after the start of menses. Only at its lowest point, during those days, did the female aviators risk equal that of the men's risk.

This is a more disturbing report and has received supporting evidence from my own facility here at the Virginia Mason Medical Center Hyperbaric Chamber. We have documented risk related to menses — but resulting from dives to pressure rather than exposure to altitude. A female diving with menses in our chamber was 7.6 times more likely to develop DCS than one diving without menses. The rate of DCS for a nonmenstruating female chamber attendant was equal to that of male chamber attendants.

Hyperbaric chamber dives as we conduct them tend to require bottom times of two hours or more. This is not a saturation dive, but it is longer than the bottom time for the typical U.S. Navy training center dive.

So, is it fat? Is it menses? Is it real? We don't know, but keep these points in mind: the menses observations have been done in dry altitude chambers from saturation or from dry chamber dives with long bottom times. The issue of fat as a risk factor for females has not been explored by any credible study and does not make good sense as presented for short duration dives. The only study of scuba divers was not well controlled and used instructors rather than medically trained technicians as the authoritative respondents.

The DAN database is an alternative source of information. In it, 29 percent of the DCS cases reported in 1992 were females. In a 1989 membership survey, 27 percent of the respondents were female. In two separate field studies, 60 of 186 participants (32 percent) were female. This suggests that the ratio of women reporting DCS is similar to the ratio of women in the overall population of divers. It is possible, however, that females dive more conservatively than men, and therefore their reported incidence does not reflect their true risk. But, again, data from the DAN field trips indicated that as a whole, males and females dive to similar depths and for similar bottom times.

Neither does the menstrual cycle appear to be a factor in sport divers. Only three female sport divers treated for DCS at Virginia Mason Hyperbaric Chamber, Seattle, Wash. (VMHC) were diving with menses — from a patient population of 37 female divers whose menstrual history is known. In a group of premenopausal women, approximately one quarter would be experiencing menses at any given time.

Do women avoid diving during menses? In a survey of 29 female sport divers, seven of 25 non-menopausal women (28 percent) indicated that the presence of menstrual flow might affect their diving habits. However, no effect of menstrual flow on diving habits was apparent when these 25 divers were followed for one year of diving.

What we are left with is a lot of loose ends and no small amount of confusion. Chamber exposures show increased risks of DCS to females. Those risks from dry chamber exposures do not seem to be related to female sport divers or female students diving in U.S. Navy chamber wet pots. Until someone can document an increased risk with reliable data on sport divers, it should be safe to assume that female sport divers are at no increased risk for DCS compared to males.

— From March/April 1994

DRUGS AND DIVING

An Overview of Drugs and Diving

BY KAREN SMITH, M.S., R.PH.

Actual numbers of divers who use multiple drug products is estimated to be extensive. Unfortunately, few well-controlled studies exist that examine the effects of drugs in the underwater environment. The following categories have been identified as being commonly utilized by divers:
- Drugs used to ameliorate problems associated with diving.
- Drugs used to treat concurrent disease processes.
- Recreational drugs.

There is evidence, however, that drug effects can be altered at depths of 50 feet / 15.2 meters. These drug effects have been described as potentiated, antagonized and in some cases totally unpredictable. Side effects can be variable and subtle. Variations in side effects can be modified by risk factors such as cold water, depth, and oxygen or nitrogen concentrations.

The following brief review is not comprehensive. Any questions regarding the potential safety and efficacy of a drug in the underwater environment should be presented to a diving physician, a pharmacist or to DAN.

Decongestants
The most commonly utilized drugs are decongestants which facilitate ear and sinus equalization. These products provide relief of ear and sinus

ROBERT R. CLEMONS

squeeze by constricting blood vessels, reducing tissue swelling, and improving middle ear and sinus gas exchange. Rebound congestion may occur with chronic use and may actually worsen congestive symptoms. Many combination products exist which contain antihistamines (Contac™, Actifed™). These pose additional problems for the diver.

Antihistamines commonly produce sedation, and decrease overall mental acuity. Individual responses vary widely. Medications containing antihistamines are contraindicated for diving. Terfenadine™ has no sedative effects and although experience with divers is limited, this medication is probably safe for diving.

Motion Sickness

Drugs designed to treat the symptoms of motion sickness frequently cause functional motor impairment.

Antihistamines are commonly utilized to control motion sickness and may cause sedation and motor dysfunction. Meclizine (Antivert™) and dimenhydrate (Dramamine™) are commonly used antihistamines utilized for motion sickness. Other agents such as the Scopolamine (TransDerm Scop™) skin patch provides a system which administers low doses at a continuous rate. Scopolamine is classified as an anticholinergic agent which has sedative properties. Additional side effects may include dry mouth and blurred vision, and its safety cannot be guaranteed while diving. Many divers use this product to control motion sickness symptoms successfully, but individual reactions vary.

Editor's note: Trans-Derm Scop was temporarily removed from the market after this article was published (January/February 1993). As of May 1997, Trans-Derm Scop is still in redevelopment. Its manufacturer states that it is hopeful the medication will be available in 1997.

Sedative and Pain Agents

Often the disease process itself, rather than the medication, prevents the individual from diving.

• Sedatives or antianxiety agents (Valium™, Ativan™, Dalmane™, Halcion™) significantly alter mental function and cannot be used safely while diving.

• Skeletal muscle relaxants (Parafon DSG™, Flexeril™, Robaxin™ also produce variable amounts of sedation and should not be used while diving.

• Analgesic preparations, especially those containing propoxyphene, codeine, oxycodone, or hydrocodone (Darvon™, Darvocet™, Tylenol #3™, Percodan™, Percocet™) are contraindicated for diving due to decreased mental and exercise performance.

Respiratory depression has also developed in individuals utilizing these medications.

Antipsychotic Agents

Drugs used to treat psychiatric disturbances such as depression or psychosis (Elavil™, Sinequan™, Haldol™) not only produce the sedative effects described with antianxiety agents, but also have been noted to cause cardiac dysrhythmias.

The effects of these agents appear to impair cognitive performance for most individuals using them. The effects of these agents underwater are unpredictable and dangerous and are considered absolutely contraindicated for diving.

Antihypertensive Agents

A variety of medications treat high blood pressure. However, many commonly used hypertension agents produce side effects which could limit diving performance, although experience is limited.

Diuretics (Hydrochlorothiazide™, Lasix™, Bumex™) produce fluid loss. This can compound dehydration and lead to electrolyte abnormalities associated with vigorous exercise underwater.

Drugs designed to reduce or limit heart rate (Inderal™, Labetalol™, Metoprolol™) could affect diver capacity. Other agents act directly on the peripheral vasculature (Minipress™, Hytrin™) or via a centrally medicated mechanism (Catapres™, Tenex™, Aldomet™) and can produce drowsiness.

These agents all pose potential dangers to the diver since exaggerated side effects may be noted in individuals under increased exercise performance requirements. Individuals for whom these medications are prescribed should talk to their physician.

Anti-Asthmatic Agents, Bronchodilators

Asthma with its respiratory ccompromise [can be] a contraindication for diving. The use of theophylline (TheoDur™, SloPhyllin™, Uniphyl™) can produce central nervous system stimulant effects and cardiac dysrhythmias.

Products which stimulate bronchodilation (Metaprel™, Alupent™, Ventolin™) also produce variable amounts of tachycardia (rapid heartbeat).

Steroids are also used to treat acute asthma and have limited side effects such as sodium retention.

Gastrointestinal Agents

Antacids (Maalox™, Mylanta™) appear to pose little to no adverse effects on the diver.

Histamine-2-antagonists (Tagamet™, Zantac™, Pepcid™, Axid™), can produce additional CNS effects such as drowsiness and headache. These agents can also produce altered cognitive performance and are not recommended for diving.

Recreational Drug Use

Illicit drugs such as narcotics and hallucinogens are not recommended for diving. Their dangerous side effects cannot be adequately predicted underwater.

Alcohol also produces dangerous side effects. These include the confusion associated with the well known sedative properties of judgment and motor reflexes. Alcohol also causes vasodilatation, which can impair heat conservation underwater, and produce diuresis and mild dehydration.

The caffeine contained in coffee, tea and soft drinks may also pose problems underwater. Caffeine can produce diuresis, which could lead to dehydration.

Summary

Over-the-counter drug use is prevalent in our society. However, the effects of these medications underwater are poorly investigated and not well understood. Divers must have both their medication regiments and underlying medical conditions carefully reviewed before diving.

Drug Use Recommendations

Recommendations for drug use and monitoring are rather empiric and are based on observed effects in a normal environment. Often times, the disease process itself excludes the individual from diving. The greatest concern for physicians is the drug's potential to cause decreased motor coordination, altered mental state, or change in respiratory or cardiovascular status.

Before taking any medications, here's what you should do:

• Know the medications you are taking (both prescription and non-prescription).

• Be aware that drug actions are variable and often unpredictable underwater.

• Ask your physician, pharmacist, or DAN about the safety of your medications.

• Limit non-prescription drug use.

— From January/February 1993

Oral Contraceptive Use in Women Divers

BY KAREN SMITH, M.S., R.PH.

Oral contraceptives, if used correctly, are very effective methods of birth control.

Use of these products is widespread among women of childbearing age due to their relative ease of use and actual pregnancy prevention rate, reported at 98 percent. To date, there are no studies available discussing an increased development of decompression sickness or other diving problems.

Recently, published discussion of the risk benefit of oral contraceptives has centered around long-term evaluations of oral contraceptives and other estrogen-containing products. Many women divers have raised legitimate concerns regarding effects of oral contraceptives in the hyperbaric environment.

These associations of disease development remain controversial, but this brief review will attempt to describe some of the documented adverse drug reactions associated with oral contraceptives and their potential implications for sport divers.

Short-Term Effects

Common side effects appear to be caused by the estrogen component in oral contraceptives.

These effects are most pronounced during the first cycle and may disappear or diminish after three to four cycles.

Conventional dose preparations (Ovral®, Demulen®, Lo/Ovral® and others) are most frequently associated with nausea/vomiting, edema/fluid retention, headache, dizziness and depression. These effects appear in 10-20 percent of women taking these medications.

Changing dosage or medications during the initial month of therapy does not appear to alleviate those symptoms. These side effects may persist despite symptomatic treatment.

The development of fluid imbalances (either retention of fluid or dehydration secondary to nausea/vomiting) may be problematic for sport divers.

Alterations in mental function and acuity are rare, but the development of dizziness or headaches early on in oral contraceptive therapy may limit diving performance. Therefore, caution is advised when diving during initial oral contraceptive therapy.

Long-Term Effects

Hypertension — Oral contraceptives have been associated with increased blood pressure.

Blood pressure elevations are usually minor, but significant elevations have occurred in some women. The risk of developing hypertension is increased in women who have used oral contraceptives five years or more, are over 35 years old and have a family history of high blood pressure.

Although a diagnosis of high blood pressure is not absolutely contraindicated for sport diving, individuals should seek a physician's evaluation to determine their fitness for diving.

Thromboembolic Disease — Oral contraceptive use has been associated with an increased risk of thromboembolic and thrombotic disorders.

These disorders involve the development of "clot-like" vein occlusions, which are usually composed of blood, platelets and other cellular matter. These occlusions can lead to the development of emboli, which can produce blockage in the veins supplying blood and oxygen to the extremities, lungs, brain and heart.

Investigators have demonstrated a 4- to 11-fold increased risk of fatal thromboembolism in oral contraceptive users compared to nonoral contraceptive users.

Additional studies also indicate that an even greater risk of cardiovascular side effects are seen in women on oral contraceptives who are over 35 years and who are considered heavy smokers (> = 15 cigarettes per day).

Any individual presenting with a history of thromboembolic or thrombotic disorders is not encouraged to dive, due to the possible risk of venous occlusion with resulting decompression sickness.

Summary

Oral contraceptives are commonly used by female divers. The effects of oral contraceptives on diving are not well documented. Although theoretical risks exist, the use of oral contraceptives alone does not appear to be an absolute contraindication to diving. Recommendations for women on oral contraceptives include strict adherence to dive depth limits and familiarity with the signs and symptoms of thromboembolic disease.

Physicians and individuals involved with the patient at the time of an injury or emergent event should be made aware of oral contraceptive use as well as other medications ingested by the diver.

— *From May/June 1990*

Shattering the Myth
of Aspirin and Diving

BY KAREN VICK, M.S., R.PH.

Take two aspirins and call me in the morning ...
This well-known and overused maxim has led many individuals to perceive that aspirin is good medicine and is great for treating just about anything that ails people.

Some divers have extended this common but erroneous belief into the realm of diving — that aspirin should be good for preventing decompression sickness (DCS) and for improving the eventual outcome of a diving accident.

However, clinical evidence does not support this leap of faith.

Aspirin, as a salicylate compound, has been shown to be effective in diminishing mild to moderate pain, reducing fevers and decreasing inflammation at the site of tissue injury. In fact, many over-the-counter preparations contain salicylates.

However, for the past 20 years the medical community has been evaluating another effect of aspirin therapy. Aspirin has a direct effect on the function of platelets (small circulating blood cells). This is an important observation since platelets are often responsible for plugging blood vessels and causing a thrombosis (blood clot) which can lead to a stroke or heart attack.

Aspirin seems to prevent the platelets' ability to "stick together" to form the clot within the blood vessel. This observation has led to the use of aspirin in patients who may be at risk for the development of thrombosis. Unfortunately, much controversy still exists regarding this therapy.

Routine use of aspirin has therefore been limited to physician discretion, and based on the risks and benefits of each particular patient.

However, just as the routine use of aspirin for individuals with documented clotting risk has not been adequately established, there is no clinical proof that aspirin can prevent decompression sickness and is therefore not recommended for routine use.

Anecdotal reports exist of individuals ingesting multiple aspirin tablets (six to 10 tablets) in an attempt to reduce their chance of acquiring DCS.

Despite the lack of clinical evidence in favor of aspirin, some divers have noted this "anti-platelet" effect of aspirin, and are using it as part of their routine dive plan.

Additionally, excessive use of aspirin by the diver may, in fact, pose other serious dangers. Aspirin, even, within normal dosage ranges, can prolong bleeding in most individuals.

The diver who is also taking other medications may enhance the effects of aspirin and be at increased risk if they are bleeding from a laceration. Bruising may also be more extensive and more frequent.

Individuals who have a history of peptic or duodenal ulcers, or have had a recent traumatic injury, are at an increased risk of bleeding again at that site.

It is fairly well known that the likelihood of bubble-related problems worsening, and hyperbaric treatment becoming more difficult, increases with delayed recognition and treatment of a problem.

Because of the pain relieving effect of preventative aspirin therapy, common early signs of DCS, such as joint and muscle pain, may not be immediately recognized. Thus hyperbaric treatment may be delayed.

Finally, some individuals cannot tolerate compounds containing the active ingredient in aspirin, salicylate. These individuals have allergic-like reactions, such as asthma or hives, and must use extra caution when taking medications.

Indiscriminate use of aspirin before divng to avoid DCS should therefore be discouraged and avoided for all of the above reasons.

If you are unsure if a preparation you are planning to use contains aspirin, read the label first or consult with your physician or pharmacist.

— From May/June 1991

DAN Takes A Look at Over-the-Counter Medications

Some of the more common questions to DAN medics concern the use of OTCs and their compatibility with safe diving.

BY DANIEL A. NORD,
AEMT-CC, CHT, DAN MEDIC

As open-water students, we all were drilled about the perils of alcohol and diving. To be sure, there is no exception to the rule that drinking and diving don't mix.

But what about other drugs and diving — specifically over-the-counter medications? Is the line so clear-cut with OTCs?

This is the stuff many dive medical questions are made of — some of the more common questions to DAN medics concern the use of over-the-counter (OTC) medications and their compatibility with safe diving.

The fact that these drugs are easily available over the counter versus a more controlled dispersal as with prescription medications carries with it a sometimes faulty assumption: that all OTCs are completely safe, whether you're topside or underwater.

Not true, say doctors, diving medical specialists — and anecdotal experiences of divers. All drugs are capable of producing some side effects, and even untoward effects in some people when above water.

So what happens when you use OTCs underwater, when you're subjected to the pressures of depth? The answer is not so clear, because little empirical evidence is documented. There has been scant research conducted on the effects of drugs used in a hyperbaric environment. Diving while using most medications is, at best, a matter for you, your doctor and DAN to discuss — before you dive.

CAN'T LIVE WITHOUT 'EM?

Three-fifths of the medications purchased in the United States are nonprescription over-the-counter (OTC) drugs, widely viewed as a cost-effective segment of personal health care. The OTC drug system supports a trend toward self-care and self-medication and is experiencing, on average, an 8- to 10-percent annual growth. Given the popularity of recreational scuba, there is often a concern that some OTCs may not be appropriate for use while diving.

By definition, OTCs are that classification of drugs considered safe for consumer use, based solely on their labeling. When used as directed, they present a minimum risk and a greater margin of safety than prescription (Rx) drugs. They are typically used to treat illnesses which can be easily recognized by the user, in contrast to conditions treated by prescription drugs, which are generally more difficult to assess. Additionally, there are about 300,000 OTC drugs currently on the market, far outnumbering the 65,000 prescription drugs.

The most commonly encountered OTCs — and probably of greatest concern for the sport or recreational diver — fall within the following categories:

- Antihistamines
- Decongestants and cough suppressants
- Anti-inflammatory agents
- Analgesics
- Anti-motion sickness preparations

PRESCRIPTION FOR THOUGHT

A diver considering the use of any medication should first give serious thought to the underlying need or reason to take the drug. Does the underlying condition disqualify the individual from diving, or does it compromise his general safety and that of other divers?

The diver, for instance, who requires decongestants in order to equalize his ears and sinuses has increased risk of serious injury from barotrauma. Another example is the seasick diver who, medicated or not, may experience in-water episodic disorientation, vomiting, loss of buoyancy control and embolism as a result of breath-holding or violent diaphragmatic movement.

No drug is completely safe, regardless of the environment. Drugs are chemicals and by design, alter body functions through their therapeutic action. Moreover, they all may have undesirable effects that vary by individual or environment — with sometimes unpredictable results.

BACKGROUND INSIGHTS

What's the first step to take in researching your medications? Review and familiarization with the active ingredients, warnings and directions provided by the manufacturer may offer good insight to the potential for a problem. Here are some examples to learn from.

• Antihistamines

Most often used to provide symptomatic relief of allergies, colds and motion sickness are antihistamines, with the active ingredients diphenhydramine hydrochloride, triprolidine hydrolochloride and chlorpheniramine maleate. The word "antihistamine" literally denotes a drug with characteristics which are antagonistic to the actions of histamine.

Histamine, in turn, is a powerful stimulant of gastric secretion, a constrictor of bronchial smooth muscle, and a dilator of capillaries and arterioles. Antihistamines, then, counteract the symptoms of allergies, colds and motion sickness, but may have side effects. In therapeutic doses, these side effects may include dryness of the mouth, nose and throat, visual disturbances, drowsiness or an undesired sedation or depression — all significant factors that, together or separately, can affect the safety of a dive. Antihistamines can also depress the central nervous system (CNS) and impair a diver's ability to think clearly and react appropriately when the need arises.

• Decongestants

These are vasoconstricting drugs that cause narrowing of the blood vessels, which often gives a temporary improvement of the nasal airways. Common active ingredients include pseudoephedrine hydrochloride and phenylpropanolamine hydrochloride. Decongestants may cause a mild CNS stimulation and can also offer numerous side effects such as nervousness, excitability, restlessness, dizziness, weakness and a forceful or rapid heartbeat.

Medications known to stimulate the central nervous system may have a significant and/or undesirable effect on the diver. Additional precautions or warnings may advise against use by individuals suffering from diabetes, asthma or cardiovascular disease.

• Anti-Inflammatories & Analgesics

As with any drug, it is wise to consider the underlying condition for taking anti-inflammatories or analgesics. These drugs are generally taken for the temporary relief of minor aches and pains, and although they may provide temporary relief, remember that the injury itself is still present. Limitations in range of movement because of the injury, swelling or pain can place a diver at risk of additional injury. In addition, they may mask mild pain due to decompression sickness, and the diver may subsequently delay seeking treatment.

Active ingredients include naproxen sodium and ibuprofen, with notable side effects such as heartburn, nausea, abdominal pain, headache, dizziness and drowsiness. Standard precautions discourage their use by those with medical disorders involving heartburn, gastric ulcers, bleeding problems or asthma.

With anti-inflammatories or analgesics, perhaps one of the most significant considerations is potential adverse drug interactions in individuals treated with anticoagulants, insulin and nonsteroidal anti-inflammatories (NSAIDs).

• Anti-Motion Sickness Preparations

It's best not to self-medicate here; specific warnings regularly prohibit the use of these medications prior to consulting a physician. It's generally agreed that — at any time — recreational divers should use these medications with caution.

As with some antihistamines, these medications may typically contain meclizine hydrochloride, dimenhydrinate, diphenhydramine hydrochloride and cyclizine. Common side effects are drowsiness and fatigue. Coupled with impairment of a diver's ability to perform hazardous activities requiring mental alertness or physical coordination, these side effects will definitely not enhance the pleasure of a dive.

UNDERWATER PRESSURES

Any medication that affects the CNS, such as anithistamines, decongestants anti-motion sickness medications, has the potential to interact with increased partial pressures of nitrogen. How? The effects of the medication may increase the chance of nitrogen narcosis. In addition, nitrogen may have a synergistic effect in enhancing the sedative or stimulant quality of the drug.

Furthermore, because of the increased intensity of these effects, a new and unexpected reaction such as panic may occur in an otherwise rational diver. These side effects will vary from diver to diver and from day to day within the same diver — it's simply not possible to predict who will have a reaction while diving.

Product Category	Active Ingredients
Antihistamines	diphenhydramine hydrochloride, triprolidine hydrolochloride, clemastine fumarate, brompheniramine maleate, chlorpheniramine maleate, pyrilamine maleate
Decongestants	pseudoephedrine hydrochloride, phenylpropanolamine hydrochloride, phenylephrine hydrochloride, oxymetazoline hydrochloride, naphazoline hydrochloride
Anti-Inflammatories & Analgesics	naproxen sodium, ibuprofen, acetaminophen, aspirin, ketoprofen
Anti-Motion Sickness	meclizine hydrochloride, dimenhydrinate, diphenhydramine hydrochloride, cyclizine

Sample Warnings

May cause drowsiness. Do not take this product
if you are taking sedatives or tranquilizers, without
first consulting your doctor. Use caution when driving
a motor vehicle or operating machinery. May cause
excitability, especially in children. Do not take
this product, unless directed by a doctor, if you have
high blood pressure, heart disease, diabetes, thyroid
disease, glaucoma, a breathing problem such as
emphysema or difficulty in urination due to enlargement
of the prostate gland.

Do not take this product if you have high blood
pressure, heart disease, diabetes, thyroid disease
or difficulty in urination due to enlargement of
the prostate gland except under the advice and
supervision of a physician. Do not take this product
if you are presently taking a prescription antihypertensive
or antidepressant drug containing a monoamine
oxidase inhibitor, except under the advice and
supervision of a physician.

Do not take this product if you have stomach problems
(such as heartburn, upset stomach or stomach
pain) that persists or recurs, or if you have ulcers
or bleeding problems, unless directed by a doctor.
if you are taking a prescription drug for anticoagulation
(thinning of blood), diabetes, gout or arthritis unless
directed by a doctor.

Do not take this product if you have asthma, glaucoma,
emphysema, chronic pulmonary disease, shortness
of breath, difficulty in breathing or difficulty in urination
due to enlargement of the prostate gland, unless
directed by a doctor. Use caution when driving a
motor vehicle or operating machinery. Not for frequent
or prolonged use except on advice of a doctor.

TOPSIDE SAVVY

What does this all mean for the recreational scuba diver? From a medical perspective, many doctors knowledgeable in diving medicine will quickly advise anyone who requires medication in order to dive to wait the illness out. Other maxims to heed follow below.

Consult your physician when you are ill — your doctor may be able to provide you with a more effective medication and counsel you on diving fitness.

Study all the information supplied with your medication and understand the warnings, precautions and what effects it may have on your body. A trial exposure of at least one or two days prior to diving may help you assess your individual reaction to the drug.

As we often experience in other day-to-day matters, the decision of whether or not to dive is personal and one of acceptable risk. The choice of acceptable risk is a matter of judgment, with careful attention given to the risk versus the benefits, as well as the ability and willingness to deal with possible negative consequences.

Diving should be a positive experience. Dive with care. Remember that both your doctor — and DAN — are there to answer any questions you may have about diving and your health.

— From May/June 1996

RESCUE

Alternative In-Water Rescue Techniques

BY JOHN LIPPMANN, EXECUTIVE DIRECTOR, DAN SOUTH EAST ASIA-PACIFIC

U.S. COAST GUARD PHOTO

The victim and his buddy were both relatively inexperienced divers. During the descent, the victim's buddy signaled to abort the dive. The victim indicated he didn't want to and continued the dive, leaving his buddy to ascend alone. The divemaster entered the water to look for the missing diver. He noticed a continuous plume of bubbles, a sure sign of a free-flowing regulator. He found the victim sitting on a rock at 70 feet. His regulator was indeed free-flowing and out of his mouth, but his mask was still in place. The diver appeared unconscious, because he fell over as the divemaster approached. The divemaster placed his octopus into the victim's mouth; it fell out immediately. At this stage he knew the situation was serious. He replaced the octopus in the diver's mouth, held it in place, and put some air into the victim's BC using the direct feed.

Tilting the victim's head back, the divemaster held the octopus in the diver's mouth. He left both weight belts in place and inflated his own BC to provide enough lift for the ascent. Grasping the diver's chin, he maintained contact and head tilt throughout the ascent.

The divemaster dumped air from his own BC to control the ascent. He also noticed bubbles and froth coming from the victim's mouth during the ascent.

Witness reports suggested that the victim had been underwater somewhere between five and 10 minutes. Since the diver was alone, no one knew how long his regulator had been displaced. The water temperature was around 65°F / 18°C, and the surface was calm. The divemaster had been in the water two minutes.

The victim was rolled onto the marlin board, his gear removed and he was dragged onto the boat. His wetsuit jacket — a quarter-inch with hood — was cut open. His eyes were very bloodshot, his skin was gray and froth was coming from his mouth and nose.

Rescuers could find neither breath nor pulse in the injured diver. They began two-operator CPR, with the divemaster performing ventilations and a dive instructor performing compressions. The procedure was difficult because the diver's jaw was clenched and only partly open, and the froth in his mouth was now mixed with vomit.

The rescuers had performed CPR for five minutes, when the victim's eyelids fluttered. Rescuers stopped giving compressions but continued with ventilations (which were continued using a bag-valve mask with supplemental oxygen).

A rescue helicopter arrived, and a paramedic was lowered onto the boat. Since the victim was now semiconscious and had difficulty breathing spontaneously, the paramedic swapped out the bag-valve mask for an oxygen resuscitator. The diver responded and eventually established his own regular breathing pattern. His pulse was steady at 85 beats per minute.

On shore, the victim was transferred to the hospital and recompression chamber. En route, paramedics continued administering 100 percent oxygen via a tight-fitting demand-valve mask.

At the hospital, the diver was recompressed to 60 feet / 18.2 meters. Over several days he received three to four hyperbaric oxygen treatments; he was released from the hospital the next week, with no apparent residual symptoms. The chamber staff believed his symptoms were probably caused by near-drowning alone, without further complications of decompression illness. The diver said he couldn't remember what caused the incident. However, the divemaster noticed the mouthpiece from the victim's second stage regulator was missing.

The divemaster stated that he regularly practiced rescue techniques and CPR and that he found this rescue to be a relatively straightforward procedure.

At some time in his diving career, a diver may find it is necessary to perform an in-water rescue of an unconscious diver. Fortunately, such situations are rare.

Rescue and resuscitation skills are valuable tools that all divers should rapidly acquire. These skills should be practiced often — at least twice annually — to maintain a high level of readiness.

In an actual emergency, the first issue to consider is the urgency of the situation. Whether the operation will be a rescue or a body recovery depends on a variety of factors:

- whether the diver is still breathing;
- how much time has elapsed since the diver stopped breathing; and
- the temperature of the water (and insulation of the diver), among other factors.

Normally, the first step is to determine whether the diver is really unconscious. Exhaust bubbles indicate that the diver is breathing and may, or may not be, conscious. The absence of bubbles for more than about five to 10 seconds indicates that a diver is not breathing. A slumped position, eyes closed or blankly staring may indicate impaired consciousness. Gently shaking the diver should elicit a response if he's fully conscious. A diver who doesn't react at all or only reacts weakly should be brought to the surface.

The rescuer should get a firm grip on the injured diver, take a couple of seconds to compose himself, and determine the best course of action to take. At the same time he should locate the diver's weight belt and BC inflate/deflate mechanisms.

Although it is important not to waste time, the few seconds taken to assess the situation may save unnecessary complications later.

Whether the diver is breathing or not, the rescuer should support the regulator in the diver's mouth and ensure that it doesn't become dislodged. Positioning the injured diver's head with a backward head tilt should maintain air passage.

Backward Head Tilt

This tilt is normally used to open the airway of an unconscious person on land. When an unconscious person is lying on his back, the tongue falls against the back of the throat and can obstruct the airway. Tilting the head back and lifting the lower jaw should allow air to enter and leave the lungs with minimal obstruction.

Some rescue protocols, however, suggest the rescuer support the victim's head in a neutral position (i.e., not tilted back or forward). Whether a neutral head position will provide an adequate airway in this situation is debatable.

It has been suggested that because the unconscious victim underwater should be brought to the surface in an upright position, airway obstruction from the tongue is less likely. Therefore, a neutral head position should be adequate to allow air to enter the lungs of an unconscious, breathing diver (with an air supply), or to vent from the lungs of a breathing or non-breathing diver.

Another argument against using the backward head tilt is that any water that had collected in the diver's mouth could enter the throat if the head was tilted back. If the diver wasn't fully unconscious, this water could cause a laryngospasm (a reflex spasm of the larynx), which could last for several minutes. The laryngospasm would abate only when the diver became deeply hypoxic (oxygen shortage). The likelihood of laryngospasm decreases as an injured diver lapses further into unconsciousness.

If laryngospasm occurred during ascent, expanding air in the lungs might not effectively escape, thus increasing the possibility of a pulmonary barotrauma. Although some physicians assert that air can still escape from an unconscious person's lungs despite laryngospasm, this has not always been supported by anesthetic experience.

In fully developed laryngospasm during anesthesia, both inhalation and exhalation may be impossible. This situation only occurs in a partially conscious person, however, and not in the fully unconscious person.

Inflating the Buoyancy Compensator & Mask and Weight Belt Removal

Some rescue protocols urge the rescuer to inspect the victim's mask. If there is no water in it, it is usually recommended to leave the mask in place (although a possible exception to this is discussed later). However, if there is water in the mask, it has been argued that the mask be removed.

If the mask contains air and water, the air will expand on the way to the surface, forcing water through the victim's nose and into the throat, and possibly causing laryngospasm if the diver is not fully unconscious.

If the mask is full of water, it can either be removed underwater or on reaching the surface. It probably won't make much difference. If the diver is breathing and the mask is removed, the rescuer can pinch the injured diver's nose to prevent water entering during ascent.

Certain rescue procedures suggest that the victim's weight belt be removed. The injured diver is often heavy (many being substantially overweighted), and it may be necessary to remove his weight belt to increase the diver's buoyancy.

It is a good idea to locate the injured diver's BC inflate/deflate mechanism, since it may save time finding it later. The weight belt may then be removed and pulled well clear to prevent its tangling with other gear, and dropped. However, not all rescuers recommend removing the victim's weight belt underwater.

To control ascent rates, some suggest adding air to the victim's BC, via the direct feed, to provide the necessary positive buoyancy. This will be impossible if there is no air in the victim's tank, and it may not be practicable even if the air supply is not depleted, especially in deep water. Various tests have demonstrated that it can take up to a minute or more to inflate certain BCs at depth, and at low supply pressures. This delay could adversely affect the outcome of the rescue.

Alternatively, the required buoyancy may be achieved if the rescuer inflates his own BC. The advantage of this is that it is usually easier for a rescuer to control buoyancy using his own familiar device. This may mean that the injured diver remains negatively buoyant, at least for some of the ascent. Again, a firm grip on the victim is essential.

Where possible, the injured diver should be positively buoyant. If the divers separate for any reason during the ascent, the victim's positive buoyancy should ensure that the victim would continue to ascend. If the victim was negatively buoyant and contact was lost, he could sink.

This is one of the potential problems with leaving the victim's weight belt on and using the rescuer's BC to provide sufficient buoyancy for ascent. It is also one reason why the removal of the rescuer's weight belt is not recommended.

Positive buoyancy may not be appropriate if it hinders direct access to the surface, such as in a cave. In a situation like this, it may be necessary to leave the injured diver's weight belt in place, try to achieve neutral buoyancy for both rescuer and victim, and swim the diver out.

There appears to be little justification for the rescuer to release both the victim's and his own weight belt, even in shallow water. Some divers forget that the risk of a lung overexpansion injury is greatest during the last few feet before the surface.

In most cases, the rescuer should retain his own weight belt, at least until after reaching the surface and after making the victim positively buoyant. The rescuer who ditches his weight belt may create an uncontrolled and rapid ascent — a danger if he encountered an entanglement, dropped the victim, or encountered some other unforeseen circumstance.

The next move is a somewhat controversial one: The rescuer has to decide whether to maintain contact with the victim throughout the ascent — which is the usual teaching — or to ensure the victim is positively buoyant, release him, and follow him up. The decision may be influenced by the depth of the water and the rescuer's own situation. The most commonly taught technique is to maintain contact with the victim throughout the ascent. In this procedure, the rescuer ensures positive buoyancy by initially removing the victim's weight belt and/or adding air to either the victim's or his own BC. The rescuer maintains physical contact with the victim while both ascend, driven by positive buoyancy. If the diver is breathing, it is possible he could regain consciousness during the ascent, become disoriented and panic. In this case, the rescuer should have a firm hold of the injured diver — better from behind, some experts say — so he can restrain the injured diver safely if the need arises.

The rescuer can control the ascent rate to some extent by releasing air from his own BC and/or the victim's. This is a time when skill acquired by prior practice — not to mention an extra pair of hands — is helpful.

The rate of ascent can vary considerably. If both divers are wearing full quarter-inch wetsuits and the victim's weight belt has been dropped, very fast ascent rates can occur near the surface, especially if expanding air hasn't been dumped from the BCs on the way up. The rescuer should ensure that he breathes in and out, possibly exhaling more than normally (although not continuously) when approaching the surface. Angling the fins and arching the body to create extra drag can also help reduce the ascent rate.

In 1974, a radically different method was suggested for retrieving a diver who is found lying on the bottom, unconscious, regulator out. It has been adopted, to varying degrees, by some rescuers, despite the absence of substantial supporting data.

When a non-breathing diver is brought to the surface, the partial pressure of oxygen in the diver's body rapidly falls because of the reduction in ambient pressure and the body's oxygen consumption.

It was argued that, as the gases in the chest expand and escape during the ascent, oxygen will be quickly drawn away from the body tissues and transported to the lungs. This depletes oxygen in the blood and tissues leading to oxygen starvation (anoxia) and death. The deeper the victim is found, the greater the potential is for oxygen drain because of the larger pressure differential and increased distance and time of ascent.

It was reasoned that the injured diver must be brought to the surface as rapidly as possible to minimize this oxygen drain from the tissues. Consequently, it was suggested that if a diver is found unconscious with his regulator out, the rescuer should remove the injured diver's weight belt and mask, raise him to the vertical position, inflate the victim's BC and let him go. The rescuer would then follow at a safe rate of ascent, retrieve the victim on the surface and then begin resuscitation. This procedure was recommended as a last-resort option in circumstances where the surface is calm and clear of obstructions, and where there may be some concern that the rescuer could not make a safe, reasonably rapid ascent.

By positioning the diver in a head-up position, the pressure on the lower chest will be greater than that on the upper chest. It was argued that this pressure differential should force excess air out from the mouth and prevent further water from entering the larynx. As the diver ascends, expanding air should vent from the lungs and out the mouth, preventing a pulmonary barotrauma.

Some preliminary tests were conducted to investigate the effect of in-water head-up positioning. The few tests conducted appeared to support the claim that the upright position encourages airflow from the lungs.

To many, the vision of an unconscious diver ascending rapidly to the surface, raises the obvious concern of pulmonary barotrauma and associated complications. However, an unconscious victim may be in less danger from a lung overpressure injury, even at the very rapid ascent rates that could be achieved with this suggested rescue procedure, than a conscious panicked diver would be under similar circumstances.

Air cannot enter the lungs when an unconscious person has his head slumped forward, though it may be able to escape. Some physicians believe that expanding air from the lungs can passively open the airway from below and escape safely. To illustrate, proponents have noted that a conscious person who takes a deep breath then tucks his head down so that his chin is firmly against his chest can still exhale easily. In addition, medical experience has shown that people with laryngeal cancers blocking the vocal cords, who have great difficulty breathing in, can vent air or oxygen introduced to the trachea satisfactorily. But, the belief that air can always escape from an unconscious person's lungs has not been verified by anesthetic experience, which is normally conducted with the patient lying flat.

The rescuer's objective is to get the victim and himself to the surface as quickly and as safely as possible. Individual circumstances will often affect each rescue.

The rescuer who was trained to leave the victim's weight belt on may in fact need to remove it to raise the victim. A rescuer who had planned to maintain contact with the victim throughout the ascent may be forced to release the victim to prevent himself rocketing to the surface.

In all cases, the rescuer should be able to quickly adapt if circumstances become unpredictable. If the rescuer planned to bring the victim to the surface in a controlled manner and then found that he was forced to allow the victim to rapidly ascend alone, he should not abort the rescue believing he had failed. Upon surfacing, the rescuer should locate the victim and continue the rescue. It is possible that the rapid ascent may have in fact increased the injured diver's chances of survival.

On the Surface

Once both divers are on the surface, it is important to establish a clear and open airway and ventilate a non-breathing victim as soon as possible.

In the water, the rescuer should ensure that both he and the victim are sufficiently buoyant before ventilations begin.

It is also essential to remove the injured diver from the water as soon as possible for the most effective evaluation and subsequent treatment. Methods may vary according to each situation.

One protocol recommends that the rescuer attempt to ventilate the victim as soon as they reach the surface and before making any buoyancy adjustments. Buoyancy is then adjusted after the first breaths are given.

Another protocol suggests that after checking for breathing and draining water from the victim's mouth, ventilations are begun prior to adjusting buoyancy. Other protocols recommend that buoyancy be increased before ventilation is attempted.

The victim's face must be supported above the surface. To do this, the rescuer can adopt the "do-si-do" position, by placing a hand under and cradling the victim's neck, and by various other means.

The amount of buoyancy required to enable the rescuer to deliver dry breaths to the victim depends on a number of factors, including the skill of the rescuer and the surface conditions.

At this stage, the victim's weight belt should be ditched underwater or on reaching the surface. Many rescuers, especially those carrying a lot of lead, may be better off ditching their own weight belt at the surface. Some divers may find it difficult to maintain their orientation in the water without a weight belt, especially if wearing a buoyant exposure suit. Occasionally, the rescuer might be reluctant to remove his weight belt in case he needs to submerge for any reason.

Partial inflation of the victim's BC usually provides sufficient support. Fully inflating the BC may restrict chest movement and may also make it more difficult to get close to the victim's head for ventilation. As long as the rescuer has ditched his own weight belt, it is usually unnecessary to inflate his own BC, although it may sometimes be useful, especially if little buoyancy is provided by the wetsuit. If both BCs are substantially inflated, it can be difficult to get close enough to the victim to ventilate him without pushing his head underwater.

On the surface, it is usually better to approach the victim from behind the shoulder, rather than from the side. This reduces the chances of pushing the victim underwater while attempting ventilations. The rescuer can often turn the victim's head slightly towards him to get a little closer, surface conditions permitting.

Above water, it may be difficult to determine whether the injured diver is breathing. If the diver was not breathing during the ascent, it is unlikely he will be breathing on the surface. In the event of choppy surface conditions, and if the diver was breathing during ascent it may be better to leave the regulator in his mouth, as long as there is enough air in the victim's tank. Holding the regulator in place (and leaving on the mask) should prevent the victim from inhaling water. The diver's head should be tilted back and chin supported, if possible, to open the airway. If the diver is breathing effectively from the regulator, the rescuer should hear the demand valve being triggered. If it is possible to bring the diver on board quickly, it may be wiser to not lose time trying to ventilate him in the water.

Over the years there has been debate as to whether the rescuer should try to drain the airway before beginning resuscitation. Although on land it is relatively easy to roll the victim onto the side to clear the airway, the situation is a lot more complicated in the water.

If the victim has vomited or if there is frothy sputum coming from his mouth, the rescuer can attempt to scoop out any obvious material with his fingers, although this will be difficult to do effectively in the water.

Despite the fact that some methods recommend the rescuer pull down the corner of the victim's mouth to allow water to drain out, this may often be unsuccessful and can allow water in from a passing wave.

The fact is, most protocols don't require the rescuer to attempt to clear foreign matter from the airway. When the rescuer commences resuscitation any foreign matter blown into the larynx will not cause laryngospasm, unless the victim is not fully unconscious. Complications caused by inhalation of foreign matter will be addressed, if necessary, when the victim arrives at the hospital.

It is important to open the victim's airway as wide as possible when delivering the breaths. The first step is to tilt the victim's head back as far as possible. Additionally, the injured diver's chin should be supported, if possible. If performing mouth-to-mouth ventilations, chin support may be more easily provided if the rescuer can use a cheek seal (rather than his fingers) to seal the victim's nose, freeing one hand for chin support. Jaw support can also be provided relatively easily if mouth-to-nose ventilations are used. It may also be easier to obtain a good contact seal with mouth-to-nose, rather than mouth-to-mouth ventilation. Mouth-to-nose ventilation may be the only alternative if the victim's jaw is clenched and the mouth cannot be opened.

Some rescuers are taught to use a snorkel as an aid to ventilation. However, the technique can be cumbersome and difficult to perform, requires regular practice, and cannot be done effectively with certain snorkels. A pocket-style resuscitation mask can be a useful adjunct. Working from behind the victim's head, the rescuer can use a jaw-thrust maneuver to lift the jaws and tilt the head back.

The American Heart Association currently recommends that rescue breathing be commenced with two full ventilations of one and a half to two seconds each, followed by a check for a carotid pulse.

If a pulse is detected, ventilations are delivered at the rate of one every five seconds.

Unfortunately, it is often very difficult and impractical to maintain the recommended sequence when rescuing an injured scuba diver in the water.

Most rescue protocols don't require a pulse check in the water because of the difficulty of detecting a pulse when hindered by cold hands and diving gear, and because in-water CPR is near-impossible. The majority of procedures make the assumption that a pulse is present and call for ventilations to be maintained until the diver is on board and further assessed.

If a pulse is in fact present, effective ventilations should provide the necessary oxygen to preserve life. However, if the victim's heart is not beating effectively (cardiac arrest), the ventilations will serve no useful purpose and are likely to delay transport of the victim to the boat or shoreline where CPR can be implemented.

If the victim has no pulse, it is critical that CPR is begun as soon as possible and to ensure that an ambulance is called without delay.

Time is crucial to the non-breathing victim, and especially to the victim with no pulse. If the rescuer suspects that the victim's heart has arrested, which is likely if he was submerged without breathing for more than about three to five minutes, it may be better not to attempt ventilations if the shore or the boat can be reached fairly quickly.

Several years ago, a study was conducted to assess whether it was possible to perform effective CPR in the water. The technique was demonstrated on an instrumented aquatic mannequin, which was ventilated with a specially modified, pressure-limited second-stage regulator. The trials were performed in full scuba gear by trained rescuers.

The results achieved on the mannequin met the minimum limits for CPR. However, the technique requires that the victim be positioned head-up in the water, and it is doubtful whether adequate circulation would reach the victim's brain in this position. In addition, the procedure requires a specially modified regulator if performed by a single rescuer. Not surprisingly, the technique never caught on.

If ventilations are continued while towing the diver to a boat or shore, the rescuer should endeavor to maintain a regular rate of ventilation and prevent water from entering the injured diver's upper airway.

It is difficult, physically tiring and time-consuming to try to maintain the sequence of one breath every five seconds as recommended by the American Heart Association. No sooner has the rescuer begun to get under way when he has to stop to ventilate the victim. Consequently, it may be a reasonable compromise to provide a sequence of two slow breaths every 10 to 15 seconds. The rescuer can tow for about five seconds before stopping to interpose the two slow breaths. If surface conditions are choppy, the rescuer can often cover the victim's mouth and nose while towing, to prevent more water from entering the airway.

The rescuer should pace the physical exertion to avoid exhaustion. Unnecessary equipment can be removed to reduce weight and drag. What gear to ditch and when to do so depends on the particular circumstances.

Any assistance that is available should be utilized to hasten the rescue and reduce rescuer fatigue. Techniques for removal of a victim from the water are important and demand regular practice beforehand. Divers need to develop and practice techniques suitable for their boat and dive sites.

Once the injured diver is landed on a solid surface, the normal resuscitation protocol should be followed. The injured diver should be rolled into the recovery (left lateral recumbent) position, the airway cleared and the breathing and pulse checked.

Resuscitation should be continued, as appropriate, until medical aid arrives and takes over the management of the victim. Oxygen, at the highest possible inspired concentration, should be administered, if available.

Key Points to Remember

The potential rescuer should have an overview of various possible rescue protocols and an understanding of the basic underlying principles. Some key points to remember are:

- Unless the victim reaches the surface he will certainly die.
- The rescuer should get the non-breathing diver to the surface as quickly as possible — without endangering himself.
- Once on the surface, sufficient buoyancy should be obtained to provide dry ventilations, if required.
- The diver should be taken to shore as quickly as possible to enable proper assessment and management.
- The rescuer should enlist help as soon as possible and ensure an ambulance is contacted with minimal delay.
- The rescue should be paced to avoid exhaustion of the rescuer.
- The introduction of 100 percent oxygen for the victim is desirable if the necessary skills and equipment are available.
- The diver should be kept in a horizontal position.
- The victim must be medically assessed, even if he appears to have recovered.

— From July/August 1993

Far-Out Emergencies

Emergency management considerations when diving in remote locations

BY RICHARD DUNFORD, M.S., DAN NORTHWEST REGIONAL
COORDINATOR, AND WESLEY HYATT, DAN COMMUNICATIONS

JOHN T. PENNINGTON PHOTO

If you plan an extended drive or boating trip somewhere exotic —
parts of Baja, Mexico, Central America, Alaska, the South Pacific — or
even if you're planning a weekend trip to a remote dive site, you may
have apprehensions about your travels. At the top of that list is that you
may have an accident that leaves you, your family or companions, or
someone else injured.

But you can be prepared. Whether you're venturing into the seas, camping in the desert, trekking through a mountain pass or exploring tropical jungles, your preparation beforehand can help turn the tide in many potentially dangerous situations.

The farther you are from medical help, however, the greater your risk. It takes longer to secure medical help and evacuation; and management of an accident can become risky after critical hours have elapsed. Adequate preparation prior to a trip to a remote area is essential. This kind of foresight is exactly what you need to manage diving accidents in remote locations.

The key to preparing for remote travel is self-sufficiency. When you're planning your trip, do the following: Make careful review of evacuation facilities and medical care, particularly in third-world countries; know the fees for services; familiarize yourself with local customs and immigration practices; know what first aid equipment is carried — whether it be on board a dive boat or in your own supplies; and investigate the local conditions for evacuation and medical care before you commence your diving.

The first step is to create an emergency assistance plan.

The Emergency Assistance Plan

It helps to have a written outline of what to do in serious emergencies, detailing the equipment and procedures you'll use. Here are basic elements of an emergency assistance plan:

Emergency Contact Information — This includes the numbers you need to call for rescue in the event of an accident. The primary number you'll need is the local emergency medical service number. It's not always going to be 911.

If you'll be at sea, be sure to get a phone number and radio frequency for the coast guard or naval patrol. In general, VHF channel 16 is for emergencies, but a little research may be in order. In some parts of the world coastal patrols and rescue fall under the jurisdiction of police departments. In other locations, there is no rescue assistance other than other vessels who are in the same area.

Another important number is listed on your DAN member card. DAN *TravelAssist* arranges 24-hour medical emergency evacuation. It covers costs, but cannot reimburse medical evacuation arranged by another party. It is available by dialing 1-800-DAN-EVAC (1-800-326-3822) toll-free in the United States, Canada, Puerto Rico, the Bahamas and the U.S. and British Virgin Islands. For assistance elsewhere throughout the world, call (202) 296-9620, collect.

Other contact information you'll need will include your health insurance company, boat or car repair and towing services, the number for the consulate (if traveling overseas), and any pertinent travel contacts like airline, hotel and expedition company phone numbers.

Emergency Communications Equipment — A critical area of importance to diving safety in remote locations is communication with the outside world on a 24-hour basis. Communications are necessary to alert what local rescue agencies and medical authorities are available and to execute evacuation plans.

In addition, good communications make it possible to obtain medical advice, be alerted to changed rescue plans, develop plans to circumvent potential obstacles, and get help from local authorities or U.S. representatives in expediting evacuation plans. Communications are needed to alert a chamber to a pending arrival and to receive medical instructions for the patient.

When you're out at sea — literally and figuratively — how do you make the call for assistance?

In most cases, a VHF (Very High Frequency) marine radio will be sufficient. VHF units have a range of approximately 25 miles/41 km and require almost line-of-site conditions to the receiving station. (This means no elevated structures, such as buildings, trees or mountains act as barriers to receiving VHF signals.)

The common strategy for communication in remote locations is to use short-distance communications such as VHF to communicate with a local radio station that has long-distance capabilities. A radio link is then patched to a distant point.

For diving applications, this would probably indicate you would hail a naval or merchant marine vessel (i.e., a cruise or cargo ship) on your VHF radio and use their single sideband or satellite system for long-distance communications.

Another alternative is a cellular phone. The phones are portable, lightweight and easy to use. Plus, you can call any telephone number in the world from your cell phone. The only drawback to cellular communications is that they are limited by the phone's service area. In some cases — especially if you're boating far away from shore or hiking through remote, mountainous regions — the phone may not work.

If a cell phone won't do the trick, another alternative for long-distance communications — those in excess of 25 miles/40 km — is your own satellite communication or single sideband radio. These systems are expensive, but if you plan on doing a large amount of remote travel (e.g., you just bought a yacht and are planning on sailing around the Pacific for the next nine months) they're worth the price. One area of critical importance in using single sideband equipment is the geographic location — with associated general atmospheric effects and the atmospheric effects occurring at the time of use (e.g., storms). These conditions will affect the range of this equipment to such an extent that under good conditions, the signal will go around the world, but in bad conditions, they may be limited to less than 500 miles/820 km.

When you're communicating with emergency services, it's important to know where you are. Lengthy delays in evacuation or rescue assistance can be avoided if you can provide rescuers with precise information on location. For this reason, a personal GPS (Global Positioning System) unit should be considered standard equipment for the adventurous traveler. GPS uses signals from a fleet of satellites orbiting the planet to determine your location, altitude, speed and even direction of travel. Hand-held GPS receivers are tiny (some about the size of a calculator), come in water- and shatter-proof designs, and will pinpoint your position anywhere on the planet to within 100 feet/30 meters. GPS units are available in a variety of models with a wide number of additional features (like moving maps, terrain charts, etc.). Some models are best for boating, while others are designed for backpacking and trekking.

First Aid Equipment

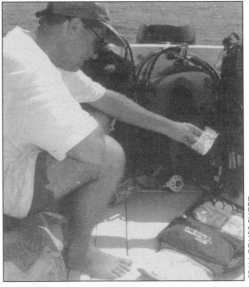

SEAN COMBS PHOTO

First Aid Kit — There are several items necessary if you're putting together a first aid kit for remote travel. Among them are: bandages, gauze pads, tape, antibacterial soap, safety pins, a folding pocket knife, thermometers, tweezers, a space blanket, steristrips, non-narcotic pain relievers, antidiarrheal medication, decongestants, motion sickness tablets, vinegar (for marine stings), alcohol, iodine solution, eyewash, eye drops, Betadine™, Neosporin™, glucose gel, sun block, hydrocortisone cream, mosquito repellent (DEET), and a waterproof light. It's a good idea to see a travel physician before your trip to get a supply of prescription medications like epinephrine (e.g.,

Epi-Pen™) or antibiotics you or your traveling companions take on a regular basis.

Remember to carry some kind of guide book on first aid. For general first aid and accident management, bring along *Medicine for the Outdoors*, by Paul S. Auerbach, M.D. (Little, Brown and Company, available at many bookstores and outfitters). For diving first aid, remember to carry your copy of the DAN *Underwater Diving Accident Manual* or its newer version know as the DAN *Dive and Travel Medical Guide*.

Finally, acclimatize yourself to the place you're visiting; don't walk in bare feet; and wear appropriate footwear for where you're walking in order to avoid cuts, snake and insect bites and parasites in the soil.

Oxygen Delivery Units — Along with the first aid kit, DAN recommends the use of an oxygen delivery system to handle suspected cases of decompression illness (DCI). Many types of oxygen delivery systems are on the market, but to choose one, consider factors such as portability, efficiency, length of oxygen delivery and operator requirements.

Oxygen delivery systems that operate on the demand principle are most efficient for conscious divers, delivering oxygen when they inhale. No intervening medical personnel are required to operate the equipment, but an oxygen provider should be present to assist the patient if needed.

With the demand system, the diver receives oxygen as he inhales it from the system — during exhalation, the system is not delivering oxygen. This system is easy to administer as long as a good face seal or mouthpiece can be provided. These systems are commercially available as a package that includes an oxygen cylinder, a demand regulator and associated face masks, and they are normally packed securely for transport.

Appropriate First Aid for Diving Accidents

If you dive — whether at home or abroad — it is imperative that you be prepared for a possible diving accident involving either air embolism or decompression sickness. The single most beneficial action you can take to aid a diving accident in situations where long delays are expected is to administer 100 percent oxygen.

Assuming the injured diver took a breath of compressed air underwater, these procedures are recommended:

Establish the ABCs. This is the first priority in any emergency, including diving rescue. Make sure the diver has a clear, open Airway; look, listen and feel for diver Breathing (respiration); check the carotid pulse to insure adequate Circulation. DAN statistics reveal that 96 percent of injured divers are breathing. If there is any difficulty in meeting any of the ABCs, initiate appropriate CPR/first aid procedures.

Administer 100 percent oxygen. Following the ABCs, this is the primary first aid measure administered at the dive site and during evacuation. Oxygen is generally considered the standard of care for diving emergencies. DAN recommends that there be enough oxygen available to get the injured diver to an appropriate medical facility.

A primary contraindication to administration of 100 percent oxygen is for anyone with severe chronic obstructive pulmonary disease (COPD). It is highly unlikely that any individual with severe COPD would be involved in any type of diving, however.

Know and understand basic cardiopulmonary resuscitation. CPR techniques may be necessary for some extreme cases of decompression sickness, air embolism and cases of near drowning. Training in the techniques of CPR is easily obtained through the American Heart Association or the American Red Cross. Learning this basic skill is valuable because it may allow a rescuer to temporarily maintain a diving accident victim's vital functions until more sophisticated techniques can be applied.

Give fluids, specifically water, to injured divers who are conscious — especially since the pathology of decompression sickness involves fluid balance. In emergency room and hospital settings, patients often get intravenous fluid (IVs), but in the field, administration of IVs is impractical for the untrained individual. Administration of fluids by mouth is good practice if the patient is awake and alert. If the patient is not awake or at least sufficiently alert to swallow, avoid fluids by mouth, because the injured diver may inadvertently suck the liquid into his lungs.

Put the injured diver in the lateral recumbent (recovery) position. The American Heart Association recommends that a diver who has serious symptoms such as severe fatigue, headache, severe pain, weakness, paralysis or any change in the level of consciousness be placed in the lateral recumbent position. This position places the diver on the side, with the head supported and the upper leg bent at the knee to secure the position. The advantage to this position is that it helps keep the airway clear. If a patient vomits, it prevents the vomitus from being aspirated back into the lungs.

Oxygen Issues in Remote Locations

Most of the basic first aid approaches just described are no problem to employ even in places far from the beaten track, with one notable exception — oxygen.

Although it's always advisable to plan ahead, it's just not always possible. If you discover inadequate oxygen supplies, you'll have to use a remote source of oxygen in the local community. This poses several difficulties. It may require adaptation to unusual or nonstandard fittings, and the amount of available oxygen cannot be guaranteed. The quality of oxygen in remote areas is an issue. Medical and industrial oxygen are produced basically the same way, but level, quantities and types of contamination are tied to the bottle's history. It's good to know what the bottle's previous contents were — preferably over the last three fills — to avoid using a contaminated cylinder.

The choice between using and not using this type of oxygen source for diving accident victims who may be deteriorating or nonbreathing is difficult — and not without risks. But given the choice of the long delays in treatment in remote locations, it is advisable to use the available oxygen.

The best way to be prepared is to carry your own oxygen into the remote locale you're visiting. In deciding what type of system you'll carry, you will have to estimate what type of situation you may have to manage. As a minimum, a 100-percent inspired oxygen demand system is required. Ideally, there should be a sufficient quantity of oxygen available to last through the evacuation, but as a practical minimum, enough oxygen to exceed the two-hour minimum should be carried.

Evacuation and Hyperbaric Chamber Treatment

After first aid, the most important thing you can do for a diver with symptoms of DCI is to get that person to a chamber. In most populated areas like the United States and Canada, it's wise to seek out emergency medical services first. In third-world countries, however, the issue becomes more problematic. It's advisable to make a thorough check of both medical facilities and chambers before your trip in case you are forced to seek a chamber right away.

Evacuations are often carried out by plane or helicopter through agencies like DAN *TravelAssist*, the Coast Guard or a military transport, depending upon location. This is especially true in more severe cases and in situations where long distances are required. But, evacuations are often carried out by automobile; it's not unusual for a diving accident victim to walk into a chamber and announce his problem.

If you're faced with evacuation, remember the primary evacuation route is usually considered the most expedient method. It's always advisable to have a backup plan that is more conservative, but reliable, in unfavorable conditions. Consider local conditions such as: the possible effects of weather, the availability and type of aircraft, the time required to complete the evacuation, and whether a member of the diving party will be required to accompany the victim to the evacuation destination.

Evacuation from a remote diving location is highly variable; it's difficult to describe — usually a "make the best with what's available" situation. The destination of the evacuation, however, deserves some consideration. There may be a local medical facility, but the level of training among the local medical authorities can leave a lot to be desired. In that event, you may need to contact DAN to talk the local medical staff through the proper care procedures.

More Remote = More Risk

It is imperative that individuals diving in remote locations understand that not all medical emergencies can be handled successfully. The more remote the location, the greater the medical risks involved.

If you choose to dive in a remote location, consider what type of diving medical emergency you're capable of handling, obtain the proper equipment and training necessary and don't carry equipment you're not trained to use.

The knowledge and equipment you have to help you manage a remote diving accident can make the difference in keeping a bad situation from turning worse. Your preparation may help save a life, perhaps even your own.

— *From July/August 1995*

The Four R's of Managing a DCI Injury

Recognize Symptoms.
Respond with Oxygen.
Relay with EMS/DAN.
Recompress Early.

BY BILL CLENDENEN, DAN DIRECTOR OF TRAINING

Oxygen is critical to supporting life. We know this as a basic tenet of biology — from our first encounters in elementary school, when we read of Joseph Priestley's "discovery" of the gas, to high school chemistry and the studies of chemical bonding, oxidation and human physiology. Oxygen is a fact of life, no matter how closely — or casually — we view it.

To a diver with decompression illness (DCI), oxygen has an even greater significance — it can mean the difference between having residual symptoms of the injury and being symptom-free after a diving accident. And it's important to act quickly: Early recognition and treatment of a diving injury has significant benefits. Besides increasing the effectiveness of recompression therapy, it improves your chances of complete resolution of symptoms.

In the unlikely event that you or your dive buddy are affected by a decompression illness accident, following these four steps will increase the chances of symptom free recovery and get you back into the water a lot sooner.

The Steps to Managing Decompression Illness (DCI)

There are four easy steps to managing DCI: Recognize the symptoms early; deploy oxygen first aid rapidly; activate emergency response services and DAN; and get recompression therapy early

It's important to follow all these steps — their combination leads to successful recovery from a diving injury. If any step is missing, it could compromise the medical outcome, whether it's you or your buddy who's injured.

1. Recognize the Symptoms

The first step to managing any diving accident is recognizing symptoms of DCI. Decompression illness is a broad term used to categorize the symptoms of both decompression sickness (DCS) and arterial gas embolism (AGE). Symptoms of either ailment can range from subtle indications like pain and numbness to more severe indications, such as unconsciousness and paralysis.

Other symptoms include dizziness, weakness, extreme fatigue, headache, nausea and itching. DCI symptoms usually manifest themselves during the first 20 minutes after surfacing from a dive, though divers experiencing more subtle cases of DCS may not recognize their symptoms until later.

However, for many divers, it's not recognizing symptoms that's the problem — it's telling someone. To admit that you might be injured is difficult. DAN statistics show that approximately 20 percent of injured divers continue to dive after noticing their symptoms.

Denial should also be considered one of the most common signs and symptoms of a decompression illness — your mind can use defense mechanisms to protect you when illness sets in. Many times, unless your injury is obvious and noted by others, it's easy to ignore your symptoms or attribute aches and pains to other, less serious problems like sports injuries.

So what can you do? You can become more aware of the various ways DCI shows itself. Remember that mild, pain-only symptoms of decompression sickness can progress into more serious stages. If you question whether you have symptoms following a dive, tell someone and get assistance — there's no harm done if your symptoms turn out to be unrelated to your dives. Remember the axiom: It's better to be safe than sorry.

2. Respond With Oxygen: The Golden Gas

The second step to managing DCI is to get oxygen. Whether it's for you, your buddy or another diver, the field delivery of emergency oxygen is an essential step in the healing process. Once you've established the airway, breathing and circulation (ABCs), your first priority is providing as close to 100 percent inspired oxygen as possible to the injured diver.

Why oxygen? By excluding nitrogen from your lungs, you will more quickly eliminate the excess nitrogen accumulated from your dive. This may also reduce nitrogen bubble size, increase oxygenated blood flow to the body's tissues and reduce blood sludging (a thickening of blood resulting from excess nitrogen). Oxygen also can help reduce tissue swelling, and for those divers in respiratory distress, it may ease breathing.

The most recognized benefit of emergency oxygen use, however, may also contribute to a delay in calling for assistance. How? Sometimes when oxygen is delivered to injured divers, symptoms are completely relieved. DAN's 1996 *Report on Diving Accidents and Fatalities* notes: "12 percent of all reported DCI cases [in 1994] were symptom-free prior to receiving recompression therapy when receiving supplemental surface oxygen, whereas only 3 percent of the DCI cases not receiving oxygen were symptom-free before recompression."

Because oxygen sometimes completely relieves symptoms, injured divers may feel that they no longer need to be evaluated and treated. However, they still require medical evaluation. Anytime you treat a diving injury, you should relay with Emergency Medical Services and then contact DAN. You need to pass the injured diver into the health care system as soon as possible to minimize the effects of the injury.

Although it's encouraging to note an increase in the percentage of injured divers who received emergency oxygen prior to recompression treatment, according to the 1996 Report, seven out of 10 injured divers still do not receive emergency oxygen prior to recompression treatment. There's much room for improvement.

3. Relay with EMS/DAN: The Handoff

Once you've recognized the symptoms of a diving accident and provided first aid for the injured diver through emergency oxygen, the next step involves getting the injured diver into the health care system. In keeping with the recommendations of the Journal of the American Medical Association (JAMA) and the American Heart Association (AHA), when you respond to an unresponsive diver, you should activate the Emergency Medical Services (EMS) after your initial assessment but before providing emergency first aid.

It's critical to establish an Emergency Action Plan for all diving activities. Know the location of the nearest telephone — and carry coins to make the call. In many communities, EMS is activated by simply calling the local emergency telephone number 911. In areas which do not have an EMS system established, you should investigate and set up procedures for handling diving emergencies. This information needs to be available to all divers in the group

Cellular phones help provide an added insurance to communications, especially from remote locales. At sea in the United States, you can call the U.S. Coast Guard on VHF radio channel 16 for assistance. Although the USCG generally responds only to life-threatening emergencies at sea, it may be added insurance in some emergencies.

If you're not sure whom to call, or if the injured diver is conscious and alert, call DAN at (919) 684-8111. Remember, you can call collect in an emergency. When you've reached DAN, state that you have a diving emergency, and you will be briefed on what to do next. DAN has a team of physicians, nurses and emergency medical personnel on call 24 hours a day to help injured divers in an emergency. DAN can also help coordinate recompression therapy. If EMS personnel or assisting physicians have questions on dive accident management and treatment, DAN is ready to help answer those questions as well.

The information that you need to provide to the EMS responder includes:

1. the location of the emergency (as precisely as possible);
2. the phone number from where the call is being made;
3. circumstances of the diving emergency;
4. how many divers are injured;
5. current condition of the injured diver(s);
6. what first aid is being given; and
7. any other information as requested.

You, the caller, should hang up the phone last to make sure the EMS and/or DAN personnel have no further questions.

This third step in the treatment of DCI is paramount to successful treatment. This is where DAN acts as a resource to both the diving and medical communities. It's critical that injured divers enter the health care system so they can be evaluated by medical professionals for stabilization and coordination of recompression treatment — the sooner the better.

4. Recompress Early: The Last Hurdle

The final step in the treatment of a decompression illness is hyperbaric therapy — as soon as possible. The longer the delay in calling for help to actual recompression, the less effective the treatment. Timely recompression can minimize the likelihood of residual symptoms and help avoid permanent injury.

Once a physician diagnoses an injured diver with DCI, DAN can recommend treatment at the nearest hyperbaric chamber. By recompressing the diver in the chamber, the size and volume of nitrogen bubbles are reduced. This, followed by a slow "ascent" in the chamber, allows a steady release of excess nitrogen, restoring the flow of blood to the tissues and relieving symptoms.

Because breathing 100 percent oxygen at treatment depths of 60 feet/18 meters (2.8 ATA) is recommended, additional washout of nitrogen occurs with the increase in the pressure gradient. This use of 100 percent oxygen in the chamber helps the injured diver avoid any more absorption of nitrogen during recompression.

Early recompression is a critical step in helping divers with DCI. This treatment, combined with early recognition, emergency oxygen and good communications with EMS and DAN, means divers have more reasons than ever to brush up on their communication and dive skills, and support DAN, the link to dive safety the world over.

Gearing Up for O2

Although it has long been documented that the use of emergency oxygen is the most beneficial first aid measure an injured diver can receive, it wasn't until DAN introduced the "Oxygen First Aid in Diving Accidents" course and associated emergency oxygen equipment in 1991 that there was a standard established for what training and equipment is necessary to provide first aid to divers with decompression illness.

What types of oxygen equipment are available? Which type will provide you with the greatest amount of inspired oxygen? There are two common kinds of emergency oxygen delivery equipment: demand and constant-flow. While both systems are capable of delivering high percentages of oxygen, only the demand valve used with a tight-fitting mask can deliver 100 percent inspired oxygen.

The demand regulator system has many other benefits for divers. It's similar to a scuba system, so training is simplified. It's also the only system that delivers 100 percent oxygen, which gives the greatest nitrogen washout benefit. The demand system conserves oxygen better than the constant-flow system, and because the demand regulator is activated by the diver's inhalation and stops delivering oxygen when the injured diver exhales, it meets 100 percent of an injured diver's inspiratory (breathing) needs.

Although the constant-flow system is not as efficient as the demand system, because its ability to deliver high percentages of inspired oxygen varies, it is still a viable system if used properly. When the constant-flow system is used in conjunction with a non-rebreather mask, it delivers upwards of 90 percent inspired oxygen. For the non-breathing diver, by using a pocket mask with supplemental oxygen, the rescuer increases the oxygen percentage to the injured diver from 16 percent to 50 percent or more when performing artificial respirations.

When in doubt, call DAN

DAN's data on how long it takes injured divers to call for help indicate that the average time to call for help is 18 hours. Many injured divers call DAN not because they have symptoms, but because their symptoms won't go away. When the symptoms of DCI are immediate, obvious and life-threatening, divers call for help right away. However, since most diving injuries are not immediately life-threatening, the delay to call can be long — 6 percent of all DCI reported to DAN in 1994 requested help more than four days after the onset of symptoms were noted.

Oxygen First Aid:
The Dive Accident Solution

In the DAN *Oxygen First Aid in Dive Accidents* course [now renamed *Oxygen First Aid for Scuba Diving Injuries*], you learn the signs and symptoms of decompression illness, trends in diving accidents, the benefits of oxygen and the hazards associated with its use. You also get the opportunity to practice using the DAN Oxygen Unit, which incorporates both the demand and constant-flow systems, while learning how to activate the EMS and DAN.

The DAN Oxygen course is an introduction for divers to learn more about the "Four R's" of managing a diving accident. Although the factors surrounding each decompression illness are unique, these four clear and consistent steps will ensure a successful outcome for the injured diver.

Recognize the symptoms of DCI. Assessment includes the subtle, constant process of observing and interacting with those with whom you dive. Remember, the denial of symptoms may be the first sign that an injury has occurred.

Respond with oxygen. Once you've established the airway, breathing and circulation (ABCs), provide oxygen. This increases the effectiveness of recompression therapy and may relieve symptoms. One hundred percent oxygen should be delivered by a demand valve and tight-fitting mask.

Relay with EMS/DAN. By activating EMS or calling DAN, you set in motion the mechanism to get the diver to advanced medical treatment. Have an Emergency Action Plan and know the location of the nearest phone.

Recompress early. Lastly, treat decompression illness in a recompression chamber. The sooner an injured diver receives definitive treatment, the better the chances of a symptom-free recovery.

The Four R's of Managing Decompression Illness are like a ladder. Just take it one step at a time and you'll find yourself with a successful recovery and complete relief of DCI symptoms. For more information on DAN's Oxygen Program, call (919) 684-2948, extension 555.

— *From January/February 1996*

First Aid

Valuable assets on any dive trip, kits and training go hand in glove for the dive traveler

BY ROBERT N. ROSSIER

When I took my first scuba course more than 20 years ago, basic diving first aid was part of the curriculum. I'll never forget the treatment suggested for subcutaneous emphysema, which involved lancing the afflicted diver's neck with a dive knife to relieve the air pressure. The concept was truly absurd, but it got us thinking about the potential for a serious diving medical problem.

Over the years, scuba instruction has changed dramatically, and so have both the training and the tools used for diver first aid.

THE NEW WAVE IN DIVER FIRST AID

When it comes to medical products and medications, improvements are made almost every day — a peek into any modern diver first aid kit reveals this truth. A carefully thought-out and well-stocked first aid kit will treat a broad range of afflictions including cuts and scrapes, colds and sore throats, ear problems, sunburn, blisters, marine life stings and bites, exposure, motion sickness and gastrointestinal distress.

The most likely type of injury on a dive trip is trauma in the form of sprains, cuts, scrapes and blisters. A good first aid kit is stocked with plenty of bandages and antiseptics like Betadine™ solution and Bactroban™ ointment. One thing we don't have to worry about today is suturing up a gash on a buddy's leg or arm. A major improvement over first aid kits of old are the various adhesive closure strips used to bind a wound after it has been thoroughly irrigated using a syringe with a disinfectant solution.

Also high on the list of diver maladies are stings and bites from close encounters with creatures such as fire coral, moray eels, and even stinging bees. A most dangerous condition is the allergic reaction called anaphylactic shock, which can follow such an episode, resulting in respiratory failure. But a product called the EpiPen™ takes more than the sting out of the situation. The pen-shaped device makes it simple for an untrained user to administer a lifesaving hypodermic shot of epinephrine to the victim. With a doctor's prescription, the EpiPen can be carried in your dive first aid kit until the fluid inside changes color, indicating the shelf life has expired.

Gastrointestinal distress is a common problem on dive trips, and numerous modern medications such as Bactrim™ and Imodium™ can be stocked in a first aid kit to remedy the symptoms. Ipecac, a medication which induces vomiting, has been used for years in the trea™ent of poisoning victims, but experts now suggest that it's often an inappropriate and dangerous treatment. In some cases, dilution of the poison is proper treatment, and in other cases activated charcoal is the best approach. More recently, activated charcoal capsules have become available, which are much easier to administer than the powdered form.

One thing we didn't find in first aid kits 20 years ago was emergency medical oxygen. Today, reasonably priced systems are available on the market, including the DAN Rescue Pak. Oxygen is now considered essential for effectively treating decompression sickness (DCS) and arterial gas embolism (AGE).

In recent years, strides have been made in tailoring first aid equipment to the user. Today manufacturers produce activity-oriented first aid kits for everything from biking and hiking to diving, but more important is the user-friendly format which make rendering first aid easier for the user who has minimal training. Good examples are the diver first aid kit distributed by DAN, the DSS-Guardian, which was developed by the DAN medical staff and designed for treatment of injuries and illness described in the DAN *Dive and Travel Medical Guide*; Adventure Medical Kits, manufactured in Oakland, Calif.; or Medical Sea Pak, in Rochester, N.Y.

FIRST AID TRAINING

While it's important to have a good first aid kit in time of need, the contents will be virtually useless unless you know how to use them. All divers should have first aid training as a bare minimum. Most training includes cardiopulmonary resuscitation (CPR) and provides the foundation for any emergency medical care. Since first aid provider skills can deteriorate over time, first aid providers should retrain every two years to refresh and update their knowledge and skills.

Although essential background, when it comes to specific dive-related injuries or situations when emergency medical services aren't a 911 call away, basic first aid training can come up short. To be prepared to effectively deal with diving emergencies, divers should consider one of the many diving first aid courses available. As modern diving first aid students learn, philosophies in the treatment of scuba accident victims have changed in recent years. As diving instructor and trainer Dennis Graver points out, "The latest advice is to always keep victims in a horizontal attitude — from when they're in the water until they get to the emergency room at the hospital."

Perhaps the most threatening injuries a diver may sustain are those related to pressure, and oxygen therapy is by far the most effective first aid a rescuer can offer. The DAN Oxygen Provider course provides divers with the skills and knowledge to safely administer emergency oxygen to an injured diver.

Even if you're well-versed in first aid, remember that the person using your first aid kit might not be you, so a key ingredient is an up-to-date text on the subject. One of the most important changes in diver first aid is the availability of practical, up-to-date reference materials.

FIRST AID REFERENCES

There are several important textbooks on the subject of first aid for divers. The DAN *Dive and Travel Medical Guide* provides concise information on the prevention and treatment of scuba diving injuries and maladies associated with travel.

In his book *Scuba Diving First Aid*, Graver points out that much of what is taught in a standard first aid course doesn't apply to the treatment of diving accident victims.

Another essential text for divers is *A Medical Guide to Hazardous Marine Life* by Dr. Paul Auerbach. This manual provides concise, understandable information on the recognition and treatment of marine life injuries. The text also covers treatment of wounds and lacerations, burns and infections.

SOME PARTING THOUGHTS

While first aid training is an important aspect of a proficient diver's background, some injuries and ailments require prompt attention from medical professionals, and the farther we are far from professional help, the more serious the concern. But as Graver points out, "We're living in the information age, and there's a virtual explosion of information available to divers. The key is getting access to the information in a timely manner."

With this in mind, an important component for any dive first aid kit is a cell phone. While a cell phone won't provide communications capability everywhere, it certainly opens up tremendously expansive regions to immediate professional medical advice. "And it's not just for summoning medical assistance," notes Graver, "it's for getting medical advice on the spot."

The best first aid kit is one which gets little use. As Dr. Auerbach explains, "When putting together a first aid kit, the key word is prevention. With a careful eye to prevention, you won't need the rest of the equipment in the kit. Items like sunblock and sunglasses should top the list of accessory items carried in a first aid kit."

Knowing how to use all the resources in your first aid kit is also important. As Richard Dunford of the Virginia Mason Medical Center, Wash., points out, "Don't assume you can use something in the field if you've never had any training in using it." You should never administer a medication unless you have been properly trained. If there's something in your first aid kit with which you're unfamiliar, its time to think about more training.

An important concept for divers to understand is that a first aid kit is something which must be tailored to a particular dive trip. As Dunford notes, "The contents of a first aid kit should change, just as the contents of your gear bag changes. The further you'll be from immediate medical care, the more you'll want to have on hand." Since first aid training and equipment go hand in hand, the more first aid equipment you carry, the more training you'll need to use it properly.

In 20-plus years of diving, I've never been called on to lance a blister on my foot, never mind perform a life-threatening ritual with a dive knife. What I'm really waiting for is someone to come up with an emergency holographic medical technician, like the doctor on the "Star Trek Voyager" television series, that fits in my first aid kit. In the meantime, it's time again to renew and update my first aid and oxygen training.

— *From January/February 1997*

AIR/NITROX DIVING

It's a Gas...

Nitrox raises fewer eyebrows than a few years back, but just as many questions.

BY CATHIE CUSH WITH REPORTS BY
DR. EDWARD THALMANN

Once upon a simpler time, divers didn't have to make many choices. Fins were black. Wetsuits were black. And tanks held air.

In today's world of art nouveau neoprene and candy-colored silicon, why settle for breathing the same old stuff — especially when it can get you bent?

Divers do have alternatives to air, most notably the gas known as nitrox, also called oxygen-enriched air. Although most divers still put plain old ordinary air in their tanks, in the last five years nitrox users have become increasingly visible, and enriched air has become a favorite topic in the dive media.

Despite often-angry debates surrounding the benefits of nitrox and its suitability for recreational divers, the gas may take even greater steps toward mainstream acceptance with the launch of PADI's Enriched Air Diver program at the 1996 Diving Equipment and Marketing Association (DEMA) trade show.

Nitrox diving, relatively new to the recreational diver, had both its rewards and hazards.

Whether nitrox is a fad or the wave of the future still depends on who's talking, but PADI's acceptance is a fairly strong sign that the gas isn't going to evaporate into thin air anytime soon.

A 53-year-old infant

Air, for the sake of this discussion, contains 19-22 percent oxygen, with the balance being nitrogen. Not coincidentally, humans on the surface generally function very well at these levels, at least physiologically speaking. But at depth, the increased partial pressure of nitrogen can lead to problems such as narcosis and decompression illness.

As early as 1943, Christian Lambertsen, M.D., of the University of Pennsylvania's Institute for Environmental Medicine, suggested that adding oxygen to air would give U.S. Navy divers physiological and operational advantages, but it wasn't until the late 1950s and early '60s that military and commercial operations began to use the gas regularly.

By 1978, the National Oceanic and Atmospheric Administration (NOAA) had adopted a mixture called NOAA Nitrox I, which contained 32 percent oxygen, to allow scientific research divers to extend their bottom times without increasing their decompression obligations. Enriched air became available to recreational divers in the late 1980s, largely through the efforts of Dick Rutkowski, a former NOAA deputy diving coordinator and founder of Hyperbarics International, Key Largo, Fla.

And that's when the Great Nitrox Debate began . . .

"Nitrox is safer than air."

"What about oxygen toxicity?"

"It reduces the risk of decompression."

"It's dangerous to produce."

"It reduces nitrogen narcosis."

"It's too technical for sport divers."

Nitrox has been credited with eliminating post-dive fatigue and generating a sense of well-being. It has been accused of deteriorating dive equipment and interfering with recompression therapy. Some of the issues that arose during the debate have clear-cut answers; others do not. A lot of them fall into that unequivocal scientific category: We have no reason to believe that it is not the case — but there's no proof that it is.

Hedging your bends

Current thinking points to nitrogen as the overwhelming factor in determining the risk of decompression sickness. With nitrox, some of the nitrogen in the breathing mix is replaced with oxygen. If two divers dive the exact same profile, the one using enriched air will have a lower risk of decompression sickness than the one breathing air. If the nitrox diver is willing to accept the same decompression risk as the air diver, he or she would be able to make a longer no-stop dive than the air diver, shorten some of the stops on a decompression dive or reduce surface interval requirements.

The choice of enriched-air dive planning tools is determined by the diver's goals. Some follow tables generated specifically for the nitrogen/oxygen mixture they are breathing. Using such tables allows the diver to take maximum advantage of the reduced nitrogen load at depth and the increased rate of nitrogen elimination during decompression, but it doesn't necessarily reduce the risk of decompression sickness.

A more conservative method is to calculate the equivalent air depth (EAD). Here, the diver computes a profile assuming he or she were breathing air with the same partial pressure of nitrogen (PN2) as the nitrox mix. For example, a diver using NOAA Nitrox I (32 percent oxygen) can dive to 121 feet/37 meters using a 100-foot/30-meter schedule. The diver would decompress according to that air schedule, but would eliminate nitrogen faster than if he or she were breathing air. This gives the diver using the EAD method an additional safety factor.

Several manufacturers now offer decompression computers that allow enriched-air users to take advantage of the hyperoxic mix. Most base their decompression schedules on an algorithm using a PN2 computed from the gas mix. Some will compute a reduced PN2 throughout the dive, but otherwise will use the same algorithm as for air breathing.

Unless the algorithm has been fully tested under these conditions, the risk of DCS could be higher, lower or the same as on air.

"Are you willing to be part of the group of divers who, by their experience, will determine which of the three possibilities applies?" asks Edward Thalmann, M.D., DAN's Assistant Medical Director.

The most conservative approach to breathing enriched air is planning the dive according to standard air tables or an air-based computer. If the diver in the example above (at 121 feet/37 meters breathing 32 percent O2) followed the U.S. Navy air tables and surfaced using the 130 fsw air no-decompression limit in 10 minutes instead of 25 using the EAD procedure, he or she would have a two-group safety margin.

"If you don't use it to stay longer, you have a built-in safety factor," says Joe Clark, co-owner of Ocean Divers in Key Largo, Fla., the first dive operator to offer enriched air to recreational divers. "It's good for people my age who like to dive a lot."

In 1993, American Nitrox Divers International (ANDI) began its Limited SafeAir User Program, which certifies recreational students to use 32 and 36 percent oxygen mixtures on no-decompression dives using air tables or air-based dive computers. ANDI's original enriched-air course, which has evolved into the Complete SafeAir User Program, teaches students to use mixes from 22 to 50 percent O2, and to use the EAD formula as well as nitrox computers and tables. Several certifying agencies have licensed the ANDI programs, and some are offering new divers the option to become certified without ever breathing standard compressed air.

Watering down Martini's law?

One controversial issue in enriched air is the claim that it reduces inert gas narcosis. Based on the equivalent air depth concept, a dive made to 100 feet/30 meters on a mix containing 36 percent oxygen is equivalent to a 75-foot/23-meter dive, and the diver should only experience the level of narcosis that he or she would at that shallower depth. Widely reported anecdotes from numerous enriched-air divers seem to support this notion. Research, however, doesn't support this theory.

"We have a small dilemma," says noted table designer, Dr. Bill Hamilton of Hamilton Research. "There's not much data, but the little data there is says that a difference in performance could not be detected when they switched between a high and a low oxygen in an oxygen-enriched air mix. That suggests, as do the properties of the gases, that oxygen is just as narcotic as nitrogen."

In *The Physiology and Medicine of Diving*, DAN Executive Director Peter Bennett, Ph.D., D.Sc., cites a 1963 study which "showed that oxygen significantly potentiated nitrogen narcosis." A 1990 study by Sweden's Karolinska Institute and Hamilton Research supports this finding, concluding that "the degree of narcosis is not significantly ameliorated when a substantial part of the N2 is substituted with O2...."

A cruel princess

The biggest potential danger with enriched air is the increased oxygen content. Oxygen toxicity is not usually a problem with air at depths that most sport divers visit. With nitrox, the "Princess of Gases" could become a raging witch without much provocation.

Researchers have long studied oxygen toxicity — both central nervous system and pulmonary effects. Enriched-air divers generally aren't concerned with pulmonary O2 toxicity, which occurs over long exposure times. The problem is Central Nervous System (CNS) O2 toxicity, which could cause a seizure underwater, leading to drowning, unless the diver is wearing a full-face mask. Enriched air divers learn to look for symptoms of high-dose/short-term oxygen poisoning, such as visual disturbances, nausea, ringing in the ears and muscle spasms. However, the greatest danger in dealing with hyperoxic breathing mixes is that epileptic-like seizures may occur without warning.

A significant amount of time in an enriched-air certification course is spent learning how to reduce the risk of O2 toxicity by staying within recommended guidelines for oxygen partial pressure limits and exposure times. The problem for enriched-air divers is that those guidelines are still a matter of controversy and even if followed will not guarantee that a convulsion will not occur.

At NOAA, where dives are highly structured and tightly supervised, the maximum allowable PO2 is 1.6 atmospheres absolute (ATAs), notes Doug Kesling, training and safety coordinator at the National Undersea Research Center (NURC) at the University of North Carolina, Wilmington. NURC is funded by NOAA and began using nitrox in 1986. The 1992 edition of ANDI's The Application of Enriched Air Mixtures states that "the area between 1.45 and 1.6 ATA PO2 is considered to be within 'the caution zone," and the agency currently recommends that divers not exceed 1.45 ATAs on high-workload dives.

"There's some confusion between how far you could go and how far you should go," notes ANDI's Stuart Masch. "No one is suggesting pushing the limit — it's like the decompression tables. Conservatism is something the diver builds in — it's not a matter of policy."

In Sweden, the law mandates a maximum exposure of 1.4 ATA, says Karl Shreeves, PADI's manager of technical development. "I'd like to know how they enforce it," he adds.

In a paper on oxygen exposure management, DAN's research director, Richard Vann, Ph.D., took a practical and conservative view, suggesting that "For air or nitrox diving, a maximum exposure limit of 1.2 bar (ATA) would appear to be conservative, while allowing a 'cushion' for partial pressure increases due to unplanned depth excursions. Perhaps 1.4 bar would be acceptable if depth could be carefully controlled. On the other hand, there are those who testify to diving safely at 1.6 bar. This may well be true, but skepticism is appropriate until these divers document their claims in the form of computer-recorded depth-time profiles with certified breathing mixtures."

Working up to trouble

In *The Physiology of Medicine and Diving*, James Clark, M.D., Ph.D., of the University of Pennsylvania's Institute of Environmental Medicine notes that high carbon dioxide levels increase blood flow to the brain, resulting in a higher oxygen dose. Exercise is one factor that could lead to CO_2 retention. So does the increased gas density that occurs when breathing at depth.

The original research on oxygen toxicity limits involved subjects using 100-percent oxygen rebreathers. Mixed-gas scuba used a nitrogen oxygen mix, which allowed greater depths to be obtained but with the same PO_2 level as using 100 percent oxygen rebreathers. What was surprising was that symptoms of oxygen toxicity occurred at lower PO_2 levels using nitrox than when breathing 100 percent oxygen.

"Hyperoxic gas mixtures would seem to increase arterial CO_2 levels compared to air at the same depth," notes Dr. Thalmann, who served as head of Diving Medicine and Physiology Research at the Naval Medical Research Institute prior to joining the DAN staff. "This is the reason that the U.S. Navy has adopted 1.3 ATA as the current maximum PO_2 level for N2O2 dives. Levels above this have increasing probabilities of O2 convulsions and, by my experience, 1.6 ATA is definitely too high."

One of the great difficulties in managing oxygen risk is the wide range of tolerance among individuals, and the wide range of tolerance that a given individual may have from day to day — or even from one minute to the next.

In British Royal Navy studies of oxygen toxicity conducted during World War II, such factors as age, weight, fitness or smoking did not seem to play a direct role in determining when an individual would experience oxygen symptoms. At the same exposure, the onset of symptoms appeared in as few as seven minutes for some divers, while others experienced no symptoms within 30 minutes. When an individual diver was studied during repeated exposures, the onset of symptoms varied from seven minutes to 148 minutes with no apparent pattern.

High O2 Mixes: Handle With Care

Diving high oxygen mixes in the U.S. Navy has been a fact of life for 50 years. The main problem has been and always will be the possibility of an underwater oxygen convulsion.

Both the Royal Navy and U.S. Navy have done thousands of exposures in order to determine what PO2 limits will minimize the chance of a convulsion. These limits are found in their diving manuals. However, every diver using high oxygen breathing mixes is taught that an oxygen convulsion may occur even if these limits are strictly adhered to. When diving, then, the buddy system is taken a step further by having divers physically tethered to each other during training dives — and for many other dives unless it would compromise the mission

If an oxygen convulsion occurs, the buddy will know right away and can take immediate action.

Only rigorous training and meticulous attention to the dive profile can minimize the chance of an oxygen convulsion. Only a buddy who knows exactly what to do if a convulsion occurs can minimize the chance of drowning from a convulsion. Even if the risk of an oxygen convulsion is, say, one in 10,000 dives, it is of little comfort if you are the one.

— *Dr. Edward Thalmann*

"Forget about the idea that O2 convulsions only occur in weak, out-of-shape wimps," Dr. Thalmann says. In a 1984 study at the U.S. Navy Experimental Diving Unit (NEDU), convulsions occurred "in well-trained SEALs perfectly capable of leaping tall buildings in a single bound."

Exercise level does seem to make a difference, however, most likely due to elevated blood carbon dioxide levels. To complicate matters further, the Royal Navy studies indicate that oxygen toxicity symptoms occur much sooner when the diver is breathing underwater than if the diver were in a hyperbaric chamber.

The possibility of an oxygen convulsion is a serious consideration when breathing higher-than-normal oxygen levels. While oxygen seizures are rare using nitrox, the consequences when they occur can be lethal. A diver drowned off the New Jersey coast in July 1992. Analysis of his home-mixed enriched air showed that he was exposed to a PO2 of 1.8 ATAs or higher at depth — higher than any organization's recommended limits. It is assumed that the diver convulsed, lost his regulator and drowned. That same month, an enriched-air diver lost consciousness and drowned in a Florida cave system. Although he maintained a PO2 of 1.4 ATAs or less throughout most of the dive, hard work swimming against a current and periods of time with an exposure from 1.5-1.7 ATAs may have led to an oxygen convulsion, although enriched air has never been verified as a contributing factor in this accident. These fatalities are marked exceptions. Tens of thousands of enriched-air dives have been completed without complications involving oxygen.

"We have never had an oxygen incident with enriched air on open-circuit scuba," says NURC's Kesling. "One seasoned diver reported odd sensations at depth, so we chose to dive her on air."

Unfortunately, enriched-air divers can't count on "odd sensations" to tip them off to an impending convulsion. "In studies done for the U.S. Navy SEALs at the Navy Experimental Diving Unit, all but one O2 convulsion occurred without any warning. In fact, in divers having other symptoms of O2 toxicity, many went on for some time without other problems before reporting them," recalls Dr. Thalmann, who performed the research. "The bottom line is, you will most likely have no warning of an impending convulsion. You will either drown or wake up in a cozy place with no memory of what happened."

For safety's sake
It should go without saying that education and training are critical if a diver wants to use nitrox. The diver mentioned above who died in New Jersey was a "self-taught" nitrox user.

It's also important to prevent having the wrong O2 mix. A mix that is too high could lead to oxygen toxicity problems, and a mix that is too low could result in decompression problems, Dr. Thalmann notes. Cylinders should be analyzed after being filled and after detaching from the filling station, and then be properly labeled.

As with decompression limits, divers should approach oxygen limits conservatively. Some observers have even suggested that divers breathing hyperoxic mixes should use full-face masks to prevent drowning in the event of an underwater convulsion.

Breathing a high oxygen-nitrox mix adds two additional risks not normally found in air diving, says Dr. Thalmann — the possibility of having an oxygen mix in your cylinder that is different than what it's supposed to be; and the possibility of an oxygen convulsion if the safe maximum depth is exceeded.

What does all this mean for the average recreational diver? For some, enriched air will be a helpful tool to minimize the risk of decompression illness or to maximize bottom time — provided that they make the commitment to getting the training and equipment to use it properly.

Other divers will determine that the benefits of high-oxygen breathing media simply aren't worth the additional risks. It's an individual decision — but as nitrox becomes increasingly available, it's likely that more and more divers will be weighing their breathing gas options.

What is air, anyway?

When you studied partial pressures in scuba class, you probably rounded the components of air to 20 percent oxygen and 80 percent nitrogen. Actually, air contains 21 percent oxygen and 79 percent nitrogen. To be more specific, air has 20.95 percent oxygen and 78.05 percent nitrogen. The remaining 1 percent includes argon, carbon dioxide, neon, helium, krypton and xenon. Compressed air may have from 19-22 percent oxygen.

What's in a name?

What do you call a mixture of oxygen and nitrogen?

You could call it nitrox, which many divers do. Nitrox refers to any mixture of oxygen and nitrogen, even air. Air, with a standard pressure of oxygen, is "normoxic" nitrox. Outside of diving, nitrox is often used to refer to mixtures with lower-than-normal oxygen content.

The term "enriched air" or "oxygen-enriched air" may be more accurate and less prone to cause confusion. It's also sometimes referred to as enriched-air nitrox, EAN or EANx. For real precision, call it "high O2 nitrogen breathing mix" or "hyperoxic N2O2 mix."

SafeAir© is a copyrighted term used by American Nitrox Divers, Inc. to refer to any enriched air mixture with an oxygen content between 22 and 50 percent.

Words for the Gas-Wise

Bar Metric equivalent of 1 atmosphere absolute (ATA).

Best mix A gas blend that contains the highest possible oxygen content that will still enable the diver to stay within oxygen limits at the deepest point in the dive. This maximizes the decompression advantages that oxygen offers.

Equivalent air depth (EAD) The depth of an imaginary air dive that would have the same nitrogen partial pressure as an actual dive on oxygen-enriched air.

fO2 An abbreviation for the fraction of oxygen in a gas mix.

Lorrain Smith effect This describes the adverse effects that the body has to elevated partial pressures of oxygen at exposures nearing 24 hours. Also called "pulmonary" or "whole body" oxygen toxicity, it has pneumonia-like symptoms.

Maximum operating depth The deepest that a breathing gas should be used based on CNS oxygen limits.

Partial pressure The pressure exerted by a component of a gas mixture. A breathing gas with 32 percent oxygen has an oxygen partial pressure of .32 ATA at the surface and a PO2 of 1.3 at 100 feet/30 meters.

Paul Bert effect Central nervous system oxygen toxicity, named after an early researcher, may involve tunnel vision, ringing in the ears, nausea, dizziness, anxiety, muscle spasms, convulsions and loss of consciousness.

PO2 An abbreviation for the partial pressure of oxygen, this is also written as PPO2.

— From January/February 1996

Note: For more information on obtaining enriched-air (EAN) training, see your dive instructor for a current listing of agencies with EAN courses.

The Air In There

Do divers need to take a closer look at what they breathe?

BY CATHIE CUSH

KEY WEST, FLA — Following the April 1994 diving death of a tourist here, the Monroe County Medical Examiner's Office determined that elevated levels of carbon monoxide (CO) in the blood contributed to the fatality. Subsequent testing of the tanks that the diver had used showed CO levels reported to be as high as 2,600 parts per million. This exposure is more than twice what is considered lethal and more than 260 times the level recommended by the Compressed Gas Association for Level F breathing air.

The role of carbon monoxide in the highly publicized death of this individual helped thrust this colorless, odorless — and potentially deadly — gas into the consciousness of the sport diving community. Although the incident was isolated, it sparked talk of government regulation of scuba. In the year since, at least two companies have developed devices that allow divers to test for CO in their tanks.

Statistically, carbon monoxide contamination doesn't seem to be a significant problem for sport divers. This case is only the second incident of its kind out of 447 scuba fatalities reported to DAN since 1989. John McAniff of the National Underwater Accident Data Center at the University of Rhode Island reports only three other fatalities involving contaminated air since 1976.

When CO is present, however, it can have fatal consequences. What's more, it raises issues regarding something that most divers ironically take for granted: the quality of the air we breathe.

According to Joel Dovenbarger, R.N., DAN's Director of Medical Services, DAN receives about 10 calls a year from divers who suspect they've received bad air. But, says Dovenbarger, "When the air is analyzed, rarely does anything come back indicating carbon monoxide, particulates or oils."

Beats oxygen to the blood

Carbon monoxide is a poisonous gas that results from the incomplete combustion of fossil fuels. Its toxicity is a result of its affinity for hemoglobin, a blood protein that carries oxygen to cells throughout the body. When inhaled, CO binds to hemoglobin some 200 times more readily than oxygen does, interfering with the blood's ability to provide sufficient fuel to the cells. After prolonged exposures, CO may interfere directly with cell function.

Divers may breathe air with unacceptable levels of carbon monoxide from a scuba tank or a surface-supplied system. A tank could become tainted if it is filled from a compressor with an improperly placed intake valve that draws in air contaminated with exhaust fumes, or from a compressor that has experienced a "flash," the burning of hydrocarbon buildup inside the system. Similarly, if the intake of a surface-supplied system is downwind of the exhaust of a boat engine, for example, CO levels in the air could rise dangerously.

When CO binds with hemoglobin, it forms a compound called carboxyhemoglobin. When blood levels of this compound rise initially, the body reacts by increasing blood flow to the heart and the brain to compensate for the decreased oxygen levels. As exposure continues, it can lead to respiratory depression, irregular heartbeat and damage to the heart muscle. Eventually, the respiratory system fails, or the amount of oxygen in the blood decreases to the point where it cannot support life.

It's difficult to pinpoint exactly when an individual breathing tainted air might begin to show symptoms, as they do not always correlate with carboxyhemoglobin levels. According to *The Physician's Guide to Diving Medicine*, edited by Shilling, Carlston and Mathias, early symptoms such as headache and dizziness "occur when divers breathe air contaminated with 800 parts per million (ppm) of carbon monoxide for an hour. At 1,600 ppm, confusion occurs, followed by collapse, and, at 3,200 ppm, unconsciousness."

Killer or contributor?

Unless the CO is several percent, it would unlikely cause death. (Very high CO can damage the brain directly, causing respiratory arrest.) More likely, the confusion or unconsciousness which may occur would be a contributing factor leading to drowning. In the Monroe County case, the cause of death was listed as air embolism. When divemasters found the body, floating face up just off the bottom in 65 feet/20 meters of water some 150 yards/137 meters from the wreck they were diving, they discovered blood in the decedent's mask and the regulator was dislodged.

"It's a difficult trail to follow," Dovenbarger says of an attempt to analyze such an accident. "Carbon monoxide poisoning is like nitrogen narcosis or taking drugs — they all affect your judgment and can lead to death."

Several divers on the boat with the decedent reported feeling weak, disoriented, nauseated or on the verge of unconsciousness. These all can be symptoms of CO toxicity. Others can include severe frontal headache, palpitations, loss of consciousness and seizures. The cherry-red lips and fingernail beds so often mentioned in association with CO poisoning are usually only seen in victims who have already died. Other victims are more likely to appear bluish.

Depending on the exposure, a victim of CO poisoning may also experience neurological problems that arise after an apparent recovery. These probably stem from trauma to the brain due to lack of oxygen. They can include depression, disorientation, loss of hearing or vision, gait disturbances, epilepsy, tremors or speech disturbances.

Hyperbaric oxygen is used to treat CO poisoning in divers and non-divers alike. Administration of 100 percent oxygen cuts the half-life of carbon monoxide from about five hours and 20 minutes to approximately an hour and 20 minutes. At three atmospheres in the chamber, the half-life is shortened to less than 25 minutes, and the tissues receive enough oxygen to perform all their metabolic functions. As in cases of decompression sickness, prompt hyperbaric treatment seems to be important in reducing both acute and long-term effects of CO exposure.

Increased air awareness

In recent years, the increased use of nitrox and mixed gases has led divers to look closely at the "ingredients" in the air they breathe. Although the initial concern was to reduce contaminants to keep nitrox and trimix blending systems' oxygen clean, the debate surrounding the specifications helped raise the awareness of both consumers and purveyors of compressed air.

The Compressed Gas Association (CGA) recommends that compressed air for scuba diving to 130 feet/40 meters meet the association's Level E specifications for such contaminants as carbon monoxide and oil. CGA makes, but cannot enforce, such recommendations. Level E allows a maximum of 10 ppm of carbon monoxide, 500 ppm carbon dioxide, 25 ppm methane and 5 mg/m3 of condensed oils. The Occupational Safety and Health Administration (OSHA) and the U.S. Navy allow 20 ppm of CO. All three allow some odor, if it is "slight," "not objectionable" or "not noxious/pronounced."

The American Conference of Government Industrial Hygienists has recommended a Threshold Limit Value-Time-Weighted Average for CO of 50 ppm at the surface. This means that an individual can be exposed to 50 ppm of CO for eight hours without suffering ill effects. As concentration increases, exposure times must decrease. Maximum short-term exposure to CO (15 minutes in 24 hours) is 400 ppm.

All these recommendations are useful, but the fact is, most recreational dive operators aren't required to test the air they're dispensing. A few states require testing on the books, but for the most part, air quality is self-regulated. Since the mid 1980s, PADI has required that its Five-Star facilities test their air quarterly and supply PADI Headquarters with the results, and it is considering making the recommendation across the board for all PADI facilities. Recently, the requirement was changed to a prerequisite, and shops must show that they have tested successfully for at least two quarters before receiving the Five-Star designation.

In the United States, the shops must meet CGA Level E. Outside the United States, shops are required to meet at least CGA Level E, unless local standards are more stringent. The specifications adopted by the technical training agencies for oxygen-compatible air are necessarily much more strict than Level E. At Tek 93, a technical diving forum held annually, representatives from American Nitrox Divers Inc. and the International Association of Nitrox and Technical Divers agreed that compressed air to be used with oxygen should contain no more than 0.1 mg/m3 of condensed hydrocarbons and no more than 2 ppm carbon monoxide (CO). Each agency requires its facilities to participate in quarterly gas analysis. Technical Divers International has announced it will enforce quarterly testing as of September 1995.

Many consumers, it seems, take all this for granted.

"Divers spend hours color-coordinating their equipment, then never give a thought to their air. It's overlooked, neglected — and it's life support under hostile conditions," observes Mike Casey, a technical sales and diagnostics representative for Lawrence Factor, Inc., a Hialeah, Fla., company that provides high-pressure compressors, filtration and purification systems, and breathing-gas testing for both the military and private sector. Working in cooperation with Jolie Bookspan, Ph.D., and Beneath The Sea/Dive Philadelphia, Casey has developed an "Air Aware" Program through which he awards certificates of merit to dive shops that test their air regularly.

Through his company's free technical information line (305-823-7174), Casey receives calls from divers who fear they may have breathed bad air, and Lawrence Factor tests tanks when divers are in doubt. Most of the time, he says, it's not the air. The flip side of the issue, he suspects, is that "a lot of incidents that might be air-related might be chalked up to other things. Some of the symptoms, like headache and nausea, may never make it into the doctor's medical report."

Air testing, Casey says, is an opportunity for education. If an air station fails to meet the specs, correcting any problems can be a learning experience. Casey says he has seen shops in strip malls place compressor air intake pipes on the roof of the building, with no concern for what might be pumped out nearby. Many operators, he notes, are unaware that a long rainy spell may shorten the effective life of an air filter. Some shops rotate filters or merely do a visual check, which is not adequate to determine if the filter is saturated. Contaminants may cling to the sides of high-pressure lines or chambers.

"It's not necessarily the guy who spends the most money, but the guy who takes care of his system," Casey says. "If there's a problem, a lot of times we can solve it over the phone. Sometimes an intake needs to be moved or filters have to be changed."

Compressed-air consumers

Divers can do more than they probably realize to ensure they are receiving air that meets CGA Level E standards. First, they can ask to see a copy of the air station's air analysis report.

"If a shop doesn't know the last time its air was tested, I would be concerned about breathing it," says Casey.

"It's up to the consumer," says Dovenbarger. "If divers want the retailer to provide the highest quality air, they need to make sure the facility is current in its testing."

A "taste test" should take place before the tank leaves the shop, not on the ocean floor. Several divers aboard the boat with the decedent mentioned earlier noted the air in their tanks smelled or tasted unusu-

---

Cigarette Smoking:

Not A Good Idea for Divers

Divers who are concerned about carbon monoxide should start by taking a look at their lifestyles. Chances are, if they're smokers, they'll inhale more CO from a cigarette than they'll ever get out of a scuba tank.

According to *The Physician's Guide to Diving Medicine,* "The smoke from a typical American cigarette contains about 4 percent carbon monoxide (20,000 ppm). The average concentration inhaled is 400-500 ppm." As a result, carboxyhemoglobin levels in a smoker are as much as 15 times higher than they are in a nonsmoker. What's more, it takes about eight hours to eliminate 75 percent of the inhaled CO from the body.

The book cites a 1963 study of smoking habits and carboxyhemoglobin rates which shows that someone who smokes between half a pack and two packs a day exhales about 27.5 ppm of carbon monoxide. As the authors note, this is higher than the 20 ppm CO limit for breathing air allowed by the U.S. Navy. A light smoker exhales about 17 ppm CO — higher than the CGA Level E breathing air limit for the poison.

---

al, yet most chose to dive anyway. Several of them complained later of weakness or nausea. Although CO is odorless, presence of an odor, taste or color indicates other contaminants which may be accompanied by carbon monoxide. Devices are available that enable a diver to test a tank for gross levels of carbon monoxide.

Some divers may have to overcome the idea that since it's air, it should be free, or virtually so. An air testing program may drive the price of a fill up 50 cents or a dollar — but it seems like a small price to pay for peace of mind.

— From September/October 1995

If You Dive Nitrox You Should Know About OXTOX

DAN discusses the dangers of oxygen toxicity when using nitrox as a breathing gas

BY DR. E.D. THALMANN, DAN ASSISTANT MEDICAL DIRECTOR;
CAPTAIN, MEDICAL CORPS, U.S. NAVY (RETIRED)

It's a fact: we need oxygen to live. It's because of the way our cells use oxygen that we are able to breathe, exercise, and even think. In each of our cells, structures called mitochondria take the oxygen which diffuses in from our blood, disassemble it into its two component atoms (remember, oxygen — O_2 — is composed of two oxygen atoms), and then hook some available hydrogen nuclei to them to form water.

The process releases energy, which is used for all functions of life. The problem is that in disassembling the oxygen molecule, it involves a step in which an extra electron is hooked on. This forms an intermediate called a superoxide anion, and this is a bad actor. It is highly reactive, and it will make mincemeat out of most other molecules it comes in contact with.

These anions are like coals in a furnace: as long as they are contained, we get lots of safe chemical energy; if they get out we get a great deal of damage. The mitochondria are designed to contain these superoxide anions, but just in case some get loose, there are a host of protective chemical reactions designed to sop them up and prevent them from doing any damage.

Besides producing excessive amounts of the superoxide anion, elevated tissue oxygen levels also affect a variety of other biochemical reactions which may affect oxygen toxicity in ways that are only beginning to be understood. Tissue-protective mechanisms and biochemical reactions are tuned to life in an atmosphere containing 21 percent oxygen, or 0.21 atmospheres absolute (ata) oxygen partial pressure. (See sidebar: "Remember Partial Pressure?", page 34.) As the partial pressure increases above this comfortable 0.21 ata, protective mechanisms are slowly overwhelmed and biochemical reactions are affected. This may eventually result in "oxtox," or oxygen toxicity.

Oxtox — What Is It?

Oxygen toxicity is a time duration phenomenon: that is, both time and partial pressure play a role. If an oxygen partial pressure of 2 ata is breathed for a few minutes, there would probably not be any problem. But, breathing it for an hour, might cause problems. This is why oxygen exposure limits are given as partial pressure/time limits. As the partial pressure gets higher, the recommended exposure time gets shorter. What kind of problems might breathing a high oxygen partial pressure cause? It is the lungs and the brain which are the target organs of major concern in diving oxygen toxicity. Oxygen toxicity in the lungs (pulmonary oxygen toxicity) is like getting a bad case of the flu, but it will rarely cause permanent damage. The most common situation in which pulmonary oxygen toxicity might occur is during very long recompression treatments.

Oxygen toxicity of the brain, commonly referred to as central nervous system (CNS) oxygen toxicity, is different. It can occur during actual diving, and when it does, it can ruin your day — and possibly more. Some symptoms of CNS oxygen toxicity include flashing lights in front of the eyes, tunnel vision, loud ringing or roaring in the ear (tinnitus), confusion, lethargy, a feeling of nausea or vertigo, areas of numbness or tingling, and muscular twitching, especially of the lips.

These CNS symptoms are inconvenient, and a warning to change to a breathing gas with a lower oxygen partial pressure as soon as possible, but do not put the diver at risk of injury at this point. The big daddy of CNS symptoms does, however. It is the full-blown grand mal convulsion. During a convulsion, a diver will thrash about, perhaps bang his head into something hard, or if underwater, may lose his mouthpiece. The result can be trauma or drowning.

The good news is that convulsions are rare; the bad news is that all the inconvenient CNS symptoms noted above do not always provide warning of an impending convulsion. In some cases, a convulsion may occur without any warning at all. One more piece of good news: the convulsion in and of itself is not harmful, so if you don't crack your head or drown, you should have no permanent damage.

By now you're probably asking where these dire descriptions are leading.

To a better understanding, we hope, of diving on nitrox. As air-breathing sport divers need to know about decompression sickness (DCS), divers using high oxygen in nitrogen mixtures (nitrox) need to know about oxygen toxicity. (To read more about nitrox, see page 207.

Both decompression sickness and oxygen toxicity are rare occurrences; they can be made rarer with good diving practices. With DCS, it's using your table or computer conservatively and keeping the ascent rate down. With oxtox, it's paying attention to the partial pressure and the amount of exposure time.

The main thing we're discussing here is CNS oxygen toxicity, because this is the most dangerous kind. Lung oxygen toxicity is unlikely to be a problem for recreational divers, so it will be mentioned only in passing.

Remember Partial Pressure?

The partial pressure of a gas is a measure of the number of molecules in a given volume — the molecular concentration. The physiological effects of a gas are due mainly to its partial pressure, no matter what the total pressure is.

If a gas has only one component, say 100-percent oxygen, the partial pressure and the pressure are the same. If there is a gas mix, then the partial pressure is the gas fraction times the total pressure. A 50 percent oxygen-in-nitrogen mix has an oxygen partial pressure (pO2) of 1.0 atmosphere absolute (ata) at a depth of 33 feet / 10 meters where the total pressure is 2 ata.

At this depth the 50 percent oxygen would have the same physiological effect as 100 percent oxygen at the surface. Breathing a 100 percent oxygen mix at a depth of 33 feet / 10 meters (2 ata total pressure) would be equivalent to breathing the 50 percent mix at 132 feet / 40 meters (4 ata total pressure).

Royal Navy Studies

The grand old man of CNS oxygen toxicity is Professor Kenneth Donald, who cut his teeth on the problem during World War II in Great Britain. (Want to know more? Read Reference 1, page 40.) At that time the Royal Navy was under pressure to develop the technology used by the Italians to severely damage the battleships HMS Queen Elizabeth and HMS Valiant in the harbor of the port city of Alexandria, Egypt, in 1941.

Italian divers wearing 100 percent oxygen rebreathers, drove a torpedo close into a ship. While submerged to avoid detection, they detached its warhead under the ship's hull, and beat a hasty retreat after a timer was set.

The Royal Navy soon began developing its own band of underwater divers called "Charioteers" to carry out similar missions. Dr. Donald was assigned as a Surgeon Lieutenant to provide medical care during training of the divers using the British 100 percent oxygen rebreathers. The accepted safe limits for breathing 100 percent oxygen at the time (2 hours at 50 feet / 15 meters, 30 minutes at 90 feet / 27 meters) produced enough convulsions that the British Admiralty decided some sort of studies were needed to define the scope of the problem and, hopefully, find a solution.

About to be transferred to the Shetland Islands, Dr. Donald had a change of fortune and proceeded instead to a facility just outside of London, where he found himself heading up a major research effort to get a handle on the problem of CNS oxygen toxicity.

Royal Navy Discoveries

Over the next three years, Dr. Donald's team conducted literally hundreds of exposures on human volunteers (remember, there was a war on). This series of studies formed the basis of what we know about CNS oxygen toxicity, namely:

• There is a large individual variation in susceptibility and time of onset to symptoms. This is what is referred to as "oxygen tolerance."

• Compared to dry exposures, immersion decreases oxygen tolerance a great deal, decreasing exposure times up to a factor of four or five.

• Exercise decreases oxygen tolerance a lot, compared to rest.

• Diving in very cold (<49°F / 9°C) or very warm (>88°F / 31°C) water seems to decrease oxygen tolerance.

The goal of the research was to develop a set of oxygen exposure limits — that is, a table that indicated how long a diver could safely breathe 100 percent oxygen at various depths. The main obstacle toward developing a good set of exposure limits was the large individual variation in oxygen tolerance. Not only did the time of onset and severity of CNS symptoms vary considerably between divers, but in a given diver there was a large day-to-day variation. One stalwart individual made dives twice a week for over three months on exactly the same dive profile (70 feet / 21 meters, 65°F / 18°C, at rest, 100-percent oxygen) until signs of oxygen toxicity developed (again, a notable contribution to the war effort!). His symptom onset time was random and ranged from seven minutes to 148 minutes!

As a result of these studies, the Royal Navy considered it unsafe to breathe 100 percent oxygen below a depth of 25 feet / 7.6 meters (an oxygen partial pressure of 1.76 ata). In fact 25 feet / 7.6 meters was the shallowest depth tested. No particular time limit was given for this exposure, but the longest time tested was two hours. The carbon dioxide absorbent canisters of the diving rigs of the day rarely lasted more than 90 minutes.

The Royal Navy made deeper dives by using nitrogen-oxygen mixtures in the newly developed semi-closed circuit rebreathers. This was the beginning of so-called "mixed-gas diving," where the breathing gas is mixed from oxygen and nitrogen rather than simply being compressed from atmospheric air.

U.S. Navy Studies

In the 1950s, Dr. E.H. Lanphier, then a Lieutenant in the U.S. Navy Medical Corps, undertook a series of studies at the Navy Experimental Diving Unit (NEDU), located at that time in Washington, D.C., to investigate whether oxygen exposure limits could be developed for 100 percent oxygen dives deeper than 25 feet / 7.6 meters. Table 1 (below) shows the limits that he recommended. The 100 percent oxygen exposure limits in Table 1 remained in use up to 1970 and with only slight modifications were used through 1991 when they were again changed. Dr. Lanphier was also charged with investigating how these limits should be applied to the oxygen partial pressures encountered in mixed-gas nitrox diving. During nitrox diving, oxygen partial pressures similar to those used in 100 percent oxygen diving may be encountered, but since nitrogen has been added, these partial pressures are reached at a greater depth and, therefore, at a greater breathing gas density.

U.S. Findings

From his studies, Dr. Lanphier concluded that the increased gas density encountered during mixed-gas nitrox diving required the exposure times at a given oxygen partial pressure to be shorter than for 100 percent oxygen rebreathers, which can be used only at shallow depths, and which result in a lower gas density. The reason for this decreased tolerance during nitrox diving was thought to be due to decreased carbon dioxide elimination at the greater depths, resulting in higher blood carbon dioxide levels. This would make the diver more sensitive to oxygen toxicity. These U.S. Navy nitrox mixed-gas nitrogen-oxygen exposure limits are shown in Table 2 (page 230). Notice that compared to those for 100 percent oxygen breathing in Table 1, these are quite a bit shorter for the same partial pressure. With the advent of closed-circuit oxygen rebreathers, the U.S. Navy no longer uses nitrox scuba and no longer publishes nitrox exposure limits in their official diving manual.

TABLE 1

USN 100 Percent Oxygen Rebreather Exposure Limits (1954)

Normal Operations

Depth (feet)	Time (min)
10	240
15	120
20	90
25	65

Exceptional Exposure Operations

Depth (feet)	Time (min)
30	45
35	34
40	25
45	15

The Conflict — and Some Good Advice

The British disagreed with Dr. Lanphier's findings, and the Royal Navy set exposure limits for nitrox diving that were no different than for 100 percent oxygen diving. This area remains controversial — Dr. Donald's case for keeping the exposure limits the same for both 100 percent oxy-

TABLE 2

USN Oxygen Exposure Limits for Nitrogen-Oxygen Mixed-Gas Diving (1959)

Normal Exposure

Oxygen Partial Pressure (ata)	Time (min)
1.6	30
1.5	40
1.4	50
1.3	60
1.2	80
1.1	120
1.0	240

Exceptional Exposure

Oxygen Partial Pressure (ata)	Time (min)
2.0	30
1.9	40
1.8	60
1.7	80
1.6	100
1.5	120
1.4	180
1.3	240

gen and nitrox diving has weaknesses and should not be accepted as proven.

Dr. Lanphier's work is certainly compelling enough that divers should be very cautious before extrapolating oxygen exposure limits based on 100 percent oxygen rebreathing directly to nitrox diving at higher gas densities. Ideally, nitrox limits should be tested at the maximum gas density anticipated for their use.

CO2 Retention

Why would carbon dioxide (CO_2) retention become a problem at increased gas densities? There have been many studies showing that as depth increases while breathing air, the high oxygen and increased gas density will normally slow the rate at which we breathe and thereby the rate at which we eliminate carbon dioxide. This will raise the blood levels of carbon dioxide. On top of this, however, is the fact that, because of individual variations, not all divers will slow their breathing in the same amounts.

Dr. Lanphier investigated the problem of divers who tended to breathe more slowly during diving than would normally be expected — so-called "carbon dioxide retainers." He felt that these individuals would be at an especially high risk of CNS oxygen toxicity when breathing high oxygen in nitrogen gas mixtures.

Should a nitrox diver be concerned about whether he is a carbon dioxide retainer? Unfortunately, there is no good test to reliably identify carbon dioxide retainers. The best strategy at present is to use conservative oxygen exposure limits.

More U.S. Studies — Oxygen Exposure Limits

In the late 1970s and early '80s, the Navy Experimental Diving Unit (NEDU) — now moved to Panama City, Fla.— conducted a series of studies to look at longer exposure times breathing 100 percent oxygen at shallow depths while exercising at levels typically encountered by combat swimmers while swimming long distances underwater. (Remember, exposure times developed using divers at rest may well cause problems for exercising divers, since exercise decreases oxygen tolerance.)

The conclusion of the study was that four-hour exposures at 25 feet / 7.6 meters (1.76 ata) had a low probability of causing CNS symptoms but were not without hazard since a convulsion was reported at this depth after 72 minutes of exercise. Because of this hazard, it was recommended that routine exposures be carried no deeper than 20 feet / 6.1 meters (1.6 ata) for up to four hours, with a single excursion between 21 and 40 feet / 6.4 and 12 meters for 15 minutes, or between 41 and 50 feet / 12 and 15 meters for five minutes.

Even this recommendation does not completely eliminate the possibility of a convulsion. One diver had a convulsion at 20 feet / 6.1 meters approximately 48 minutes after making a 15-minute excursion to 40 feet / 12 meters at the beginning of the dive. These studies had their share of oxygen convulsions and verified their unpredictability as observed by Dr. Donald some 40 years earlier. One feature of these convulsions that deserves mentioning is that they usually occurred with little or no warning.

With the advent of nitrox diving it is wise to consider these studies. Dr. Andrea Harabin, a scientist at the Naval Medical Research Institute (NMRI) in Bethesda, Md., analyzed the human oxygen exposures from the NEDU studies and used a mathematical model to predict the probability of CNS oxygen toxicity symptoms occurring. (See Reference 2, page 240 for details.)

When she considered all symptoms which resulted in the diver stopping his dive, she found that the model had a threshold at 1.3 ata; that is, the probability of a CNS symptom occurring at or below this level should be essentially zero.

Some of the CNS symptoms that caused dives to be halted could have been due to many other reasons besides oxygen toxicity and were classified as "Probable." In contrast, with "Convulsions" and "Definite Symptoms" (see Table 3, page 232), there is usually no question that oxygen toxicity is the culprit. When Dr. Harabin considered just the convulsions and definite symptoms, she found the thresholds to be 1.7 ata. This analysis again reflects the large degree of uncertainty inherent in these types of human exposures.

What Oxygen Level Is Safe?

So, what levels of oxygen can be breathed safely? Currently, the U.S. Navy is using 1.3 ata as the maximum limit in its closed-circuit rebreathers — the more conservative threshold found by Dr. Harabin for exercising divers. Using these closed-circuit rigs, exposures exceeding eight hours are possible, and at the 1.3 ata level the chance of CNS oxygen toxicity should be very rare.

TABLE 3
Symptoms of CNS Oxygen Toxicity Encountered in NEDU Studies
Convulsions: the most serious symptom and the one to avoid at all cost.
Definite: muscle twitching, tinnitus (ringing in the ears), blurred or tunnel vision, disorientation, aphasia (inability to express oneself by speaking), nystagmus (rapid side-to-side motions of the eye), or incoordination.
Probable: more equivocal signs which could be due to oxygen toxicity as well as other causes: light headdress apprehension, dysphoria ("just didn't feel right"), lethargy, and transient nausea.

Very long exposures, however, may put the diver at risk for some lung toxicity symptoms. The National Oceanic and Atmospheric Administration (NOAA) takes a slightly more conservative approach, recommending 180 minutes at 1.3 ata for normal exposures and 240 minutes only for exceptional exposures (see Table 4, page 40). This additional conservatism, according to NOAA, "take(s) operational safety considerations into consideration and are sufficient in duration for anticipated NOAA dives."

The NOAA limits shown in Table 4 are based on the results of the NEDU oxygen exposure limit studies done in the '80s, taking the increased gas densities encountered in nitrox diving into account. The "normal exposure limits" are longer than the nitrox limits proposed by Dr. Lanphier in Table 2 (page 230) but are quite a bit shorter than the 240 minutes, 1.6 ata exposure, currently allowed by the U.S. Navy for 100 percent oxygen diving. However, the "exceptional exposure limits" are virtually the same as originally recommended by Dr. Lanphier, showing that there has not been much change in opinion as to what is safe at these higher partial pressures.

PADI, the Professional Association of Diving Instructors, has proposed a limit of 1.4 ata for open-circuit nitrox scuba diving. Because open-circuit scuba diving would not expose divers to this level continuously, in practice it should be as safe, or safer, than the 1.3 ata U.S. Navy limit for continuous exposures. (See sidebar "Continuous vs. Intermittent Exposures," page 238.) In fact, the shallow exposure times in the 1.3- to 1.4-ata range are mainly to avoid lung oxygen toxicity; the likelihood of CNS toxicity at these levels is very low and probably not much different over this range.

Is it possible to breathe oxygen at a higher oxygen partial pressure (pO2)? The answer is yes, but! Dr. Harabin's analysis gave a threshold limit of 1.7 ata (23 feet / 7 meters) for an exercising diver when considering only "convulsions" and "definite" symptoms. This is uncomfortably close to the 25-foot / 7.6-meter (1.76 ata) depth where a convulsion was reported, so backing off to 20 feet / 6.1 meters(1.6 ata) gives a little more breathing room.

Currently the U.S. Navy would allow an exercising exposure at this partial pressure for up to four hours, but that assumes breathing 100 percent oxygen at 25 feet / 7.6 meters by trained combat swimmers. A depth excursion of only 5 feet / 1.5 meters would put the diver in an area where convulsions have been reported, and divers who tend to retain carbon dioxide during exercise may be at increased risk.

The NOAA limit for nitrox diving at 1.6 ata is 45 minutes for normal diving and 120 minutes for exceptional exposure diving. Again, some conservatism is built into these limits and consideration given to the fact that this partial pressure may be breathed at higher gas densities than would be encountered by the divers using 100 percent oxygen.

During a nitrox dive done at Duke University's F.G. Hall Hypo/Hyperbaric Center at 100 feet / 30 meters, breathing 1.6 ata pO2 (oxygen partial pressure) during heavy exercise, a convulsion occurred after 40 minutes. Perhaps this would not have occurred had there been a lower level of exercise, but it does seem to indicate that the NOAA limit of 45 minutes for 1.6 ata nitrox diving is not overly conservative.

Breathing 100 percent oxygen during the 20-foot / 6.1-meter decompression stop is common practice, and at this depth, the partial pressure will be about 1.6 ata. At this shallow depth, under conditions of rest, the chance of CNS oxygen toxicity should be very low. But, like most things in life, this is not certain, as evidenced by a recently reported oxygen convulsion at 20 feet / 6.1 meters during decompression by a technical diver after completing a dive on the Lusitania.

Recommendations

One thing you should be impressed with by now is that oxygen toxicity is fickle; convulsions have occurred at shallow depths under conditions where most experts would not have expected them to occur.

So, as an air sport diver, how should you view nitrox diving? The answer is: carefully.

Experts rationalizing why particular oxygen exposure limits do or do not cause oxygen toxicity are like investment analysts rationalizing movements in the stock market — everyone has a reason, but know one really knows why!

First, whenever a gas is breathed with an oxygen fraction above 21 percent, you should assume that oxygen toxicity is a possibility and have appropriate training. This not only means having a buddy clearly visible at all times but also knowing what action to take should oxygen toxicity occur.

Second, using equipment designed to compress high oxygen mixtures can be hazardous in itself and requires special training.

Third, what you get in your tank may not be what you expect. A method of analyzing the amount of oxygen in the tank independent of the filling station must be available. Fourth, if you are attracted to rebreathers, remember that they are complex pieces of life-support gear, requiring much more care and feeding than the good old scuba regulator. If you get into rebreathers, expect to get hit with good-sized training and maintenance costs.

Finally, there is the matter of keeping the possibility of oxygen toxicity to a minimum.

Moving Ahead

For open-circuit scuba diving, consider the "green light" region any oxygen partial pressure of 1.4 ata or less (this is about 82 feet / 25 meters on a 40-percent oxygen mix.) As long as this level is never exceeded, other limitations of open-circuit scuba diving will limit the exposure time to lengths where CNS oxygen toxicity is unlikely to be encountered, even for exposures approaching four hours.

Proceeding With Caution

Between 1.4 ata and 1.6 ata (this is 99 feet / 30 meters on a 40-percent mix) is the "yellow light" region. The possibility of oxygen toxicity at 1.6 ata is low, but the margin of error is very slim compared to 1.4 ata. Individual variation, the likelihood of an unplanned depth excursion causing an increase in oxygen partial pressure, and the possibility of having to perform heavy exercise in an emergency put the possibility of oxygen toxicity at levels where caution should be exercised. Thus, levels of 1.5 to 1.6 ata should be reserved for conditions where the diver is completely at rest, such as during decompression. Again, as noted previously, the dive team must still be prepared for the possibility of an oxygen convulsion at these levels.

Stop!

Above 1.6 ata is the "red light" area. Just don't do it.

Yes, there is evidence that short exposures at higher levels of pO2 (oxygen partial pressure) are possible but so are convulsions. At these levels, oxygen exposure depth/time limits must be adhered to. Even mild exercise may put divers breathing high-density nitrox mixes at increased risk; and even open-circuit scuba divers can achieve durations likely to get them into trouble at these levels. Diving using these high partial pressures of oxygen should be left to the trained professionals who can weigh the risks and benefits and who have the necessary training and support structure in place, if an oxygen convulsion occurs.

Finally . . .

Nitrox diving may extend bottom times or decrease the possibility of decompression sickness, depending on how it's used, but it adds to the risk of oxygen toxicity. Decompression sickness rarely occurs in the water and is rarely life-threatening. When it happens underwater, however, life support is usually not an issue — instead, attention is focused on getting to a treatment chamber.

If an oxygen convulsion occurs, it almost always occurs underwater, greatly complicating treatment. So while the probability of a convulsion may be low, the possibility of severe injury or death is high if it does occur. Taken together this makes it a risky occurrence, and each diver needs to consider that risk whenever nitrox is used. Experience and good training are essential. This is an area that requires team diving, with the whole team full trained in nitrox diving.

What do you do if oxygen toxicity or a convulsion happens?

Editor's Note: After reading the article on nitrox in the January/February '96 Alert Diver, a DAN member asked what the recommended procedure was in the event of an underwater oxygen convulsion.

An oxygen convulsion in the water is rare but potentially life-threatening. Like learning CPR, practicing the proper handling of an oxygen convulsion is maintaining a skill you hope you'll never use. The organization with the most experience with 100 percent oxygen diving is the United States Navy. Its recommendations for managing oxygen toxicity is as follows:

According to the USN Dive Manual sections 14.9.1.1 and 14.9.1.2 the suggested procedure for dealing with seizures is:

Management of Nonconvulsive Symptoms. The stricken diver should alert his dive buddy and make a controlled ascent to the surface. The victim's life preserver should be inflated (if necessary) with the dive buddy watching him closely for progression of symptoms.

Management of Underwater Convulsion. The following steps should be taken when treating a convulsing diver:

a. Assume a position behind the convulsing diver. Release the victim's weight belt unless he is wearing a drysuit, in which case the weight belt should be left in place to prevent the diver from assuming a face-down position on the surface.

b. Leave the victim's mouthpiece in his mouth. If it is not in his mouth, do not attempt to replace it; however, if time permits, ensure that the mouthpiece is switched to the surface position.

c. Grasp the victim around his chest above the underwater breathing apparatus (UBA) or between the UBA and his body. If difficulty is encountered in gaining control of the victim in this manner, the rescuer should use the best method possible to obtain control. The UBA waist or neck strap may be grasped if necessary.

d. Make a controlled ascent to the surface, maintaining a slight pressure on the diver's chest to assist exhalation.(see commentary below)

e. If additional buoyancy is required, activate the victim's life jacket. The rescuer should not release his own weight belt or inflate his own life jacket.

f. Upon reaching the surface, inflate the victim's life jacket if not previously done.

g. Remove the victim's mouthpiece and switch the valve to SURFACE to prevent the possibility of the rig flooding and weighing down the victim.

h. Signal for emergency pick-up.

I. Once the convulsion has subsided, open the victim's airway by tilting his head back slightly.

j. Ensure the victim is breathing. Mouth-to-mouth breathing may be initiated if necessary.

k. If an upward excursion occurred during the actual convulsion, transport to the nearest chamber and have the victim evaluated by an individual trained to recognize and treat diving-related illness.

Deciding whether to ascend with a diver who is convulsing can be tricky. In section 8-2.4 of Volume 1 of the U.S. Navy diving manual it states:

"If a diver convulses, the UBA should be ventilated immediately with a gas of lower oxygen content, if possible. If depth control is possible and gas supply is secure (helmet or full face mask), the diver's depth should be kept constant until the convulsion subsides. If an ascent must take place, it should be done as slowly as possible. If a diver surfaces unconscious because of an oxygen convulsion or to avoid drowning, the diver must be treated as if suffering from arterial gas embolism."

Obviously, a full face mask is the best way to perform diving with high oxygen mixes because the diver can be kept at depth until the convulsion subsides. If the diver is breathing from a mouthpiece and it comes out of his mouth, there is no option but to surface the diver, since when the convulsion stops he will try to take a breath. Training and practice are the only ways to ensure that divers will know how to bring a convulsing diver to the surface, using a slow, controlled ascent, if that be-comes necessary.

In the section on the management of underwater convulsions, the reference to switching the mouthpiece to the surface position would refer only to rebreathers where an open mouthpiece which inadvertently becomes submerged can flood the UBA.

Also, step g should be modified if the victim is breathing nitrox using open-circuit scuba. If someone is convulsing, you won't be able to remove the mouthpiece; and this should never be done by force. Once the convulsion subsides, if the mouthpiece is secure (or if the diver is wearing a full face mask) and if the diver is still in the water and breathing, then leave everything in place until you can get the injured diver out of the water. If he is not breathing, then remove the mouthpiece once on the surface and begin rescue breathing.

The main goal while the injured diver is in the water is to keep him from drowning. Next is to ensure that his airway is open after the convulsion stops by keeping the neck extended.

Finally, be on the lookout for foreign bodies in the trachea. It is possible to bite off the parts of the mouthpiece between the teeth during a convulsion, which can find their way into the trachea, blocking the airway. In these cases, the injured diver will begin coughing as he returns to consciousness, or he may try to breathe but not get any air into his lungs. Here you need to institute the standard procedures taught in CPR classes for foreign body obstruction of the trachea.

Continuous vs.
Intermittent Oxygen Exposures

Remember that CNS oxygen toxicity symptoms are a time-duration phenomenon. They will not suddenly occur the minute a particular partial pressure is exceeded — it takes time. As you can see from the exposure limits in the tables (Table 4), as the inspired oxygen partial pressure increases, the exposure time decreases.

The U.S. Navy limit of 1.3 ata for continuous exposures reflects their desire to keep the risk of CNS symptoms essentially zero, no matter how long the dive.

In nitrox diving, however, divers breathe from open-circuit scuba with a fixed fraction of oxygen in the breathing mix. PADI has chosen 1.4 ata as the maximum open-circuit scuba limit; the limitations placed on duration by open-circuit scuba will ensure that the likelihood of CNS oxygen toxicity is no greater than would be experienced by the U.S. Navy closed-circuit divers.

When using open-circuit scuba, the 1.4 ata maximum oxygen partial pressure is reached only at the maximum depth, and for the vast majority of recreation divers, the time spent at this maximum depth will be limited to times where CNS oxygen toxicity is unlikely to be encountered. At all shallower depths, the oxygen partial pressure will be lower, and the overall exposure during the entire dive is unlikely to have physiological effects significantly different than a continuous 1.3 ata exposure.

Be careful when extending this analogy to higher partial pressures, however. Formulas are available for integrating the exposures at various depths to predict overall exposure times when looking only at lung oxygen toxicity. This concept does have some support research done at Dr. C.J. Lambertsen's laboratory at the Institute of Environmental Medicine in Philadelphia, Pa.

The case for CNS oxygen toxicity is much more complicated. Research done at the Navy Experimental Diving Unit (NEDU) in 1986 specifically looked at how brief exposures to oxygen partial pressures of 2.0 ata or greater would impact the overall exposure time at 20 feet / 6.1 meters of sea water (fsw). The results were not clear, and it was obvious that no formula could be developed which would allow integration of oxygen exposures at various depths into a single indicator which would help the diver avoid CNS oxygen toxicity. The best that could be said is that a single 15-minute excursion to 40 fsw/12 msw, or for five minutes at 50 fsw/15 msw, probably had no significant effect. This formed the basis of the current U.S. Navy recommendations. No such research has yet been carried out for high oxygen nitrox diving, to my knowledge.

— Dr. E.D. Thalmann

TABLE 4

Oxygen Partial Pressure and Exposure Time Limits for Nitrogen — Oxygen Mixed-Gas Working Dives (from NOAA 1991 Diving Manual)

Normal Exposure Limits

Oxygen Partial Pressure (ata)	Maximum Duration for a Single Exposure (min)	Maximum Total Duration for any 24-Hour Day (min)
1.6	45	150
1.5	120	180
1.4	150	180
1.3	180	210
1.2	210	240
1.1	240	270
1.0	300	300
0.9	360	360
0.8	450	450
0.7	570	570
0.6	720	720

Exceptional Exposure

Oxygen Partial Pressure (ata)	Time (min)
2.0	30
1.9	45
1.8	60
1.7	75
1.6	120
1.5	150
1.4	180
1.3	240

References

Donald KM. Oxygen and the Diver. England: Images, 1993. Available through Best Publishing Co., Flagstaff, Ariz. (This reference also covers all of the NEDU studies mentioned and gives full citations for them.)

Harabin AL, Survanshi SS. A statistical analysis of recent Navy Experimental Diving Unit (NEDU) single-depth human exposures to 100-percent oxygen at pressure. Bethesda, M.D. Naval Medical Research Institute Report NMRI 93-59, 1993.

Note: Both NEDU and NMRI Reports are available through: National Technical Information Service, 5385 Port Royal Road, Springfield VA 22161.

— From *May/June 1997*

FOOD FOR THOUGHT

Editor's Note: This section contains a selection of messages from DAN Executive Director Dr. Peter B. Bennett, from the "Director to You" section of past Alert Divers.

Heart to Heart

Dr. Bennett explores cardiac-related deaths versus diving deaths.

This past winter [1996 — Ed.] gave many of us record snowfalls in many parts of the Northeast and Midwest — resulting in much snow shoveling! The deep snow is well behind us now, and divers will be back in the warm water having the fun they love best. The heavy snows of the recent past, however, have prompted me to write about a common factor in both diving and shoveling snow — cardiac-related deaths.

Although shoveling light snow is safe, excess cardiac-related deaths have been reported in medical literature and the press. Possible mechanisms for this increased risk of myocardial infarction, or heart attack, include increased arterial blood pressure; coronary spasm, or vasoconstriction; and increased clot formation — all precipitated by strenuous physical exertion.

Recent evidence confirms that such activity can trigger myocardial infarction, especially in habitually sedentary individuals. This occurs with sudden increases in systolic blood pressure (198 ± 17) and heart rate (175 + 15), which researchers have hypothesized will disrupt atherosclerotic plaque and lead to the blockage of the coronary vessels.

Recently DAN fatality reports have begun to show two recurring themes: lack of experience and cardiovascular disease. I will discuss lack of experience in another editoral, but for some years now cardiovascular disease has been one of the leading causes of death. Physical exertion increases the relative risk by six times. The facts remain that surviving a cardiac arrest or myocardial infarction while underwater, or even on the surface, is less likely than while shoveling snow. This is due not only to the risk of drowning, but because of the often relatively poor medical resources available in remote diving areas.

In Caucasian men aged 25 to 34, this risk of cardiovascular disease is about 1 in 10,000, but by age 55 to 64 it is 1 in 100. It is therefore not surprising that the DAN data indicate excessive mortality due to coronary disease in divers over the age of 40. With many baby boomers now reaching age 50, this is a pertinent issue.

What can you do? Be as fit as possible with normal blood pressure, control obesity (less than 20 percent over standard height/weight charts), exercise regularly and eat a sensible, low-fat diet.

Taking it a step further, a well-known cardiologist and diver, Dr. Fred Bove, recommends that all individuals over the age of 40 who have significant risk factors (such as mild diabetes, hypertension or high cholesterol) be approved for sports diving by a cardiologist only after successfully completing an exercise test with electrocardiogram and blood pressure monitoring to a metabolic equivalent of 13 METS (metabolic equivalents). The metabolic equivalent of snow shoveling is only 6. You can see that he is suggesting a pretty high level of physical activity which, to be honest, I am not sure most could reach unless we are regular runners or maintain a regular exercise schedule. You would need 8 METS, for example, to swim against a 1-knot current.

Besides these physical considerations, another factor arises in connection with a cardiovascular death underwater — what about insurance and/or litigation? In such a death, is it considered a diving or a cardiac death? In many diving cases, an autopsy may clearly indicate plaque, leading to the pathologist noting coronary artery disease, severe atherosclerotic disease or myocardial infarction as the cause of death.

Control your cardiac risks. It will not only increase your dive safety, but next year when the snow returns, you can shovel snow more safely, too!

— From July/August 1996

Reporting Diving Incidents

This edition of *Alert Diver* [January/February 1994 — *Ed.*] concentrates on potentially dangerous marine creatures. That there are indeed dangerous creatures beneath the sea there is no doubt. But what we perceive as hazardous to us as divers — and there's no denying that danger in some cases — is used primarily for the animals' own protection.

However, rather than concentrate completely on dangerous marine creatures, I prefer to address the overall dangers to divers — and, subsequently, scuba diver incident reporting.

By using the term incident, I refer specifically to a mishap caused by any error of: the diver, the buddy, another diver or the equipment; or by flaws in the dive preparation, entry, exit or post-dive procedures.

In Australia, Dr. Chris Acott has promoted incident reporting and analysis. The British Sub Aqua Club has a similar project. Gathering such data is believed to help in the analysis of the causes of diving accidents as much as, for example, DAN's *Report on Diving Accidents and Fatalities* statistics — and may be better in some cases.

Although DAN has been very interested in incident reporting, we have been cautious because of the potential problem of handling and analyzing the enormous amount of data. And by virtue of the amount and variety of incidents, the data is less rigorously controlled than our accident and mortality statistics. However, we have decided to see what happens with our own DAN members. DAN has developed a Diving Incident Reporting Form, available by calling DAN's Medical Services Dept. at (919) 684-2948. If you — or a buddy — are involved in a diving incident, complete the form and return it to the Medical Services Department of DAN at our headquarters in Durham, N.C.

In reviewing some of the data from the analysis of the first 125 incidents reported by Acott in Australia, we find contributing factors in diver mishaps: anxiety, failure to understand dive tables, alcohol and drugs, insufficient training and medical problems not compatible with diving have caused most of the complications in these incidents. And these factors were equally distributed between the experienced and inexperienced divers.

Most incidents occurred during (46) or after (25) the dive, and a total of 30 of the 40 incidents which required treatments (75 percent) occurred during ascent or following the dive. Out-of-air situations occurred in 18 cases — a situation which should not occur and is definitely preventable.

Equipment problems predominated in this incident series, which, in my own observations of more than 20-plus years of recreational diving, is common. When we get to accident and death reports, however, equipment becomes less of a factor. The majority of such incidents (67) involve the regulator or buoyancy device. Seventeen of those were due to equipment failure — and with this it seems there is no doubt that divers today are not checking either their own equipment or their buddy's sufficiently before entering the water.

We can identify the need for an independent alternative air supply such as a pony bottle or Spare Air™ by the fact that 13 of the 18 out-of-air divers felt that such a source would have helped them.

It is interesting, however, that of those, three of the 10 using an octopus (due to poor clearing of the second stage) — and one of the three buddy breathers — still suffered saltwater aspiration, which can easily result in drowning.

We will see what we can learn from our own Diving Incident Reporting Forms. But as Acott has suggested, every diver could benefit by carrying and using an equipment checklist. This might include a first check before putting on the gear and then another before entering the water. DAN will investigate making such checklists available. The fact that our own accident data see a disproportionately higher number of accidents in divers with less than two years' experience or 20 dives, also — like Acott — suggests the need for either additional training or changes to existing training programs.

— From January/February 1994

Thermal Facts

Dr. Bennett explores the relationships between cold, exercise and DCS risks

I have recently returned from tropical Moorea, French Polynesia, teaching a DAN physicians course — DAN's 30th diving and hyperbaric medicine course. While there, one of the wives of a diving physician mentioned how cold she was on the boat after diving in the 70-degree waters. She suggested that DAN provide protective clothing for such situations during these classes.

She has a valid point: often hypothermia is not mentioned sufficiently in relation to diving risks. But being cold — as well as where and when you are cold — are important when you dive. Interestingly, as many of you have probably noticed, it is often the female diver who complains the most about getting chilled. Although women do have about a 10 percent higher body fat content than men, they also have some 17 percent less muscle mass — which helps to generate heat during activity. Women also have a higher surface area to lean body mass, which increases the area of conductive heat loss.

It is equally important to know in what part of the diving cycle the diver becomes cold. For example, if a diver becomes cold on the run out to a dive site and then dives in comparatively warm water, he may take up less nitrogen in the peripheral tissues of the body. Less total nitrogen, then, means less decompression risk than if the diver were warm before and during the dive. This is because it takes time during the dive for the peripheral blood vessels to change from vasoconstriction due to the cold and vasodilatation due to warmth — the larger the vessel the more nitrogen-containing blood can be carried to the tissues.

Now let us theorize a typical case: the diver who makes a warm run out to the dive site, dives in warmer water and so takes on a good nitrogen load. During the run to the second dive site, however, he becomes cold. Now, instead of offgassing during the surface interval, much of the gas elimination in his body may be reduced — because of the peripheral vessel vasoconstriction which results from the cold. Also, during the second dive, additional gas is taken into the tissues; and on ascent, the total nitrogen in the tissues may be higher than if the diver had properly offgassed during the surface interval. The end result is that the diver is probably at increased risk of decompression sickness (DCS).

On this basis, clearly it may be good from a decompression standpoint to be cold during the dive rather than on the surface afterwards where you should be warm for maximum gas elimination.

Exercise is also an important consideration in DCS. DAN Research Director Dr. Richard Vann has shown that at depth, exercise increases the risk of decompression illness. Exercise during decompression, on the other hand, seems to reduce decompression risk by 30 percent. Another point about exercise is that today many divers run and do other exercises routinely. Due to tissue surfaces such as muscles and tendons rubbing against each other, micronuclei are produced which are the "seeds" for bubbles to develop from. Thus, if you are expecting to dive that day, it is wiser to reduce the amount of exercise you do both before and after diving, to help reduce your risk of decompression illness. I usually suggest rather arbitrarily that you should reduce such exercise by at least 50 percent or, better still, take a time out from your routine exercises and regard your diving activity as the exercise for the day.

For the lowest risk during diving, then, it may be best to not get too warm during the dive, not to spend all your time finning and to exercise gently during the ascent (photographers hanging around for macrophotographs probably have lower risk of decompression sickness compared to the aggressive swimmer). Rather than simply hanging on a bar for three to five minutes at 15 feet or so, I prefer to swim gently around the bar before a drift to the surface. Once on board, keep warm before the next dive. Dives become more comfortable and safer, too. A need remains to have more data on the effects of exercise and cold on diving. We will also investigate some form of cold protection for divers on boats.

— *From January/February 1997*

Long-Term Effects of Diving

The latest news isn't exactly new.

As a result of a recent paper published in the British Medical Journal *Lancet* in early June 1995, a number of subsequent articles have surfaced which question the long-term consequences of recreational diving. This has caused a considerable amount of inquiry among scuba divers — and many divers have looked to DAN for a response.

The paper, by Dr. Jurgen Reul and colleagues from the Technical University of Aachen, Germany, is titled "Central nervous system lesions and cervical disc hemiations in amateur divers." These scientists studied 102 subjects — 52 amateur divers and 50 from other sports — using magnetic resonance imaging (MRI) of the brain and cervical spinal cord.

Of the divers, one had a history of decompression sickness (DCS) and two others reported situations which almost caused DCS. In the MRI results, 27 of 52 divers had a total of 85 lesions; of the 50 non-divers, 14 lesions were found in 10 people. In addition, 32 of the divers showed at least one abnormality of a cervical disc, compared to nine in the nondivers.

What does this show? First, that all of this should be put in context — these findings are not new. Whether sport and commercial divers have changes in their brains as a result of diving has been a question for many years, but as yet there has been no substantive proof.

The supposition of any damage to the brain rests on the occurrence of so-called "silent bubbles" occurring in the blood or brain and spinal cord. That such bubbles do exist has been well demonstrated by Doppler technology in blood and tissue studies of animals' spinal cords. Whether these silent bubbles are the cause of changes in the brain remains as yet unproven.

In most cases, the lungs filter out bubbles — except when there is a hole in the heart, or patent foramen ovale (*Alert Diver*, March/April 1995), when bubbles can pass to the arterial side to reach the brain and spinal cord. Spontaneous growth of bubbles in tissue during ascent is another question and relies on an adequate tension of gas in the neurological tissues accompanied by too rapid an ascent. Hence, it is more likely in deeper dives and more rapid ascents.

On the commercial front in diving, the Norwegians have organized two workshops: the first in 1983 called "Long-Term Neurological Consequences of Deep Diving," and another two years ago whose proceedings and consensus opinions were published in 1994. The 1993 consensus by international physicians and scientists was: "There is evidence that changes in bone, the central nervous system and the lungs can be demonstrated in some divers who have not experienced a diving accident. The changes are, in most cases, minor and do not influence the diver's quality of life. However, the changes are of a nature that may influence the diver's future health. [There is no evidence to support this.] The scientific evidence is limited, and future research is required to obtain adequate answers to the questions of long-term health effects."

More recent research by Dr. P.A. Rinck reported MRI studies in 70 professional divers and 47 nondiving controls. Focal areas of high-signal density (called unidentified bright objects, or UBOs) like the lesions reported by Dr. Reul were seen in 34 percent of the divers and 42 percent of the nondivers. These UBOs are often seen in all MRIs — and more often as we age. They do not indicate scarring of the brain, but, on the other hand, we do not know exactly what they mean.

The issue of brain lesions remains unproven; and if there are effects, they do not appear to materially affect the individual. As more sensitive tests become available, it is inevitable that unusual results will be found, not only in diving, but in many other unusual environments. We must, therefore, probably rely on the quality of life as the standard.

More research is needed, but the world is filled with divers — including diving medicine physicians and scientists like myself — who have been diving for over 40 years who show no unusual effects or early aging processes. Meanwhile, the research will continue.

— *From July/August 1995*

Surprising Up & Down Currents

Upwellings and downward surges can cause panic and injury among new divers.

During a recent trip to the Caribbean, I spoke to some new divers when the issue of drift diving arose. Our talk raised the issue of a more challenging and dangerous issue in diving — the down or up current.

I first encountered this in Palau while diving Blue Corner. Those who have dived this awe-inspiring wall will know that the "corner" is the entrance between the deep coral walls to the very large shallows and Rock Islands behind the wall. Depending on tides, the ocean is either going in or out through this opening, so you drop in, swim quickly down to the beautiful reef and drift in either direction. Time between tides is short.

On one of these dives, I noticed midway through the drift that the current had changed and I was beginning to move back toward where I had entered. Guessing the tide had changed, I swam upward, close to the reef, to check and met a very strong water current pressing down on me as the water came over the reef like a tremendous waterfall.

As I moved down deeper, this disappeared. On ascent from the dive, however, I was surprised to notice from my depth gauge and bubbles that as I swam away from my gentle drift dive along the reef out toward the boats, I was going deeper instead. I then increased my buoyancy and kicked my fins to break through this down current. I had forgotten that under the waterfall current close to the wall there was little problem, but in swimming away from the wall, I met the full force of the "waterfall" over the reef.

Another diver who was less able to deal with the problem found herself going from 60 feet/18 meters to 130 feet/40 meters at a fast clip, resulting in panic and a subsequent arterial gas embolism on trying to extract herself.

I am reminded of this as I recently reviewed the latest *South Pacific Underwater Medicine Society Journal*, which carried two letters reprinted from *Undercurrent*, referring to similar downwellings and upwellings in Cozumel during drift dives at the Santa Rosa Wall.

These currents in Cozumel have a seasonal source. In mid-April the ocean is changing temperature, which generates extreme underwater currents and waves. The divers in the first letter wrote that they were at 80 feet/24 meters drifting, when suddenly they were forced down to 125 feet/38 meters, then rapidly upward toward the surface. On their return to the boat in an otherwise choppy sea, there were large areas of calm water, 30-100 feet/9-30 meters in diameter, with what looked like an underwater tornado below.

The other divers were diving in January on Cozumel's Chancanab Reef. There were no unusual surface conditions, they wrote. During the 50-foot/15-meter dive, four of the group hit a down current which was more subtle than the current in the previous incident. Their only real guide was their depth gauges, which showed them at 70 feet/21 meters when they were supposedly ascending. Vigorous finning and swimming finally enabled them to ascend. At 10-15 feet/3-4.6 meters, these divers also noted a slow circular motion on the surface and a glass-flat circular area of about 70 feet in diameter with a vortex below — as in the previous report.

Such events can be very disturbing, especially for inexperienced divers. Good advice should you be caught in a downward current or upwelling is to stay calm — don't panic or swim directly against it. Instead, swim out of it at an angle in order to avoid the direct force — common sense if you have considered your plan of action beforehand, but a possible panic situation if you have not.

Familiarizing yourself with your upcoming dives and any challenges they may hold, such as these vertical currents, is an important safety factor. It also increases your enjoyment of the dive.

But remember that drift diving is still for me — and many other divers — the most enjoyable form of diving, where the ocean does the work and one is left to enjoy its beauty!

— *From March/April 1996*

No Fast Ascents — No Bends!

What do we really know about the causes of decompression illness and how to prevent it? My lifelong work in diving medicine leads me to say, "Not much!"

Consider the range of so-called decompression tables available to the recreational diver today. We have the U.S. Navy, PADI DSAT, NAUI, Buehlmann, DCIEM (Canadian) and the RNPL BSAC (British) Tables, to name a few. Add that to the dozens of dive computers — also equipped with different theoretical concepts for their decompression models — and it is clear we do not know much because all cannot be correct.

I have seen many mathematicians and physiologists over the years claim to have "the secret." Later they are amazed to find their pet new tables — like all the others before — still produce decompression sickness in divers who do everything right!

Most of these theories are based on Haldane's concept that nitrogen at increased pressures enters tissues in amounts according to fast (e.g., five minutes) or slow (e.g., 75 minutes) "tissues" — this measurement representing half the time to saturate the tissue with gas. Some divers think these half times relate to blood or fat, but in reality these "tissues" are just mathematical numbers. In the past, when the researcher discovered that bends still occurred, the solution was to add more tissues — from Haldane's initial five to Buehlmann's 16. Yet bends still occur.

Other areas of dispute are where bubbles form — spontaneously in the spinal cord, for example, or in the blood — and the role of perfusion (gas delivery by the blood) or diffusion (gas delivery through tissues). Now add to this the biological variability of recreational divers — they may be heavy, thin, male, female, old, young — plus environmental factors such as cold or warm water, currents, etc., and you have a wide variety of possibilities.

Looking at the DAN accident data over the years, I have noticed that the incidence of decompression illness of one to two divers per 10,000 is amazingly consistent and correlates with the distribution of divers for sex, age and training.

So what is going on? I believe we are up the wrong creek! True, nitrogen buildup in the body is a critical component to bubble generation, but the tissue half-time models seem irrelevant. Much more important is the rate of ascent.

It is quite likely that due to rapid ascent rates, discrete ruptures occur in lung tissue from overexpansion, causing bubbles to be produced which find their way to the spinal cord and brain. So much of what we call neurological decompression illness may well be arterial gas embolism. Due to a rapid ascent, bubbles can also spontaneously occur in the neurological tissues.

The 60-feet / 18-meter-per-minute ascent rate recommended in the past by the U.S. Navy is purely arbitrary and has no relation to gas physiology. Indeed, in the new USN tables it is slowed to 30 feet / 9 meters per minute, a further verification that slower may be safer.

Further credence to this hypothesis is given by recent research by DAN researcher, Donna Uguccioni, on the value of the three-to-five-minute stop at 15 feet / 4.5 meters (which acts like slowing the ascent). This has been shown to significantly decrease the formation of bubbles detected by Doppler monitoring.

Another fascinating piece of research on the subject was delivered by Dr. Wong at the [1995] UHMS conference in Denver, Colo. He observed Australian pearl divers who make up to 10 dives per day for up to eight consecutive days. Using Doppler devices, Wong titrated dive profiles with the least bubbles formation and found rate of ascent a most critical factor. Thus, their rate of ascent now is only about 10 feet / 3 meters per minute.

Unfortunately, many divers have trouble holding to 60-feet- / 18-meters-per-minute ascents rates, let alone 30-feet- / 9-meters-per-minute or even 10-feet- / 3 -meters-per-minute. But it may be much better to slowly drift to the surface with the safety stop at 15 feet/4.5 meters for three to five minutes.

You will, I am sure, be hearing more about ascent rates and the general move to slow them. It is a wise idea, for such slow rates should reduce the likelihood of possible discrete ruptures of the lung or even spontaneous bubble growth in tissues which may be responsible for the neurological type decompression illness seen in recreational divers today.

— *From January/February 1995*

Rate of Ascent Revisited

*Good advice is often worth repeating —
especially when new data arrives.*

In last year's January/February 1995 edition of *Alert Diver*, my editorial, "No Fast Ascents — No Bends," emphasized the importance of slow ascents in diving safety. Its thesis: Much of the past work on decompression tables based on tissue half-times was not as critical to recreational divers in preventing decompression sickness (DCS) as rate of ascent. The guiding philosophy here is that our rate of ascent at 60 feet/18 meters per minute is too fast.

In this vein, I would like you to consider some additional data. As discussed before, the Haldane hypothesis postulates gas uptake in the body at various exponentials predicated on a tissue half-time (half the time for a "tissue" to saturate with gas). Haldane postulated five theoretical half-times, later changed by the U.S. Navy to six half-times of 5, 10, 20, 40, 80 and 120 minutes.

When DCS occurred with such tables, the table builders immediately surmised the most likely cause was that gas in the "slowest" tissue was unable to come out quickly during ascent. Thus, bubbles formed and caused DCS, so they added a slower tissue half-time. Because of this, the Buehlmann tables ended up with 16 tissue half-times, from four to 635 minutes — and still DCS occurred.

Let us think more carefully. The fastest tissue is likely to be the blood; next is the highly perfused neurological tissue of the spinal cord and brain. In fact, the perfusion here is so good that such tissues saturate in a matter of minutes, whereas connective tissues at the joints (which have few blood vessels) require a much longer time to take up gas.

In a diver making a 100-foot/30-meter dive for 20 minutes, for example, the tissues with the most saturation are the blood and the neurological tissues of the brain and spinal cord. Upon ascent to the surface at 60 feet per minute, the gas may not have sufficient time to come out. This supersaturation generates bubbles (often called silent bubbles) in the blood and neurological tissues. One would expect such dives to result in neurological DCS, or Type II in the old diagnosis category.

If you dive to 40 feet/12 meters for 60 minutes, the blood and neurological tissues are certainly saturated, but the slow tissues are now also filling up. On the now-short ascent to surface, the tension in the blood has degassed to the point that the remainder is not critical, but the slow tissue is unable to release gas quickly. The critical tension of supersaturation is reached in this tissue, and pain-only (Type I) bends can occur in the joints.

With this hypothesis, slowing the ascent to 30 feet / 9 meters per minute or slower allows a reduction in blood and neurological tissue tensions during ascent to less-than-critical values, and incidence of neurological DCS should be reduced.

We know that 67-70 percent of DCS in recreational divers is neurological DCS and only 17-23 percent is pain-only. In contrast, the U.S. Navy sees mostly pain-only DCS, but the Navy does not make the deep, short dives that we do — and perhaps it is the way we dive. Not all recreational divers ascend 60 feet/18 meters per minute, let alone 30 feet/9 meters per minute. With a fully inflated BC, rates of 70-250 feet/ 21-76 meters per minute have been measured.

Finally, there is some confirmation of this hypothesis in a paper by Drs. Lehner, Ball, Lanphier, Gammin, Nordheim and Crump entitled "Dive Profiles Control the Manifestations of Decompression Injury in Diving." Presented at the 1995 Annual Meeting of the Undersea and Hyperbaric Medical Society, it outlined their use of sheep to study 528 dives, 151 of which resulted in DCS. Short, deep dives showed more frequent neurological DCS (Type II) than long, shallow dives. Pain-only incidents were more frequent after long, shallow dives.

Therefore, to improve your dive safety, I repeat: Make ascents slowly — at 30 feet / 9 meters per minute or less — and make a safety stop at 15-20 feet / 4.5-6 meters for three to five minutes (I prefer the longer) to help remove any silent bubbles. These procedures should help to reduce the incidence of all forms of decompression illness.

— From January/February 1996